1001 SHORT, EASY, INEXPENSIVE RECIPES

Cookbook Resources, LLC
Highland Village, Texas

1000 Short, Easy, Inexpensive Recipes

1st Printing - August 2009
2nd Printing - April 2010

International Standard Book Number: 978-1-59769-005-8

Library of Congress Control Number: 2009030365

Library of Congress Cataloging-in-Publication Data:

    1001 short, easy, inexpensive recipes. -- 1st ed.
      p. cm.
    Includes index.
    ISBN 978-1-59769-005-8
    1. Quick and easy cookery. 2. Low budget cookery. I. Cookbook Resources, LLC. II. Title: One thousand one short, easy, inexpensive recipes.

    TX833.5.A1777 2009
    641.5'55--dc22

                    2009030365

Edited, Designed, Published and Manufactured in the United States of America by Cookbook Resources, LLC
541 Doubletree Drive
Highland Village, Texas 75077

Toll free 866-229-2665

www.cookbookresources.com

cookbook
≋*resources*® LLC
Bringing Family and Friends to the Table

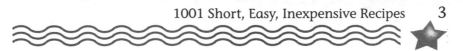

Introduction

We can always save money, but it is a lot easier to spend it than it is to save it. In *1001 Short, Easy, Inexpensive Recipes* you will find recipes and tips to help you save money and to get in a groove for effortless saving.

As an example, coupons are probably easier than ever to get. We don't have to subscribe to newspapers or wait for flyers and ads. All we have to do today is to spend some time on the Internet and find the coupons we know we will use.

Saving at the grocery store can be a game, especially when we keep track of our savings. One of the handiest things we should create for ourselves is a spreadsheet with prices for commonly purchased items. It lets us know when we're getting a good deal or when it just *looks* like a good deal.

There are so many ways we are tempted to buy that it's almost scary. We have to use a lot of common sense, restraint and discipline to get to the winner's circle of big-time savings, but it's very doable.

Be sure to read all the **"Save-A-Penny"** ideas at the bottom of many of the pages and select the ones that appeal to you. Make it a game and enjoy playing.

> *Home life ceases to be free and beautiful as soon as it is founded on borrowing and debt.*
>
> –Henrik Ibsen

Contents

Appetizers are an easy way to entertain a crowd. They add a festive touch to everyday meals, too.

How often we hear that a hearty breakfast is a great way to start the day. But many of these dishes are terrific for supper, too!

Serve for company – serve for family. These delectable beverages are super for special occasions from a wedding to a good report card!

Easy and inexpensive to fix, sandwiches can please a crowd or a couple – and these recipes add lots of flavor and interest.

Bread is an attractive accompaniment to a meal. It makes the meal complete and fills up hungry appetites.

Fresh and savory, sweet and fruity, salads take many forms and flavors to delight the senses and complement a lunch or supper.

Nothing warms the body and the soul like good soup. Soups are not only full of flavor, they are very filling and fit the budget.

Vegetables and other side dishes fill out a menu – as well as a family. Tasty and attractive, they add vitamins and other nutrients.

Contents

Dedication

With a mission of helping you bring family and friends to the table, Cookbook Resources strives to make family meals and entertaining friends simple, easy and delicious.

We recognize the importance of sharing meals together as a means of building family bonds with memories and traditions that will be treasured for a lifetime. It is an opportunity to sit down with each other and share more than food.

This cookbook is dedicated with gratitude and respect for all those who show their love with homecooked meals and bring family and friends to the table.

> More and more statistical studies are finding that family meals play a significant role in childhood development. Children who eat with their families four or more nights per week are healthier, make better grades, score higher on aptitude tests and are less likely to have problems with drugs.

 This icon indicates a slow cooker recipe.

 This icon indicates a microwave recipe.

Pocketbook Pleasers

Appetizers are an easy way to entertain a crowd. They add a festive touch to everyday meals, too.

Artichoke Dip

1 (14 ounce) can artichoke hearts, drained, chopped	395 g
1 cup grated parmesan cheese	100 g
1 cup mayonnaise	225 g

- Preheat oven to 350° (175° C). Combine all ingredients and mix well. Pour into sprayed baking dish and bake for 20 to 30 minutes.

- Serve with fresh vegetables, chips or crackers. Yields 3 cups.

• • • • •

Bean and Corn Salsa

1 (15 ounce) can black beans, drained	425 g
1 (8 ounce) can whole kernel corn, drained	225 g
1 (16 ounce) jar thick-and-chunky salsa	455 g

- Combine all ingredients in bowl and mix well. Refrigerate.

- Serve with chips, enchiladas or other Mexican food. Yields 1 quart.

• • • • •

Broccoli-Mushroom Dip

1 (5 ounce) roll garlic cheese	145 g
1 (10 ounce) can golden mushroom soup	280 g
1 (10 ounce) box frozen chopped broccoli, thawed, drained	280 g
Raw vegetables or chips	

- Melt cheese with soup. Stir constantly and add broccoli; heat thoroughly. Serve with raw vegetables or corn chips. Yields 1½ cups.

• • • • •

Broccoli-Cheese Dip

½ cup (1 stick) butter	115 g
1 (16 ounce) package cubed Velveeta® jalapeno cheese	455 g
1 (10 ounce) package frozen chopped broccoli, thawed, drained	280 g
Tortilla chips	

- Combine butter and cheese in saucepan on low heat until cheese melts. Cook broccoli according to package directions, drain and stir into cheese mixture. Heat until broccoli is hot.

- Serve with tortilla chips. Yields 3 cups.

• • • • •

Cheese Fondue

1 (16 ounce) package cubed Velveeta® cheese	455 g
1 (10 ounce) can cheddar cheese soup	280 g
1 (6 - 8 inch) round loaf bread	15 - 20 cm

- In saucepan, melt cheese with soup. Stir constantly to prevent scorching.

- Cut center from bread to form bowl. Cut removed bread into cubes.

- Pour cheese fondue into bread bowl and surround bread bowl with bread cubes.

- Use cubes to dip into fondue. (You can also eat the bread bowl.) Yields 3 cups.

● ● ● ● ●

Chili con Queso

1 (16 ounce) package cubed Velveeta® cheese	455 g
1 (10 ounce) can diced tomatoes and green chilies	280 g
2 green onions, chopped	
Corn or tortilla chips	

- Melt cheese in double boiler with tomatoes and green chilies. Place in serving dish and sprinkle with chopped green onions over top.

- Serve with corn or tortilla chips. Yields 3 cups.

● ● ● ● ●

Hamburger Cheese Dip

2 (16 ounce) packages cubed Velveeta® cheese	2 (455 g)
1 (10 ounce) can diced tomatoes and green chilies	280 g
1 pound ground beef, browned, drained	455 g
Large corn chips	

- Melt cheese with tomatoes and green chilies. Stir in meat.

- Serve hot with large corn chips. Yields 1 quart.

● ● ● ● ●

Hot Chili Dip

1 (15 ounce) can chili without beans	425 g
1 (4 ounce) can chopped green chilies	115 g
1 (8 ounce) package shredded cheddar cheese	225 g
Tortilla chips	

- Combine all ingredients and mix well. Microwave on HIGH until bubbly or bake at 350° (175° C) for 30 minutes. Serve with tortilla chips. Yields 3 cups.

• • • • •

Cottage Dip with Veggies

1 (16 ounce) carton small curd cottage cheese, drained	455 g
1 (1 ounce) packet dry onion soup mix	30 g
½ cup mayonnaise	110 g
½ teaspoon garlic powder	2 ml
Veggies:	

    Broccoli florets
    Carrot sticks
    Celery sticks
    Cauliflower

- Blend all dip ingredients well and serve with veggies. Yields 1½ cups.

• • • • •

Jezebel Dip

1 (10 ounce) jar apple jelly	280 g
1 (5 ounce) jar horseradish	145 g
1 (12 ounce) jar pineapple preserves	340 g
Ham cubes or sausage balls	

- Mix jelly, horseradish and preserves in saucepan until mixture melts; cool.

- Serve with ham cubes, sausage balls, etc. Yields 2 cups.

• • • • •

Mexico City Dip

1 (16 ounce) carton sour cream	480 g
1½ cups thick-and-chunky salsa	395 g
4 green onions, chopped	
Corn chips	

- Combine sour cream, salsa and green onions and mix well. Refrigerate. Serve with corn chips. Yields 3½ cups.

Guacamole

3 avocados, peeled, seeded, mashed
1 cup thick-and-chunky salsa   265 g
½ cup cottage cheese, drained   110 g

- Combine all ingredients and ¼ teaspoon (1 ml) salt and mix well.
  Refrigerate.

- Serve as salad with Mexican food or as dip with tortilla chips.
  Yields 2 cups.

• • • • •

Creamy Guacamole

4 avocados
1 (8 ounce) package cream cheese, softened   225 g
1 (10 ounce) can diced tomatoes and green chilies   280 g
1½ teaspoons garlic salt   7 ml
1 tablespoon lemon juice   15 ml
Tortilla chips

- Peel avocados and mash with fork. In mixing bowl, beat cream
  cheese until smooth.

- Add avocados, tomatoes and green chilies, garlic salt, and lemon
  juice and mix well. Serve with tortilla chips. Yields 2½ cups.

• • • • •

Men's Favorite Pepperoni Dip

1 (8 ounce) package pepperoni   225 g
1 (8 ounce) carton sour cream   225 g
¼ teaspoon seasoned salt   1 ml
Unsliced loaf of French or Italian bread

- Finely chop pepperoni and mix with sour cream and seasoned salt.

- Cover and refrigerate for 2 days to allow flavors to blend and
  pepperoni to soften.

- Serve in hollowed out loaf of bread surrounded by chunks of bread
  for dipping. Yields 2 cups.

• • • • •

 Cottage cheese is cheaper than sour cream. *Just process
in a blender until smooth and use as a delicious topping for
potatoes or add to other dishes.*

Olive-Cheese Dip

1 (7 ounce) jar stuffed green olives, finely chopped	200 g
1 (8 ounce) package cream cheese, softened	225 g
½ cup chopped pecans	55 g
Crackers or chips	

- Drain olives on paper towels.

- Beat cream cheese until smooth and creamy.

- Combine olives, cream cheese and pecans and refrigerate. Serve with crackers or chips. Yields 2 cups.

• • • • •

Red Cabbage Basket Dip

1 (1 ounce) packet dry onion soup mix	30 g
1½ cups sour cream	360 g
1 small head red cabbage, washed	
Fresh vegetables	

- Combine soup mix with sour cream and mix well.

- Cut off red cabbage top and hollow it out to form basket or cup. (Cut off bottom so it will sit level.) Fill with dip mixture.

- Place in center of platter and surround with carrot sticks, celery, olives, zucchini sticks or corn chips. Yields 1½ cups.

• • • • •

Easy Cheese Ball

2 (5 ounce) jars Old English® cheese spread, softened	2 (145 g)
2 (3 ounce) packages cream cheese, softened	2 (85 g)
1 cup chopped nuts	165 g
Crackers, chips or breads	

- Combine cheese and cream cheese in mixing bowl and beat well. Shape into ball and refrigerate for 4 to 6 hours.

- Roll cheese ball in chopped nuts and wrap in plastic wrap until time to serve. Serve with crackers, chips or breads. Yields 2½ cups.

 If purchasing expensive snacks such as chips, buy the bigger packages and divide the big bag into small plastic bags for lunches.

Beefy-Cheese Ball

1 (8 ounce) package cream cheese, softened	225 g
1 bunch green onions, finely chopped	
2 (2.25 ounce) jars chipped beef, chopped fine	2 (65 g)
Crackers or chips	

- Beat cream cheese until smooth and creamy.

- Combine all ingredients in bowl and mix well. Shape into ball and refrigerate. Serve with crackers or chips. Yields 1 pint.

TIP: Roll ball in ½ cup (55 g) finely chopped pecans.

• • • • •

Chicken Ball

2 (8 ounce) packages cream cheese, softened	2 (225 g)
2 (6 ounce) cans chunk white chicken, drained,	
finely shredded	2 (170 g)
Garlic salt	
Crackers	

- Beat cream cheese until smooth.

- Combine cream cheese and chicken and blend well. Add garlic salt to taste.

- Shape into ball and serve with crackers. Yields 3½ cups.

TIP: As a special touch, roll ball in chopped pecans.

• • • • •

Raspberry-Cheese Ball

2 (8 ounce) packages cream cheese, softened	2 (225 g)
¼ cup raspberry preserves	80 g
1 cup finely chopped pecans	110 g
Crackers	

- Beat cream cheese until creamy. Mix cream cheese and raspberry preserves until they blend well.

- Shape into a ball and roll in chopped pecans. Serve with crackers. Yields 3 cups.

• • • • •

Cheese Squares

1 (16 ounce) package cubed Velveeta® cheese	455 g
1 cup finely chopped nuts	165 g
3 - 5 teaspoons hot sauce	15 - 25 ml
Crackers	

- Melt cheese in top of double boiler over hot water. Stir in nuts and hot sauce and mix well.

- Pour into sprayed 9 x 13-inch (23 x 33 cm) pan and refrigerate until firm.

- Cut into squares and serve with crackers. Yields 3 cups.

• • • • •

Cheese Sticks

1 (5 ounce) jar Old English® cheese spread	145 g
½ cup (1 stick) butter, softened	115 g
1 (16 ounce) loaf unsliced French bread	455 g

- Preheat oven to 350° (175° C).

- Combine cheese and butter and beat until smooth and soft enough to spread.

- Slice bread 1-inch (2.5 cm) thick. Spread slices with cheese mixture. Cut each slice into 3 sticks and place on cookie sheet; bake for 10 minutes. Yields 36 to 45 sticks.

• • • • •

Cheese Straws

1 (5 ounce) package piecrust mix	145 g
1 (8 ounce) package shredded cheddar cheese	225 g
½ teaspoon red pepper	2 ml

- Preheat oven to 350° (175° C).

- Prepare piecrust dough according to package directions. Roll out dough on floured board into rectangular shape.

- Sprinkle cheese over dough and sprinkle red pepper over cheese.

- Fold dough over once to cover cheese, then roll out again to rectangle ½-inch (1.2 cm) thick.

- Cut dough into 3 x ½-inch (8 x 1.2 cm) strips and place on lightly sprayed baking sheet. Bake for 10 to 15 minutes. Yields 25 to 30 straws.

Cheese Wedges

1 (10 ounce) package refrigerated biscuits	280 g
¼ cup (½ stick) butter, melted	55 g
⅓ cup shredded cheddar cheese	40 g

- Preheat oven to 400° (205° C).

- Cut each biscuit into 4 wedges. Roll in melted butter, then cheese.
  Bake for 10 minutes. Yields 40 wedges.

• • • • •

Cheese Chex

⅓ cup (⅔ stick) butter	75 g
6 cups bite-size crispy corn cereal squares	185 g
⅓ cup fresh grated parmesan cheese	55 g

- Melt butter in large pot, add cereal squares and stir well.

- Add cheese and mix well over low heat until mixture blends well.

- Pour on foil and separate to cool. Yields 6 cups.

• • • • •

Chili Snacks

1 (15 ounce) can chili without beans	425 g
1 cup shredded cheddar cheese	115 g
Party rye bread slices	

- Preheat oven to 350° (175° C).

- Combine chili and cheese in saucepan and heat, stirring constantly,
  until cheese melts. Spread on party rye bread.

- Place slices on baking sheet and bake for 10 to 15 minutes.
  Yields 15 to 20 slices.

• • • • •

Check out the stores within driving distance. *Periodically, check out different stores in your area to see what they offer and compare prices. Learn where to find the best quality produce, the best store brands and the best meats.*

Quesadillas

1 - 1½ cups shredded cheddar cheese   **115 - 170 g**
10 flour tortillas
1 small onion, finely chopped
½ cup (1 stick) butter   **115 g**

- Place desired amount cheese and onion in center of flour tortilla.

- Fold over and secure with wooden toothpicks.

- Fry both sides of quesadillas in butter until golden brown.
  Yields 10 quesadillas.

*TIP: For heartier quesadillas, add cooked, shredded chicken breast on top
        of cheese and onion.*

• • • • •

Jalapeno Bites

1 (12 ounce) can jalapeno peppers, drained   **340 g**
1 (8 ounce) package shredded cheddar cheese   **225 g**
4 eggs, beaten
¼ cup milk or cream   **60 ml**

- Preheat oven to 375° (190° C).

- Seed and chop peppers and place in 9-inch (23 cm) pie pan.
  Sprinkle cheese over peppers.

- Combine eggs and milk and pour over cheese. Bake for about
  22 minutes. Cut into small slices to serve. Serves 6 to 8.

• • • • •

Bacon-Stuffed Mushrooms

1 pound large fresh mushrooms   **455 g**
1 (8 ounce) package cream cheese, softened   **225 g**
8 slices bacon, fried crisp, crumbled

- Preheat oven to 300° (150° C).

- Clean mushrooms and remove stems.

- Beat cream cheese until creamy. Mix cream cheese and crumbled
  bacon and stuff mushrooms with mixture.

- Place on foil-lined baking sheet and bake for 5 to 10 minutes or until
  hot. Broil a few seconds to lightly brown. Serves 6 to 10.

• • • • •

Creamy Stuffed Mushrooms

2 (8 ounce) cartons large fresh mushrooms	2 (225 g)
1 pound sage-flavored sausage	455 g
1 small onion, minced	
1 (8 ounce) package cream cheese	22 g

- Preheat oven to 300° (150° C).

- Remove stems from mushrooms. Brown sausage, onions and chopped mushroom stems.

- Drain sausage, add cream cheese and stir until it melts.

- Stuff mushrooms with sausage mixture. Place on cookie sheet and bake for 30 minutes. Serves 4 to 6.

• • • • •

Olive Wraps

1 (12 ounce) can buttermilk biscuits	340 g
1 (5¾ ounce) jar small stuffed green olives	145 g
Grated parmesan cheese	

- Preheat oven to 350° (175° C).

- Cut each biscuit into quarters and wrap dough around 1 olive.

- Roll in grated parmesan cheese and place on sprayed baking sheet. Bake for 6 to 8 minutes. Yields 30 to 40 pieces.

• • • • •

 # Microwave Potato Skins

4 baking potatoes	
1 cup shredded cheddar cheese	115 g
4 - 6 slices bacon, fried crisp, drained, crumbled	

- Slice potatoes lengthwise and microwave for 3 minutes.

- Scoop out potato, leave ¼-inch (6 mm) skins and fill each with cheese and bacon.

- Place on plate, cover with paper towel and microwave for 30 seconds or until cheese melts. Yields 4 servings of 2 potato skins per person.

• • • • •

Chinese Chicken Wings

3 pounds chicken wings	1.4 kg
1 (10 ounce) bottle soy sauce	280 g
½ cup sugar	100 g

- Clean wings, snip tips and discard tips.

- Mix soy sauce and sugar in 9 x 13-inch (23 x 33 cm) glass dish or pan. Add chicken wings and turn to coat.

- Cover dish and marinate wings for 24 hours in refrigerator. Turn often.

- When ready to bake, preheat oven to 250° (120° C).

- Remove from refrigerator after 24 hours and let stand for 15 minutes. Pour off most of sauce and discard.

- Cover dish tightly with foil and bake for 2 hours.

- Remove foil during last 15 minutes of baking time to brown wings. Serves 8 to 12.

Little Smokie Crescents

1 (8 ounce) can refrigerated crescent rolls	225 g
24 little smokies	
1 cup barbecue sauce	265 g

- Preheat oven to 400° (205° C).

- Unroll crescent roll dough and spread out flat. Cut the 8 triangles into 3 triangles each (so you have 24).

- Starting at wide end of each dough triangle, place 1 smokie on dough, roll up and repeat.

- Place rolls on baking sheet and bake for 10 to 15 minutes or until golden brown. Serve with barbecue sauce. Yields 24.

Apricot Smokies

½ cup apricot preserves	160 g
1 tablespoon mustard	15 ml
1 (16 ounce) package cooked little smokies sausages	

- In saucepan, combine and heat apricot preserves and mustard.

- Add smokies and heat until bubbly.

- Pour into serving dish and serve with toothpicks. Serves 6 to 10.

• • • • •

Bacon Wraps

8 bacon slices, divided
12 tater tots
12 smoked cocktail sausages

- Cut 4 bacon slices in thirds and wrap around tater tots.

- Arrange in circle on paper towel-lined platter, cover with paper towel and microwave on HIGH for 3 minutes.

- Rotate plate one-quarter turn and microwave for 2 to 4 minutes or until bacon is crisp.

- Cut remaining 4 bacon slices in thirds and wrap around cocktail sausages. Microwave as shown above. Yields 24.

• • • • •

On Top of Old Smoky

1 (16 ounce) package sliced bacon	455 g
2 pounds little smokies sausages	910 g
1 (16 ounce) box brown sugar	455 g

- Preheat oven to 350° (175° C).

- Cut bacon slices into halves. Wrap smokies in bacon halves and secure with wooden toothpicks.

- Place in baking dish and top with brown sugar spread evenly over smokies.

- Bake until sugar melts, then broil until bacon browns.
  Serves 18 (5 links per person).

• • • • •

Saucy Barbecued Sausages

1 (18 ounce) bottle barbecue sauce	510 g
1 (12 ounce) jar grape jelly	340 g
2 (16 ounce) packages cooked cocktail sausages	2 (455 g)

- Pour barbecue sauce and grape jelly into large saucepan. Cook and stir until jelly melts and mixture is smooth.

- Add cooked sausages and heat on low for 20 minutes. Stir often. Serve hot. Serves 18 (5 links per person).

• • • • •

Pigs in Blankets

1 (10 count) package hot dogs
3 (12 ounce) cans biscuits   3 (340 g)
Dijon-style mustard

- Preheat over to 425° (220° C).

- Spread biscuits with mustard. Cut hot dogs into thirds and wrap in biscuits.

- Bake for 8 to 10 minutes. Yields 30.

• • • • •

Sausage-Cheese Snacks

40 slices party rye bread, frozen
1 pound hot spicy sausage   455 g
1 (16 ounce) package sliced American cheese, quartered   455 g

- Freeze bread to make it easier to spread sausage mixture.

- Preheat oven to 350° (175° C).

- Spread raw sausage on top of frozen bread slices and top with slice of cheese.

- Place on sprayed baking sheet and bake for 20 minutes. Serves 20 to 30.

• • • • •

Sausage-Chestnut Balls

1 pound hot pork sausage   455 g
1 (8 ounce) can sliced water chestnuts, drained   225 g
1 cup barbecue sauce   265 g

- Preheat oven to 400° (205° C).

- Shape sausage into small balls.

- Cut water chestnuts in half and put 1 chestnut half in middle of each sausage ball.

- Place on sprayed baking sheet and bake for 20 minutes.

- Drain, place in serving dish and pour heated barbecue sauce over sausage balls. Use wooden toothpicks to serve. Serves 14 to 16.

• • • • •

Sausage-Cheese Balls

1 (8 ounce) jar Velveeta® cheese spread	225 g
1 pound sausage	455 kg
1½ cups flour	180 g

- Preheat oven to 350° (175° C). Combine all ingredients in bowl with wooden spoon or with your hands. Shape mixture into small balls and place on sprayed baking pan.

- Bake for 15 to 20 minutes or until brown. Serves 12 to 16.

TIP: Try hot sausage or Mexican Cheez Whiz® to give it a different taste.

TIP: These freeze well.

• • • • •

Bacon-Wrapped Chestnuts

1 (8 ounce) can whole water chestnuts, drained	225 g
¼ cup soy sauce	60 ml
½ pound bacon slices, halved	225 g

- Marinate water chestnuts for 1 hour or more in soy sauce.

- When ready to bake, preheat oven to 375° (190° C).

- Wrap ½ bacon slice around each water chestnut and fasten with toothpick. Bake for 15 to 20 minutes. Yields 15 to 20.

• • • • •

Cocktail Ham

1 cup hickory-flavored barbecue sauce	265 g
¼ cup packed light brown sugar	55 g
1 pound cooked ham, cubed	455 g
1 dozen prepared dinner rolls	

- Pour barbecue sauce and sugar into saucepan and mix well. Heat and dissolve sugar in barbecue sauce.

- Add ham and heat thoroughly. Cool, then reheat. (This improves flavor.)

- Place in chafing dish and serve on rolls. Yields 12.

• • • • •

Ham-Stuffed Tomatoes

1 pint cherry tomatoes	300 g
2 (2 ounce) cans deviled ham	2 (55 g)
2 tablespoons prepared horseradish	30 ml

- Slice tops from tomatoes. Scoop out pulp and mix with ham and horseradish; fill tomatoes. Refrigerate for about 3 hours before serving. Serves 12 to 16.

• • • • •

Glazed Ham Bites

⅓ cup chunky peanut butter	95 g
1 large slice cooked ham	
⅓ cup packed brown sugar	75 g

- Spread peanut butter over ham slice and sprinkle brown sugar over top.

- Place ham under broiler for 2 to 3 minutes or until peanut butter and sugar form brown crust.

- Cut ham into 1-inch (2.5 cm) squares. Serve hot with toothpicks. Serves 8 to 10.

• • • • •

Ham and Cheese Pick-Ups

1 (8 ounce) package cream cheese, softened	225 g
1 (1 ounce) packet dry onion soup mix	30 g
2 (3 ounce) packages thin sliced ham	2 (85 g)

- Beat cream cheese until creamy and stir in soup mix. (If needed, add a little mayonnaise or milk to make cream cheese easier to spread.)

- Lay out slices of ham and carefully spread thin layer of cream cheese mixture over each slice of ham.

- Roll ham slices into log and refrigerate for 1 to 2 hours.

- When ready to serve, slice into ¾-inch (1.8 cm) slices and place toothpick in each slice for easy pick-up. Serves 8 to 10.

• • • • •

Ham Pinwheels

9 thin slices cooked ham
1 (5 ounce) jar olive-pimento spread   145 g
9 kosher spears

- Spread ham slices with olive-pimento spread.

- Lay pickle on ham and roll; slice or serve as pinwheels. Secure with toothpicks. Serves 8 to 10.

• • • • •

Salami Roll-Ups

1 (8 ounce) package cream cheese, softened   225 g
¼ pound thinly sliced salami   115 g
Green olives, chopped, drained

- Spread cream cheese evenly over salami slices.

- Sprinkle olives over cream cheese and press into cream cheese.

- Roll and secure with toothpicks. Serves 8.

• • • • •

Salami Wedges

2 (8 ounce) package cream cheese, softened   2 (225 g)
¼ cup prepared horseradish   60 g
36 thin salami slices

- Beat cream cheese until smooth. Combine cream cheese and horseradish and mix well.

- Spread on salami slices and make 3-decker sandwiches (1 slice on top of other). Refrigerate for 1 hour.

- Cut into wedges or quarters and spear with wooden toothpicks. Serves 10 to 14.

• • • • •

Make friends at your grocery store. *Someone may tell you if something is going to be on special soon. They also may look in the back for additional stock when you can't find something.*

Tuna Melt Snackers

6 eggs, hard-boiled
2 (6 ounce) cans tuna, drained   2 (170 g)
1 (8 ounce) package shredded Velveeta® cheese   225 g
¼ cup sweet pickle relish   60 g
¼ cup chopped onion   40 g
1 cup mayonnaise   225 g
2 dozen mini hamburger buns

- Preheat oven to 350° (175° C

- Chop eggs and flake tuna. Combine all ingredients except buns.
  Spoon into buns and bake for 15 minutes. Serves 15 to 20 as
  appetizers or snacks.

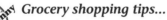

Grocery shopping tips...

*1. Don't be in a hurry. You have to have enough time to
    compare prices.*

*2. Big is not always cheaper. Check the prices on the larger sizes to
    make sure they are cheaper than the smaller sizes. They may not
    be less, especially if the smaller size is on sale.*

*3. Try store brands and generics. Many times store brands are made
    by the same manufacturers who make brand name products.*

*4. Make a list. People who have a list generally save money on every
    trip to the store.*

Budget Breakfast & Brunch

How often we hear that a hearty breakfast is a great way to start the day. But many of these dishes are terrific for supper, too!

Breakfast Shake

1 cup milk	250 ml
½ cup banana or strawberry yogurt	115 g
1 tablespoon honey	15 ml
1 banana, cubed	

- Blend all ingredients in blender until smooth. Yields 1 large shake.

TIP: You can add 1 cup ice before blending.

• • • • •

Granola Sundae

1 cup vanilla yogurt	225 g
1 cup granola mix	110 g
2 cups sliced bananas	360 g
2 cups strawberries, sliced	360 g

- Layer yogurt, granola and fruit in 4 (8 ounce/235 ml) stemmed glasses or bowls. Refrigerate until ready to serve. Serves 4.

• • • • •

Wake-Up Fruit

1 small honeydew melon or cantaloupe	
½ cup soft-style cream cheese	85 g
½ cup vanilla yogurt	115 g
1 tablespoon honey	15 ml
1½ cups fresh raspberries	185 g

- Peel and slice melon into wedges. Arrange on plate. Whip cream cheese, yogurt and honey until smooth. Drizzle mixture across melon wedges. Top with raspberries. Serves 4 to 6.

• • • • •

Yogurt-Granola-Fruit Medley

2 bananas, sliced	
1 (8 ounce) carton vanilla yogurt	225 g
1 cup granola, divided	110 g
1¼ cups seedless grapes, halved, divided	190 g

- Layer half banana slices in serving bowl. Spread with half yogurt, sprinkle with one-fourth granola and half the grapes. Sprinkle with one-fourth more granola. Repeat these layers.

- Cover and refrigerate up to 3 hours before serving. Serves 4.

Fresh Fruit Dip

1 (8 ounce) package cream cheese, softened	225 g
1 (7 ounce) jar marshmallow creme	200 g
¼ teaspoon ginger	1 ml
Fresh fruit	

- Beat cream cheese until smooth. Add marshmallow creme and ginger; mix well.

- Serve with your favorite fresh fruits such as strawberries, banana slices or apple slices. Yields 1 pint.

TIP: You can also add ¼ teaspoon (1 ml) of cinnamon.

• • • • •

Orange-Fruit Dip

1 (8 ounce) package cream cheese, softened	225 g
½ cup chopped pecans	55 g
1½ tablespoons dry orange-flavored drink mix	22 ml
Sliced apples	

- Beat cream cheese until smooth and creamy. Combine all ingredients, mix well and refrigerate.

- Serve in small bowl in middle of platter surrounded by sliced apples. Yields 1 cup.

TIP: Slice off top of an orange. Scoop fruit out of peel. Fill fruit cup with dip.

• • • • •

Baked Grapefruit

2 ruby red grapefruit	
¼ cup sugar	50 g
4 teaspoons ground cinnamon	20 ml
Fresh fruit or mint leaf	

- Preheat oven to 200° (95° C).

- Combine sugar and cinnamon.

- Cut each grapefruit in half. Cut between and loosen grapefruit sections. Sprinkle 4 teaspoons (20 ml) sugar-cinnamon mixture on each half. Bake until grapefruit is warm. Remove and garnish each half with fresh fruit or mint leaf. Serves 4.

• • • • •

Blueberry Muffins

1½ cups flour	180 g
½ cup sugar	100 g
2 teaspoons baking powder	10 ml
¼ cup oil	60 ml
1 egg, slightly beaten	
½ cup milk	125 ml
¾ cup blueberries	110 g

- Preheat oven to 350° (175° C).

- Sift dry ingredients with ½ teaspoon (2 ml) salt. Add oil, egg and milk. Stir until they mix well. Gently fold in blueberries.

- Pour into sprayed or paper-lined muffin cups. Bake for 20 to 25 minutes. Serves 4 to 6.

• • • • •

Honey-Peanut Butter Muffins

1 cup whole wheat flour	130 g
1 cup flour	120 g
1 cup chopped salted peanuts	150 g
1 tablespoon baking powder	15 ml
1⅓ cups evaporated milk	325 ml
1 cup honey	340 g
1 cup peanut butter	290 g
1 egg, beaten	

- Preheat oven to 350° (175° C).

- Combine flours, peanuts, baking powder and ¼ teaspoon (1 ml) salt.

- In separate bowl, combine milk, honey, peanut butter and egg. Add honey mixture all at once to dry ingredients and stir only until moist. Spoon into lightly sprayed or paper-lined muffin cups. Bake for 20 to 25 minutes. Serves 4 to 6.

• • • • •

The only way to buy cereal at a reasonable price is when it's on sale or you have a coupon. Just watch the newspapers or get a free coupon on the Web. Make sure the larger boxes of cereal are cheaper per ounce than the smaller sizes. Bagged cereals are cheaper than boxed cereals. Compare prices of your favorites.

Vanilla Muffins

2 cups biscuit mix	240 g
2 tablespoons sugar	30 ml
1 egg	
⅔ cup milk	150 ml
1 teaspoon vanilla	5 ml

- Preheat oven to 400° (205° C).

- Combine all ingredients and beat 30 seconds. Fill 12 sprayed or paper-lined muffin cups two-thirds full.

- Bake for about 15 minutes or until golden brown. Serves 6 to 8.

• • • • •

Freezer French Toast

4 eggs	
1 cup milk	250 ml
2 tablespoons sugar	30 ml
1 teaspoon vanilla	15 ml
¼ teaspoon nutmeg	1 ml
8 (¾-inch thick) slices day-old French bread	8 (1.8 cm)
Melted butter	

- In medium bowl, beat eggs, milk, sugar, vanilla and nutmeg. Put bread slices in sprayed 9 x 13-inch (23 x 33 cm) baking dish, pour egg mixture over bread and let stand for a few minutes. Turn slices over and let stand until all egg mixture is absorbed.

- Freeze uncovered on sheet of foil until firm, put in air-tight package and return to freezer.

- When ready to bake, preheat oven to 400° (205° C).

- Place bread slices on lightly sprayed cookie sheet. Brush each slice with melted butter. Bake for 8 minutes. Turn slices over, brush with melted butter and bake for additional 10 minutes. Serves 4 to 6.

• • • • •

Always check the expiration dates on milk and other dairy products. *It's a downer to have milk expire too soon and be a waste of money.*

French Toast on the Town

½ cup (1 stick) butter	115 g
1 cup packed light brown sugar	220 g
3 tablespoons corn syrup	45 ml
7 slices white bread, crusts removed	
6 eggs, beaten	
1½ cups half-and-half cream	375 ml
½ teaspoon vanilla	2 ml

- In saucepan melt butter and add brown sugar and corn syrup; stir until they blend well. Pour mixture into 9 x 13-inch (23 x 33 cm) baking dish.

- Place bread slices over butter-sugar mixture in single layer. (Six slices will fit in baking dish. Cut 1 remaining bread slice to fit around edges of dish.)

- Combine eggs, cream, vanilla and ½ teaspoon (2 ml) salt and mix until they blend well. Slowly pour over bread slices. Cover and refrigerate overnight.

- When ready to bake, preheat oven to 350° (175° C).

- Uncover and bake for about 35 minutes or until golden brown. Cut into squares and lift up with square spatula so brown sugar mixture comes with each serving. Serves 4 to 6.

• • • • •

New Orleans French Toast

2 eggs, beaten	
½ cup milk	125 ml
4 pieces French bread	
Oil	
¼ cup packed brown sugar	55 g
¼ cup finely chopped pecans	30 g
2 tablespoons butter, melted	30 ml

- Preheat broiler.

- Combine eggs and milk and soak bread in mixture. Fry bread in small amount of oil.

- Combine brown sugar, pecans and butter; spread over fried bread slices and place on baking sheet. Toast under broiler until mixture bubbles. Serves 4.

• • • • •

Vanilla French Toast

5 eggs, beaten
1 (12 ounce) can evaporated milk   355 ml
1 cup sugar   200 g
1 teaspoon ground cinnamon   5 ml
1½ tablespoons vanilla   22 ml
¼ cup (½ stick) butter, melted   55 g
1 large loaf sliced French bread
Powdered sugar

- Mix eggs with milk. Add sugar, cinnamon, vanilla and butter. Dip
  bread in egg mixture and place on 350° (175° C) griddle or in skillet
  on medium-high heat. Grill until brown on both sides. To serve,
  dust with powdered sugar. Serves 6 to 8.

• • • • • •

One Big German Pancake

½ cup flour   60 g
3 eggs, slightly beaten
½ cup milk   125ml
2 tablespoons butter, melted   30 g
Powdered sugar
Additional melted butter
Maple syrup

- Preheat oven to 425° (220° C).

- Beat flour and eggs together. Stir in remaining ingredients and
  ¼ teaspoon (1 ml) salt.

- Pour into sprayed 9-inch (23 cm) pie pan. Bake for 20 minutes.
  (Pancake will puff into big bubbles while baking.)

- Cut into wedges and dust with powdered sugar. Serve with melted
  butter and maple syrup. Serves 3 to 4.

• • • • • •

Use day-old bread to make French toast. *Spice it up with
a touch of cinnamon and/or orange or lemon zest.*

Silver Dollar Pancakes

2 eggs, beaten	
2 cups buttermilk*	500 ml
¼ cup oil	60 ml
2 cups flour	240 g
2 tablespoons plus 2 teaspoons sugar	30 ml/10 ml
2 teaspoons baking powder	10 ml
1 teaspoon baking soda	5 ml
Butter	
Maple syrup	

- Combine all ingredients plus ½ teaspoon (2 ml) salt. Beat just until smooth. Drop by tablespoons onto hot griddle and cook. Serve with butter and warmed maple syrup. Serves 4 to 6.

TIP: To make buttermilk, mix 1 cup (250 ml) with 1 tablespoon (15 ml) lemon juice or vinegar and let milk stand about 10 minutes.

• • • • •

Fruity Waffles

1 (10 count) box frozen waffles, thawed	
1 cup sliced bananas	180 g
1 cup blueberries	150 g
1 cup maple syrup	250 ml

- Cut waffle into 6 wedges and arrange in star shape on individual serving plate. Toss bananas and blueberries with maple syrup and spoon ½ cup (125 ml) mixture over waffle pieces on each plate. Serves 3 to 5.

• • • • •

Crunchy Peach Waffles

1 (10 count) box frozen waffles, thawed, lightly toasted	
½ cup cottage cheese	110 g
½ cup fruit and bran cereal with peaches, raisins, almonds	30 g
1 (15 ounce) can peach slices, drained	425 g

- Top each waffle with cottage cheese, cereal and peaches. If desired, substitute favorite fruit for peaches. Serves 3 to 5.

While bottled fresh fruit juice is convenient, *frozen concentrate is a better buy.*

Orange Biscuits

1 (12 ounce) can refrigerated biscuits
Sugar cubes
Orange juice

- Separate biscuits and place on sprayed baking sheet. Press 1 sugar cube into dough and pour 1 teaspoon (5 ml) orange juice on each biscuit.

- Bake biscuits according to package directions. Serves 4.

• • • • •

Orange Butter

1 cup (2 sticks) butter, softened	230 g
2 tablespoons grated orange rind	30 ml
¼ cup orange juice	60 ml

- Beat butter and grated rind until fluffy. Gradually add orange juice and beat until it blends well. Store in refrigerator and serve with hot biscuits. Yields 1¼ cups.

• • • • •

Buttermilk Biscuits

½ cup (1 stick) butter, softened	115 g
2 cups flour	240 g
¾ cup buttermilk*	175 ml

- Preheat oven to 425° (220° C).

- Cut butter into flour with pastry blender and process until mixture resembles coarse meal. Stir in buttermilk and mix until dry ingredients are moist.

- Turn dough out onto floured surface and knead 3 or 4 times. Roll dough to ¾-inch (1.8 cm) thickness and cut with biscuit cutter. Place on lightly sprayed baking sheet and bake for 12 to 15 minutes. Brush with additional melted butter, if desired. Serves 4 to 6.

TIP: To make buttermilk, mix 1 cup (240 ml) milk with 1 tablespoon (15 ml) lemon juice or vinegar and let milk stand for about 10 minutes.

• • • • •

Monkey Bread

¾ cup sugar, divided   150 g
¼ cup (½ stick) butter, melted   55 g
2 teaspoons plus extra ground cinnamon   10 ml
1 (12 ounce) can refrigerated biscuits, quartered   340 g

- Preheat oven to 350° (175° C).

- Bring ½ cup (100 g) sugar and butter to boil for 1 minute while stirring constantly.

- Combine remaining sugar and cinnamon in plastic bag. Add biscuits and shake to coat. Arrange biscuits in sprayed, floured 8-inch (20 cm) cake pan.

- Pour liquid mixture over biscuits and sprinkle a little extra sugar and cinnamon on top. Bake for 35 minutes. Serves 4 to 6.

Mini-Sweet Rolls

¼ cup (½ stick) butter, divided   55 g
¼ cup packed brown sugar, divided   55 g
1 (8 ounce) package crescent rolls   225 g

- Preheat oven to 375° (190° C).

- Place 1 teaspoon butter and 1 teaspoon brown sugar in each of 12 sprayed miniature muffin cups.

- Roll out crescent rolls. Take 2 squares and press together at the crease. Roll tightly.

- Slice each roll into 6 slices. Lay 1 slice in each muffin cup over butter and brown sugar. Bake for 10 to 12 minutes. Yields 12 rolls.

 Make a spreadsheet for grocery prices with the item in the first column and additional columns for each grocery store you visit. Record prices of commonly purchased items, so you can really see which store is best for the basics.

Apple-Cinnamon French Bread

8 large eggs	
3½ cups milk	875 ml
1 cup sugar, divided	200 g
1 tablespoon vanilla	15 ml
1 large loaf unsliced French bread	
4 - 5 medium cooking apples, peeled, sliced	
1 tablespoon ground cinnamon	15 ml
⅓ cup (⅔ stick) butter, melted	75 ml

- Beat eggs, milk, ½ cup (100 g) sugar and vanilla for 30 seconds.

- Slice bread 1½ inches (3 cm) thick and place in sprayed 9 x 13-inch (23 x 33 cm) baking dish. Pour 1½ cups (375 ml) egg-milk mixture over bread. Place apples on top. Pour remaining mixture over apples.

- Combine remaining sugar, cinnamon and butter; sprinkle over top. Cover and refrigerate overnight.

- Bake at 350° (175° C) uncovered for 1 hour. Serves 4 to 6.

• • • • •

Cheese Strudel

1 cup (2 sticks) butter, softened	230 g
1 cup sour cream	240 g
2½ cups flour	300 g

- Mix ingredients and refrigerate dough for about 3 hours. Divide in half.

Filling:

2 (8 ounce) packages cream cheese, softened	2 (225 g)
½ cup sugar	100 g
1 teaspoon vanilla	5 ml

- When ready to bake, preheat oven to 350° (175° C).

- Beat cream filling ingredients thoroughly and divide in half.

- Take half of dough mixture and roll into rectangular shape. Spread half filling down middle. Fold over sides toward middle and place on sprayed baking sheet.

- Repeat with second half of dough and filling. Place on baking sheet and bake for 30 to 35 minutes. Slice in 1-inch (2.5 cm) serving pieces. Serves 4 to 6.

• • • • •

Brunch Casserole

1 (6 ounce) package herb croutons	170 g
1 pound bulk sausage	455 g
6 eggs, beaten	
1 medium onion, chopped	
1 (10 ounce) can cream of chicken soup	280 g
1 (10 ounce) can cream of mushroom soup	280 g
1 cup milk	250 ml
1 (8 ounce) shredded Monterey Jack cheese	225 g

- Sprinkle croutons in sprayed 9 x 13-inch (23 x 33 cm) pan.

- Brown sausage in skillet and drain fat. Crumble sausage over croutons.

- In mixing bowl, mix eggs, onion, soups, milk and a little salt and pepper. Pour over croutons and meat. Top with cheese. Cover and refrigerate overnight.

- Bake at 325° (165° C) for 45 minutes. Serves 6 to 8.

• • • • •

Breakfast Sausage Casserole

2 (8 ounce) cans refrigerated crescent rolls	2 (225 g)
1 pound bulk sausage	455 g
1 (8 ounce) package shredded cheddar cheese	225 g
6 eggs	
2 cups milk	500 ml

- Preheat oven to 350° (175° C).

- Spread dough in bottom of sprayed 9 x 13-inch (23 x 33 cm) baking pan.

- Brown and drain sausage. When cool, sprinkle sausage over dough, then sprinkle with cheese.

- Beat eggs with milk. Pour mixture over sausage and add a little salt and pepper. Bake for 35 to 40 minutes. Serves 4 to 6.

• • • • •

 Buy eggs on sale and freeze for later use by breaking into plastic ice cube trays. When the eggs are frozen, remove from the trays and put in plastic bags for use as needed.

Cheese Omelet Casserole

12 eggs	
1 cup milk	250 ml
2 drops hot sauce	
1 (8 ounce) package shredded sharp cheddar cheese	225 g
1 (8 ounce) package shredded Monterrey Jack cheese	225g

- Preheat oven to 325° (165° C).

- Beat all ingredients with ⅛ teaspoon (.5 ml) salt. Pour into unsprayed 9-inch (23 cm) baking dish. Bake for one hour or until puffy. Serves 4 to 6.

Green Chilie Squares

2 cups diced green chilies	480 g
1 (8 ounce) package shredded sharp cheddar cheese	225 g
8 eggs, beaten	
½ cup half-and-half cream	125 ml

- Preheat oven to 350° (175° C).

- Place green chilies in sprayed 9 x 13-inch (23 x 33 cm) baking pan. Cover with cheese.

- Combine eggs, half-and-half cream and a little salt and pepper. Pour over chilies and cheese. Bake for 30 minutes. Let stand at room temperature for a few minutes before cutting into squares. Serves 6 to 8.

Baked Eggs

1 pound pork sausage	455 g
10 eggs, beaten	
⅓ cup flour	40 g
¾ teaspoon baking powder	4 ml
1 (16 ounce) package shredded Monterey Jack cheese	455 g
1½ cups cottage cheese, drained	330 g
¾ cup sliced fresh mushrooms	55 g

- Preheat oven to 375° (190° C).

- Cook sausage in skillet. Drain and crumble when cool. Beat eggs, flour and baking powder. Add sausage, cheeses and mushrooms. Mix well.

- Pour into sprayed 9 x 13-inch (23 x 33 cm) baking dish. Bake for 35 to 40 minutes. Serves 4 to 6.

• • • • •

Fiesta Eggs

1 pound bulk sausage	455 g
1 (10 ounce) can diced tomatoes and green chilies	280 g
½ cup hot chunky salsa	130 g
1 (4 ounce) package cubed Velveeta® cheese	115 g
10 eggs, slightly beaten	
½ cup sour cream	120 g
⅔ cup milk	150 ml

- Preheat oven to 325° (165° C).

- Brown sausage and drain on paper towels.

- Pour tomatoes and green chilies, salsa, and cheese in skillet and cook, stirring constantly, until cheese melts. Remove from heat.

- Beat eggs in bowl with 1½ teaspoons (7 ml) salt, sour cream and milk. Fold in sausage and tomato-cheese mixture. Transfer to sprayed 7 x 11-inch (18 x 28 cm) baking dish. Bake uncovered for about 25 minutes or until center is set. Serves 4 to 6.

• • • • •

Ranch Sausage and Grits

1 cup instant grits	155 g
1 pound hot sausage	455 g
1 (8 ounce) package shredded sharp cheddar cheese, divided	225 g
½ cup hot salsa	130 g
¼ cup (½ stick) butter, melted	55 g
2 eggs, beaten	

- Preheat oven to 350° (175° C).

- Cook instant grits according to package directions.

- In skillet, brown sausage and drain. Combine cooked grits, sausage, half of cheese, salsa, melted butter and eggs and mix well. Pour into sprayed 9 x 13-inch (23 x 33 cm) baking dish.

- Bake uncovered for 50 minutes. Sprinkle remaining cheese over casserole. Bake for 10 additional minutes. Serve with hot biscuits. Serves 4 to 6.

• • • • •

An Ounce of Prevention: Slip a clear plastic bag over your cookbook (or use plastic wrap) to protect the book from splatters.

Gold Rush Casserole

1 (5 ounce) box dry hash brown potato mix	145 g
¼ cup (½ stick) butter	55 g
¼ cup flour	30 g
2 cups milk	500 ml
1 (8 ounce) carton sour cream	240 g
8 slices Canadian bacon	
8 eggs	

- Preheat oven to 300° (150° C).

- Prepare potatoes according to package directions.

- In skillet, melt butter and blend in flour and ½ teaspoon (2 ml) salt and stir constantly. Gradually stir in milk. Cook, stirring constantly until thick, and remove from heat.

- Add sour cream and hash browns; mix well. Spoon into sprayed 9 x 13-inch (23 x 33 cm) baking dish. Arrange bacon on top. Bake for 20 minutes. Make depressions with spoon and add 1 egg in each depression. Bake for 15 additional minutes or until eggs set. Serves 4 to 6.

Slow Cooker Breakfast

1 (32 ounce) package frozen hash browns	910 g
1 pound cooked cubed ham	455 g
1 onion, diced	
1 green bell pepper, seeded, diced	
1½ cups shredded cheese	270 g
12 eggs	
1 cup skim milk	250 ml

- Layer one-third of each: potatoes, ham, onion, green bell pepper, cheese in sprayed slow cooker. Repeat to make several layers.

- Beat eggs, milk, and ½ teaspoon (2 ml) each of salt and pepper; pour over layers in slow cooker. Cover and cook on LOW for 10 to 12 hours overnight. Serves 6 to 8.

Buy bell peppers on sale, seed and chop or julienne. They will freeze well for later use.

Ham and Cheese Bars

2 cups biscuit mix	240 g
1 cup cooked, finely chopped ham	140 g
1½ cups shredded cheddar cheese	170 g
¼ cup sour cream	60 g
1 teaspoon garlic powder	5 ml
1 cup milk	250 ml
1 egg	

- Preheat oven to 350° (175° C).

- Combine all ingredients and mix by hand. Spread in sprayed 9 x 13-inch (23 x 33 cm) pan. Bake for 30 minutes or until light brown. Cut in rectangles, about 2 x 1-inch (5 x 2.5 cm). Serve hot or at room temperature. Serves 4 to 6.

• • • • •

Ham Quiche Biscuit Cups

1 (8 ounce) package cream cheese, softened	225g
2 tablespoons milk	30 ml
2 eggs	
½ cup shredded Swiss cheese	55 g
2 tablespoons chopped green onion	30 ml
1 (10 count) can refrigerated flaky biscuits	
½ cup finely chopped ham	70 g

- Preheat oven to 350° (175° C).

- Beat cream cheese, milk and eggs until smooth. Stir in Swiss cheese and green onions.

- Separate dough into 10 biscuits. Place one biscuit in each of 10 sprayed muffin cups. Firmly press bottom and sides, forming ¼-inch (6 mm) rim.

- Place half of ham in muffin cups. Spoon about 2 tablespoons (30 ml) egg mixture over ham. Top with remaining ham and bake for about 25 minutes or until filling sets and edges of biscuits are golden brown. Remove from pan. Serves 4.

• • • • •

Commercial snack foods are very expensive. Use cheese sliced from a bulk block, fresh fruit, fresh veggies or air-popped popcorn for easy and healthy snacks for your family.

Sausage Quiche

1 (9 inch) frozen deep-dish piecrust shell	23 cm
1 (7 ounce) can whole green chilies, split, seeded	200 g
1 pound hot bulk sausage, cooked, crumbled	455 g
4 eggs, slightly beaten	
1 (1 pint) carton half-and-half cream	475 ml
1¼ cups shredded Swiss cheese	135 g

- Preheat oven to 350° (175° C).

- Line piecrust with split green chilies. Sprinkle sausage over chilies. Combine eggs, half-and-half cream, cheese, and ¼ teaspoon (1 ml) each of salt and pepper. Slowly pour over sausage.

- Cover edge of pastry with thin strip of foil to prevent excessive browning. Bake for 35 minutes or until center sets and is golden brown. Allow quiche to stand at room temperature for 5 minutes before slicing to serve. Serves 4 to 6.

• • • • •

Sausage-Apple Quiche

½ pound pork sausage	225 g
1½ cups chopped apple	190 g
1 teaspoon ground cinnamon	5 ml
1 cup shredded cheddar cheese	115 g
4 eggs, beaten	
1 cup half-and-half cream	250 ml
½ cup biscuit mix	60 g

- Preheat oven to 375° (190° C).

- Cook sausage until brown, stir to crumble and drain. Combine apple, cinnamon, cheese and sausage. Place in sprayed 9-inch (23 cm) quiche dish or pie pan.

- Combine eggs, half-and-half cream and biscuit mix in large bowl; mix well. Pour over apple-sausage mixture. Bake for 40 minutes or until set. Serves 4 to 6.

• • • • •

Buy bread at bakery thrift stores. *Day-old bread is better for toast and for sandwiches and there are also many other bakery products available – all of which can be frozen for later use.*

Bitsy Quiches

1 (16 ounce) container cottage cheese	455 g
½ cup ricotta cheese	125 g
3 tablespoons sour cream	45 g
½ cup biscuit mix	60 g
3 eggs, beaten	
½ cup (1 stick) butter, melted	115 g
1 (8 ounce) package shredded Swiss cheese	225 g

- Preheat oven to 350° (175° C).

- Mix all ingredients. Fill sprayed muffin cups almost full. Bake for 30 minutes. Serves 4 to 6.

• • • • •

Bacon-Onion Casserole

¼ cup (½ stick) butter, divided	55 g
2 small onions, chopped	
4 eggs	
1½ cups milk	375 ml
¾ pound bacon, fried crisp	340 g
1 (8 ounce) package shredded Swiss cheese	225 g

- Preheat oven to 325° (165° C).

- Spread 1 tablespoon (15 ml) butter evenly in 9-inch (23 cm) pie pan. Melt remaining butter in skillet. Add onions and saute until soft but not brown. Beat eggs, milk, and a little salt and pepper until they blend. Stir in onions.

- Place bacon strips in pie pan and sprinkle cheese on top. Pour in egg mixture. Bake for 25 to 30 minutes or until custard is brown and is set in center. Serves 4 to 6.

• • • • •

 Check prices on milk and dairy products at local convenience stores. Many times they are less than grocery store prices, even though that may seem counterintuitive.

Faux Cheese Souffle

Butter, softened
8 slices white bread, crusts removed
4 slices ham
4 slices American cheese
2 cups milk   500 ml
2 eggs, beaten

- Butter bread on both sides. Make 4 sandwiches with ham and cheese. Place sandwiches in sprayed 8-inch (20 cm) square baking pan.

- Beat milk and eggs with a little salt and pepper. Pour over sandwiches and soak for 1 to 2 hours.

- Bake at 375° (190° C) for 45 to 50 minutes. Serves 4.

• • • • •

Chiffon Cheese Breakfast Souffle

No one will even think about meat when you serve this.

12 slices white bread, crusts removed
2 (5 ounce) jars Old English® cheese spread   2 (145 g)
6 eggs, beaten
3 cups milk   750 ml
¾ cup (1½ sticks) butter, melted   170 g

- Cut each slice of bread into 4 triangles. Place dab of cheese on each triangle and place triangles evenly in layers in sprayed 9 x 13-inch (23 x 33 cm) baking dish.

- Combine eggs, milk, butter, and a little salt and pepper. Pour over layers, cover and refrigerate for 8 hours.

- Remove casserole from refrigerator 10 to 15 minutes before baking. Bake uncovered at 350° (175° C) for 1 hour. Serves 6.

• • • • •

Make a detailed shopping list based on the menus.
Put the staples in one place in the pantry and refrigerator so you can check your supply easily. Have paper and pen handy to take notes or keep a master checklist organizing all ingredients in categories.

Bacon-Sour Cream Omelet

2 eggs
2 strips bacon
3 green onions, chopped
⅓ cup sour cream   80 g
1 tablespoon butter   15 ml

- Beat eggs with 1 tablespoon (15 ml) water. Fry bacon and crumble when cool. Save pan drippings to saute green onions. Mix bacon, onions and sour cream.

- Melt butter in omelet pan. Pour in egg mixture and cook. When omelet sets, spoon sour cream mixture along center and fold omelet on top of bottom half onto warm plate. Serves 1.

• • • • •

Bacon Nibblers

1 (1 pound) package sliced bacon   455 g
1½ cups packed brown sugar   330 g
1½ teaspoons dry mustard   7 ml

- Preheat oven to 325° (165° C).

- Cut each slice of bacon in half. Combine remaining ingredients and ¼ teaspoon (1 ml) pepper in shallow bowl. Dip each half slice of bacon in brown sugar mixture and press down so sugar coats well on bacon. Place each slice on sprayed baking sheet with sides.

- Bake for 15 minutes, turn bacon over and cook until bacon browns. Immediately remove with tongs to several layers of paper towels. Bacon will harden and can be broken in pieces. Serves 4 to 6.

• • • • •

Maple-Bacon Bake

1 pound hickory-smoked bacon   455 g
Cracked black pepper
Maple syrup

- Preheat oven to 325° (165° C). Separate bacon, lay slices across broiler pan and brush with maple syrup. Sprinkle each slice with pepper. Bake for 45 minutes. Serves 6 to 8.

• • • • •

Low-Cost Liquids

*Serve for company – serve for family.
These delectable beverages are super
for special occasions from a
wedding to a good report card!*

Apricot-Orange Punch

1 (46 ounce) can apricot juice, chilled	1.4 L
1 (2 liter) bottle ginger ale, chilled	1.9 L
1 (½ gallon) carton orange sherbet	1.9 L

- When ready to serve, combine juice and ginger ale in punch bowl. Stir in scoops of orange sherbet. Serve in 4-ounce (125 ml) punch cups. Yields 32 to 36 punch cups.

Holiday Punch

1 (1 ounce) package cherry fruit-flavored drink mix	30 g
1 (2 liter) bottle ginger ale, chilled	
1 (46 ounce) can pineapple juice, chilled	1.4 L

- Combine all ingredients and mix well. Add more ginger ale, if needed. Serve in punch bowl. Yields 24 to 36 punch cups.

Chilly Fruit Fizz

2 cups cranberry juice, chilled	500 ml
2 cups club soda, chilled	500 ml
1 cup pink grapefruit juice, chilled	250 ml

- Combine all ingredients in pitcher and mix. Refrigerate. Serves 6.

Mock Pink Champagne

2 quarts cranberry juice, chilled	1.9 L
1 (1 quart) bottle ginger ale, chilled	1 L
1 (1 quart) bottle 7UP®, chilled	1 L

- When ready to serve, combine cranberry juice, ginger ale and 7UP® in punch bowl. (Do not prepare punch ahead of time.) Serve in 4-ounce (125 ml) punch cups. Yields 30 punch cups.

Cranberry Sherbet Punch

1 (½ gallon) carton cranberry juice, chilled	1.9 L
1 (1 quart) bottle ginger ale, chilled	1 L
1 (½ gallon) carton pineapple sherbet	1.9 L

- Combine juice and ginger ale in punch bowl. Stir in sherbet. Yields 14 to 16 punch cups.

• • • • •

Cranberry Punch

2 quarts cranberry juice, chilled   1.9 L
2 (1 quart) bottles ginger ale or 7UP®, chilled
1 (12 ounce) can frozen lemonade concentrate   355 ml

- Combine all ingredients in punch bowl. Add 2 cans ice water.
  Yields 20 to 24 punch cups.

• • • • •

Party Fruit Punch

2 quarts cranberry juice, chilled, divided   1.9 L
1 (46 ounce) can fruit punch, chilled   1.4 L
1 (46 ounce) can pineapple juice, chilled   1.4 L

- Pour half cranberry juice into ice trays and freeze as ice cubes.

- In punch bowl, combine fruit punch, pineapple juice and remaining
  cranberry juice and mix well. Refrigerate.

- When ready to serve, add cranberry juice ice cubes. Yields 32 to
  36 punch cups.

• • • • •

Cranberry Cream Drink

1 cup cranberry juice cocktail, chilled   250 ml
1 large scoop vanilla ice cream
1 (8 ounce) carton vanilla yogurt   225 g

- Combine all ingredients. Serve in sherbet glasses or punch cups.
  Serves 6.

• • • • •

Cranberry-Grape Frost

1 (48 ounce) bottle cranberry juice, chilled   1.4 L
1 (46 ounce) can grape juice, chilled   1.4 L
1 (½ gallon) carton raspberry sherbet   1.9 L

- Combine cranberry and grape juices in punch bowl. Add scoops of
  raspberry sherbet and mix well. Yields 32 to 36 punch cups.

TIP: *Add 1 (2 liter) bottle chilled ginger ale or 7UP®, if you want to add
something bubbly.*

• • • • •

Frosty Grape Punch

1 (2 quart) bottle grape juice, chilled	1.9 L
1 (½ gallon) carton raspberry sherbet	1.9 L
2 (2 liter) bottles ginger ale, chilled	

- Combine grape juice and sherbet in punch bowl. When ready to serve, add ginger ale. Yields 32 to 36 punch cups.

Purple Passion Punch

3 (1 quart) bottles grape juice, chilled	2.8 L
1 (1 quart) bottle cranberry juice, chilled	945 ml
1 (1 quart) carton raspberry sherbet	945 ml

- Combine juices in punch bowl and mix well. Stir in sherbet and serve immediately. Yields 20 to 26 punch cups.

Sunny Hawaiian Punch

1 (46 ounce) can Hawaiian Punch®, chilled	1.4 L
1 (2 liter) bottle ginger ale or 7UP®, chilled	
1 (12 ounce) can frozen lemonade concentrate	355 ml

- Combine ingredients in punch bowl. Mix in 2 cups (500 ml) cold water and serve immediately. Serves about 32 to 36 punch cups.

Lemonade

2 cups lemon juice (about 8 lemons)	500 ml
6 cups water	1.4 L
1 cup sugar	200 g

- Combine all ingredients in 2-quart (2 L) pitcher and mix until sugar dissolves. Serve over ice. Yields 8 servings.

Limeade

4 - 6 large limes	
1 cup sugar	200 g

- Rinse limes and roll on cutting board or on countertop to soften. Cut limes in half and squeeze juice.

- Combine juice, sugar and 2 quarts (1.9 L) water in pitcher and stir until sugar dissolves. Yields 6 to 8 servings.

● ● ● ● ●

Lime Punch

2 (2 liter) bottles 7UP®, chilled
1 (2 liter) bottle ginger ale, chilled
1 (½ gallon) carton lime sherbet   1.9 L

- Combine 7UP® and ginger ale. When ready to serve, add lime sherbet and stir until it mixes well. Yields 32 to 36 punch cups.

Emerald Punch

2 (1 ounce) packages lime fruit-flavored drink mix   2 (30 g)
1 (46 ounce) can pineapple juice, chilled   1.4 L
1 (2 liter) bottle ginger ale, chilled

- Prepare drink mix according to package directions. Refrigerate several hours. Pour into punch bowl and stir in pineapple juice.

- When ready to serve, add ginger ale. Yields 32 to 36 punch cups.

TIP: *Make an ice ring with additional ginger ale and add to punch bowl. If you don't have a round gelatin mold, pour ginger ale into any nicely shaped container and freeze.*

Fizzy Orange Lemonade

2 quarts orange juice, chilled   1.9 L
2 quarts lemonade, chilled   1.9 L
1 (2 liter) bottle 7UP ®, chilled

- Combine all ingredients in punch bowl. Yields 32 to 36 punch cups.

Lemon-Pineapple Drink

1 (12 ounce) can frozen lemonade concentrate, diluted   355 ml
1 (46 ounce) can unsweetened pineapple juice, chilled   1.4 L
1 (2 liter) 7UP®, chilled

- Combine all ingredients in punch bowl and mix well. Yields about 22 punch cups.

TIP: *If you have time, add ice ring to punch bowl by freezing 7UP® in gelatin mold.*

• • • • •

You might try diluting apple juice with water (equal amounts of juice and water) to make it go further and also cut down on the sugar. Juice can ruin a baby's teeth.

Happy Orange Slush

1 (6 ounce) can frozen orange juice concentrate	175 ml
1 teaspoon vanilla	5 ml
¼ cup sugar	50 g
½ cup dry non-fat milk powder	35 g

• Combine all ingredients in blender with 12 ice cubes and 1¾ cups (425 ml) water and process. Serves 4.

Orange-Strawberry Drink

2 cups orange juice, chilled	500 ml
1½ cups apricot nectar, chilled	375 ml
1 cup frozen sweetened strawberries, thawed	255 g

• Combine all ingredients in blender and mix well. Serves 2.

TIP: Blend with ice cubes for an "icy" drink.

Frosty Orange-Pineapple Punch

2 (46 ounce) cans pineapple juice, chilled	2 (1.4 L)
1 (½ gallon) carton orange sherbet	1.9 L
1 (2 liter) bottle ginger ale, chilled	

• Pour juice in punch bowl and stir in sherbet. Add ginger ale and serve immediately. Yields 32 to 36 punch cups.

Orange-Grapefruit Cooler

1 (46 ounce) can orange juice, chilled	1.4 L
1 (46 ounce) can grapefruit juice, chilled	1.4 L
1 (2 liter) bottle ginger ale, chilled	

• Combine and mix juices in punch bowl. Add ginger ale when ready to serve. Yields 32 to 36 punch cups.

Five-Alive Punch

2 (12 ounce) cans frozen Five-Alive® juice concentrate	2 (355 ml)
1 (12 ounce) can frozen pink lemonade concentrate	355 ml
1 (2 liter) bottle ginger ale, chilled	

• Dilute frozen concentrates according to can directions and mix in punch bowl. When ready to serve, add ginger ale. Yields 32 to 36 punch cups.

• • • • •

Peach Nectar Punch

1 (46 ounce) can apricot nectar, chilled   1.4 L
1 (2 liter) bottle peach soda, chilled
1 (½ gallon) carton peach ice cream   1.9 L

- When ready to serve, combine apricot nectar and peach soda in punch bowl. Stir in peach ice cream. Yields 32 to 36 punch cups.

Pineapple Punch

4 (1 quart) bottles ginger ale, chilled   4 (1 L)
1 (½ gallon) carton pineapple sherbet   1.9 L
1 (15 ounce) can pineapple tidbits, chilled   425 g

- Combine ginger ale, pineapple sherbet and pineapple tidbits and mix. Serve in punch bowl. Yields 28 (4-ounce/125 ml) punch cups.

Pina Colada Punch

1 (2 quart) can pineapple-coconut juice, chilled   1.9 L
2 (1 liter) bottles 7UP®, chilled
1 (20 ounce) can pineapple rings with juice   565 g

- Combine pineapple-coconut juice, 7UP® and juice from pineapple rings in punch bowl. Float pineapple rings in punch bowl. Yields 24 punch cups.

Slushy Pineapple Punch

1 (46 ounce) can pineapple juice   1.4 L
1 (46 ounce) can apple juice   1.4 L
2 (28 ounce) bottles 7UP®, chilled   2 (830 ml)

- Freeze pineapple juice and apple juice in cans. Set out juices 1 hour before serving. When ready to serve, combine all ingredients in punch bowl. Yields 32 to 36 punch cups.

Christmas Punch

1 (46 ounce) can pineapple juice, chilled   1.4 L
1 (1 liter) bottle ginger ale, chilled
1 (2 liter) bottle strawberry soda, chilled

- Combine all ingredients in punch bowl. Use extra ginger ale or 7UP®, if desired. Yields 20 punch cups.

• • • • •

Spritely Punch

2 (2 liter) bottles Sprite®, chilled
1 (½ gallon) carton pineapple juice, chilled   1.9 L
1 (1 gallon) carton orange sherbet   3.8 L

- Combine Sprite® and juice in punch bowl. Spoon in sherbet and mix
  well. Yields 32 punch cups.

• • • • •

Pink Grapefruit Punch

1 (46 ounce) can pink grapefruit juice, chilled   1.4 L
1 (46 ounce) can pineapple juice, chilled   1.4 L
1 (1 liter) bottle 7UP®, chilled

- Mix juices and 7UP® in punch bowl. Serve immediately.
  Yields 32 to 36 punch cups.

• • • • •

Strawberry Cooler

1 (6 ounce) can frozen limeade concentrate   175 ml
1 (10 ounce) package frozen strawberries, thawed   280 g
1 (2 liter) bottle strawberry soda, chilled

- Prepare limeade according to directions on can and refrigerate.
  Blend berries in blender until smooth.

- Combine limeade and berries in punch bowl. When ready to serve,
  stir in strawberry soda. Yields 24 to 28 punch cups.

• • • • •

Strawberry Cream

1 (½ gallon) carton strawberry ice cream, softened   1.9 L
2 (2 liter) bottles ginger ale or 7UP®, chilled
1 (10 ounce) package frozen strawberries, thawed   280 g

- Combine all ingredients in punch bowl and stir well. Serve
  immediately. Yields 26 punch cups.

If you can't cut down on sodas, try the store brands.
They are significantly less expensive.

Strawberry Spritzer

3 (10 ounce) packages frozen strawberries, thawed, divided   3 (280 g)
2 (24 ounce) bottles white grape juice, chilled, divided   2 (750 ml)
1 (28 ounce) bottle club soda, chilled   830 ml

- Place 1 package strawberries with 2 cups (500 ml) juice in blender. Cover and blend until smooth. Repeat for remaining 2 packages of strawberries.

- When ready to serve, stir in club soda. Yields 32 to 36 punch cups.

• • • • •

Strawberry Lemonade

2 (10 ounce) packages frozen strawberries   2 (280 g)
1 (12 ounce) can frozen pink lemonade concentrate, chilled   355 ml
1 (2 liter) bottle 7UP® or ginger ale, chilled

- Thaw berries until slushy and mix in blender. Mix lemonade according to can directions and pour into punch bowl; stir in berries. Add 7UP® or ginger ale and stir until they blend well. Serve immediately. Yields 32 to 36 punch cups.

TIP: If this punch is too tart, add sugar.

• • • • •

Agua de Sandia

4 cups cubed watermelon   615 g
1 cup sugar   200 g

- Place watermelon in blender and process at high speed until smooth. Pour into 2-quart (2 L) container and add enough cold water to make 2 quarts (2 L).

- Add sugar and stir until it dissolves. Yields 24 to 28 punch cups.

TIP: You can play with this a little by substituting 4 cups (620) fresh cubed pineapple, juice of 4 oranges or 4 cups (885 g) frozen strawberries for watermelon.

Keep a big pitcher of water in the refrigerator. *The whole family will be more likely to drink more water if it's icy cold and ready to drink. Also, most tap water has added fluoride which helps prevent tooth decay. Did you know that a lot of bottled water actually comes from our municipal water supplies?*

Shirley Temple

¼ cup grenadine syrup	60 ml
4 cups ginger ale, chilled	1 L
4 maraschino cherries	

- Put 1 tablespoon (15 ml) grenadine syrup in each of 4 glasses. Add ginger ale and stir. Garnish with maraschino cherry. Serves 4.

• • • • •

Winter Punch

1 (46 ounce) can cocktail vegetable juice, chilled	1.4 L
1 tablespoon lemon juice	15 ml
½ teaspoon dried dill weed	2 ml

- Combine all ingredients and mix well. Refrigerate until ready to serve. Serves 8 to 12.

TIP: *Place long celery stick in each glass for stirring. Several drops of hot sauce may also be added.*

• • • • •

Cider Tea

2 (family size) orange-pekoe tea bags	
3 cups apple cider	750 ml

- Pour 3 cups (750 ml) boiling water over tea bags, cover and steep for 8 minutes. Discard tea bags.

- Stir in cider and mix well. Serves 6.

• • • • •

English Tea Punch

1 (12 ounce) can frozen orange juice concentrate, thawed	355 ml
1 (½ gallon) container prepared lemon tea, chilled	1.9 L
1 (46 ounce) can pineapple juice, chilled	1.4 L

- Dilute orange juice with water according to can directions. Combine all ingredients in punch bowl and stir. Yields 32 to 36 punch cups.

• • • • •

Pineapple Tea

1 (46 ounce) can pineapple juice	1.4 L
2 (1 ounce) packages sweetened lemon-lime flavored drink mix	
1 tablespoon instant tea	15 ml

- Place all ingredients in 1-gallon (4 L) jar and fill with water. Stir and refrigerate overnight. Add more tea to taste if necessary. Serves 8.

• • • • •

Refrigerator Iced Tea

8 (regular-size) tea bags
8 lemon slices

- Rather than boiling water on hot, humid days, just add tea bags to 2 quarts (2 L) cold water. Refrigerate for 3 to 4 hours. Remove tea bags and serve over ice with lemon slices. Serves 6 to 8.

• • • • •

Sun Tea

8 (regular-size) tea bags
10 lemon slices or mint springs

- Put tea bags in 1-gallon (4 L) jar and fill with cold water. Set jar in sunshine for 3 to 4 hours. Serve over ice with lemon slice or sprig of mint. Serves 6.

• • • • •

Hot Apple Cider

2 quarts prepared apple cider	2 L
½ cup cinnamon Red Hots® candies	115 g
1 apple, sliced	

- Pour apple cider into large pan. Stir in red hot candies. Simmer until candy dissolves. Serve hot in mugs and garnish with half apple slice. Serves 6 to 8.

Smaller bottles or cans of soda are always more expensive than the larger bottles. A 20-ounce bottle of soda is the best buy, but the best way to save money on sodas is to drink water.

Mocha Punch

1 quart coffee, chilled	1 L
1 quart chocolate milk, chilled	1 L
1 (1 quart) carton vanilla or chocolate ice cream	1 L

- Mix coffee and milk until they blend well. Just before serving, stir in ice cream and mix until creamy. Serves 8.

• • • • •

Chocolate Eggnog

1 - 2 (1 quart) cartons eggnog, chilled	1 - 2 (1 L)
¼ cup chocolate sauce	60 ml
Ground nutmeg	

- Combine eggnog and chocolate sauce, sprinkle with nutmeg and serve cold. Yields 8 to 12 punch cups.

TIP: Add more chocolate sauce, if desired.

• • • • •

Cocoa Mix

3 cups dry non-fat milk powder	210 g
1 cup sugar	200 g
⅓ cup cocoa	40 g

- Combine all ingredients and mix well. Use 6 level tablespoons (90 ml) to 1 cup (250 ml) hot water for 1 cup (250 ml) hot chocolate. Yields 4 cups mix.

• • • • •

Fruit Smoothies

2 - 3 bananas	
1 (15 ounce) can peaches, drained	425 g
1 cup orange juice	250 ml
1 (16 ounce) box frozen strawberries, thawed	455 g
2 tablespoons sugar	30 ml
Frozen vanilla yogurt	

- Place bananas, peaches and orange juice in blender and process until smooth. Add strawberries and sugar and continue to blend. Place scoop of frozen yogurt in each glass and pour smoothie mixture over it. Serves 2 to 4.

TIP: Ripe, overly ripe and frozen bananas work great.

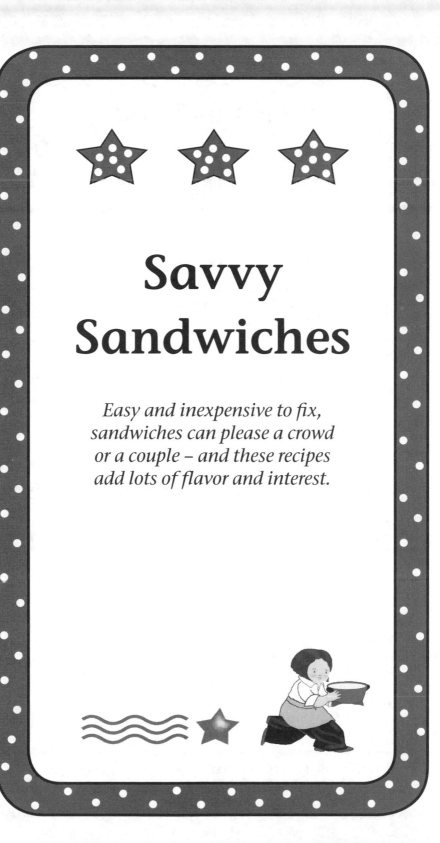

Savvy Sandwiches

*Easy and inexpensive to fix,
sandwiches can please a crowd
or a couple – and these recipes
add lots of flavor and interest.*

Pimento Cheese

1 (12 ounce) package shredded Velveeta® cheese	340 g
1 (2 ounce) jar diced pimentos, drained	55 g
⅓ - ½ cup mayonnaise	75 - 110 g

- Combine all ingredients and mix thoroughly. Refrigerate.
  Yields 1 pint.

• • • • •

Ribbon Sandwiches

8 slices sandwich bread, crusts removed*	
1 (5 ounce) jar Old English® cheese spread	145 g
½ cup (1 stick) butter, softened	115 g

- Beat cheese spread and butter until smooth.   Spread mixture on
  4 slices bread and top with 4 more slices.

- Cut each sandwich into 3 or 4 strips, wrap tightly with plastic wrap
  and refrigerate before serving. Serves 4.

*TIP: This makes a two-tone ribbon look if you use 1 slice of white bread
        and 1 slice of wheat bread for each sandwich.

• • • • •

Pinwheel Spread for Sandwiches

1 (3 ounce) package cream cheese, softened	85 g
½ cup crushed pineapple, well drained	125 g
¼ cup finely chopped pecans	30 g
White bread, crusts removed	
Butter, softened	

- Beat cream cheese until light and fluffy. Stir in pineapple and
  pecans; mix well.

- Roll each slice of bread with rolling pin to flatten. Spread each
  slice with a little softened butter and cream cheese mixture.
  Roll tightly and place in pan. Cover pan in plastic wrap and
  refrigerate for several hours or overnight. When ready to serve,
  cut rolls into ¾-inch (1.8 cm) slices and place on serving trays.
  Yields 1 cup (250 ml) spread.

 Day-old bread is the best bread for sandwiches. *Not
only can you take advantage of bakery thrift stores, bread
freezes well, too.*

Cherry-Cheese Sandwich Spread

1 (8 ounce) jar maraschino cherries	225 g
1 (8 ounce) package cream cheese, softened	225 g
½ cup finely chopped pecans	55 g
White bread	

- Drain cherries and dice very fine.

- Beat cream cheese until creamy and combine with chopped cherries and pecans. Mix until they blend well.

- Trim crusts from several slices white bread.

- Use filling for open-face sandwiches or make into 3-layered ribbon sandwiches. Yields 2 cups.

• • • • •

Black Olive Spread

1 (3 ounce) package cream cheese, softened	85 g
1 (2 ounce) can chopped black olives, drained	55g
1 (8 ounce) package shredded cheddar cheese	225 g
Party rye or pumpernickel bread	

- Beat cream cheese until smooth and stir in olives and cheddar cheese.

- Spread on slices of party rye or pumpernickel bread.

- Serve cold or broil and serve hot. Yields 1 cup.

• • • • •

 One of the best money-saving tips is to brown-bag-it at lunch. If you take your lunch to work, not only are you saving money, but you're probably getting better nutrition.

Cucumber Tea Sandwich Spread

1 (8 ounce) package cream cheese, softened   225 g
2 cucumbers, peeled, seeded, grated
¾ teaspoon seasoned salt   4 ml
White bread, crusts removed

- Beat cream cheese until smooth.

- Drain grated cucumbers well, squeezing with paper towels to remove excess moisture.

- Combine cream cheese, grated cucumbers and seasoned salt and mix well. Spread on bread and cut sandwiches into triangles or bars. Yields 1½ cups spread.

• • • • •

Olive-Egg Salad Spread for Sandwiches

6 eggs, hard-boiled
12 stuffed green olives, finely chopped
¼ cup mayonnaise   55 g
Whole wheat bread

- Rinse hard-boiled eggs in cool water, peel shells and chop eggs. Combine eggs, olives and mayonnaise. (If desired, add more mayonnaise.) Refrigerate until ready to use. Spread on bread and cut in half for sandwiches. Yields 1½ cups spread.

TIP: This spread is also good with ½ cup (55 g) chopped pecans.

• • • • •

Beef Spread for Sandwiches

1 (5 ounce) jar dried beef, chopped   145 g
1 (8 ounce) carton sour cream   225 g
¾ cup shredded Swiss or cheddar cheese   85 g
White bread, crusts removed

- Combine all ingredients and mix well. Cover and refrigerate.

- Spread on bread and cut into finger sandwiches. Yields 2 cups spread.

Freeze individual slices of sandwich meat with wax paper between slices so they are easy to remove.

Sloppy Joes

½ pound lean ground beef	225 g
1 (15 ounce) can stewed tomatoes	425 g
¼ cup ketchup	70 g
¼ teaspoon dried oregano	1 ml
5 hamburger buns	

- Brown ground beef and drain. Add tomatoes, ketchup and oregano and cook uncovered 20 minutes. Spoon onto hamburger buns. Serves 4 to 5.

• • • • •

Barbecue Beef Sandwiches

1 pound ground beef or ground sirloin	455 g
½ cup packed brown sugar	110 g
1 (16 ounce) bottle barbecue sauce	455 g
Hamburger buns	

- Brown, crumble and drain meat. Stir in brown sugar and barbecue sauce.

- Cover and simmer for 15 minutes; stir often. Spoon onto warm hamburger buns. Serves 6.

• • • • •

Zesty Roast Beef Party Sandwiches

1 (4 pound) chuck roast	1.8 kg
Worcestershire sauce	
Mustard	
Dinner rolls	

- Preheat oven to 325° (165° C).

- Rub roast with Worcestershire sauce and mustard.

- Brown roast, then add ½ cup water to keep it from burning. Bake for 3 hours to 3 hours 30 minutes. Occasionally baste with drippings and more Worcestershire sauce.

- Let roast rest 15 minutes before slicing. Slice very thin and serve on rolls. Serves 8.

TIP: Check the meat aisle for meats that are marked down for quick sale.

• • • • •

Chili-Cheese Dogs

1 (8 ounce) package shredded cheddar cheese	225 g
¼ cup chili sauce	70 g
¼ cup pickle relish	60 g
8 franks	
8 hot dog buns	

- Preheat oven to 400° (205°C).

- Combine cheese, chili sauce and relish and mix well. Split franks lengthwise and fill with mixture. Place franks in buns. Place on individual foil rectangles and seal. Heat for 15 minutes. Serves 6 to 8.

Chicken-Almond Spread

2 cups cooked finely shredded chicken	280 g
½ cup finely chopped almonds, toasted	60 g
½ cup finely diced celery	50 g
¼ cup mayonnaise	
Thinly sliced bread	

- Combine chicken, almonds, celery and mayonnaise. If desired, add more mayonnaise.

- For sandwiches, spread chicken mixture on thinly sliced bread. Serves 6.

Chicken Salad

1 (12 ounce) can chicken breast meat, drained	340 g
⅓ cup mayonnaise	75 g
1 tablespoon dijon-style mustard	15 ml
1 rib celery, finely chopped	
3 tablespoons minced green onions	45 ml
Shredded lettuce	

- In medium bowl, combine chicken, mayonnaise, mustard, celery, green onions and a little salt and pepper. Serve chicken salad over shredded lettuce. Serves 4 to 6.

TIP: You can also serve in hallowed out tomatoes or on sandwiches.

Don't waste leftovers. *Cream cheese, softened and mixed with nuts and/or chopped meat, is a quick and easy spread. Tuna, chicken, turkey, ham, roast beef or hard-boiled eggs also make delicious spreads. Use minced onions, relish or chopped pickles and chopped celery and moisten with salad dressing or mayonnaise.*

Turkey Surprise Sandwich

Mayonnaise
1 (24 ounce) loaf oatnut bread or whole wheat bread	680 g
1 pound thinly shaved smoked turkey slices	455 g
1 (8 ounce) package provolone cheese slices	225 g
2 - 3 avocados, sliced	
2 green apples	

- To make 6 sandwiches, spread very slight amount of mayonnaise on 6 slices of bread. Place several pieces of turkey on each slice and layer provolone cheese and several slices avocado with dash of salt.

- Now for the surprise! Peel and core apples and with your very best knife, cut very, very thin slices of apple and place over avocado. Spread mayonnaise on 6 more slices bread to top each sandwich. Serves 6.

• • • • •

Turkey Croissants

1 (8 ounce) package cream cheese, softened	225 g
¼ cup orange marmalade	80 g
6 large croissants, split	
1 pound thinly sliced deli turkey	455 g

- Beat cream cheese and orange marmalade in mixing bowl with mixer. Spread mixture evenly on cut sides of croissants and add turkey slices. Place top on croissant. Serves 4.

• • • • •

Turkey Burgers

2 pounds ground turkey	910 g
1 (16 ounce) jar hot chipotle salsa, divided	455 g
8 slices Monterey Jack cheese	
Hamburger buns	

- Preheat broiler.

- In large mixing bowl, combine ground turkey with half salsa. Mix well and shape into 8 patties. Place patties on broiler pan and broil for 12 to 15 minutes. Turn once during cooking.

- Top each patty with cheese slice and broil just long enough to melt cheese. Place patties on bottom buns, spoon heaping tablespoon (15 ml) salsa over cheese and top with other half of bun. Serves 6 to 8.

• • • • •

A Different Sandwich

1 (9 inch) round loaf focaccia bread	23 cm
3 ounces deli ham slices	85 g
6 slices Swiss cheese	
⅓ cup bottled roasted red bell peppers, drained*	85 g
1 (6 ounce) package baby spinach	170 g
3 tablespoons Italian or romano-basil vinaigrette	45 ml

- Preheat oven to 350° (175° C).

- Slice bread horizontally. Place layer ham and cheese on bread and top with red bell peppers and heavy layer of spinach. Top with remaining bread.

- Drizzle with vinaigrette and wrap in foil. Bake for 16 minutes. Cut into six wedges and serve immediately. Serves 2 to 4.

TIP: *Roast your own red bell peppers by holding peppers over an open flame with long metal fork or broil in the oven and turn often, until the outside skin blisters and turns dark brown on all sides. (Be careful not to burn holes through skin.) Place peppers in plastic bag, seal and allow to sweat for about 15 minutes. Skin will slide off easily.*

• • • • •

Ham Sandwiches

½ cup (1 stick) butter, softened, divided	115 g
8 onion dinner rolls, split	
1 small onion, chopped	
1 teaspoon dry mustard	5 ml
1 pound shaved ham	455 g
8 ounces sliced Swiss cheese	225 g

- Preheat oven to 350° (175° C).

- Set aside 1 tablespoon (15 ml) butter. Spread remaining butter on cut sides of rolls. Saute onion in set aside butter in skillet until translucent, about 5 minutes. Add dry mustard and mix well.

- Layer ham, cheese slice and some of onion mixture on bottom half of each roll. Replace roll tops and wrap in foil. Place on baking sheet and bake for 20 minutes. Serves 8.

Leftover meats make great sandwiches and you can use those homemade dressings on them too. Sandwiches are good not only for brown-bagging it, but for quick suppers and hearty snacks.

Hot Bunwiches

8 hamburger buns
8 slices Swiss cheese
8 slices ham
8 slices turkey
8 slices American cheese

- Lay out all 8 buns. On each bottom bun, place slice of Swiss cheese, ham, turkey and American cheese. Place top bun over American cheese. Wrap each bunwich individually in foil and place in freezer.

- Take out of freezer 2 to 3 hours before serving.

- Leave bunwiches in foil and bake at 325° (165 ° C) for 30 minutes. Serve hot. Serves 6 to 8.

Hot Cornbread Sandwich

2 (8 ounce) packages corn muffin mix	**2 (225 g)**
2 eggs, beaten	
⅔ cup milk	**150 ml**
12 slices American cheese	
6 slices deli ham	

- Preheat oven to 400° (205° C).

- In bowl, combine muffin mix, eggs and milk and mix well. Pour half of mixture into sprayed 7 x 11-inch (18 x 28 cm) baking dish.

- Carefully place 6 slices cheese, then ham slices and remaining cheese slices on top of ham. Spoon remaining cornbread batter over top of cheese. Bake for 25 minutes or until cornbread is golden brown. Cut into squares and serve hot. Serves 4 to 6.

Deviled Ham Spread

1 (4.5 ounce) can deviled ham	**130 g**
⅓ cup sour cream	**80 g**
⅓ cup shredded cheddar cheese	**40 g**
White bread	
Butter, softened	

- Preheat oven to 400° (205° C).

- Combine deviled ham, sour cream and cheese; mix well. Remove crusts from 4 slices white bread and butter lightly.

- Spread ham mixture on bread. Cut each slice into 4 squares. Bake sandwich squares for 5 minutes or until hot and bubbly. Serve as open-face sandwiches. Serves 2 to 4.

Broiler Sandwiches

5 slices bacon, cooked, crumbled	
2 eggs, hard-boiled, chopped	
1 (8 ounce) package shredded Velveeta® cheese	225 g
½ cup chopped onion	80 g
1 cup chili sauce	270 g
8 sandwich buns, split	

- Preheat broiler.

- Combine bacon, eggs, cheese, onion and chili sauce. Spread mixture on bun halves. Toast under broiler until brown. Serves 8.

Grilled Bacon and Banana Sandwiches

Peanut butter
4 English muffins, halved
2 bananas
8 slices bacon, cooked crisp
Butter, softened

- Spread layer of peanut butter over 8 muffin halves. Slice bananas and arrange on top of 4 halves. Place 2 strips of bacon on each of the 4 muffin halves. Top with remaining muffin halves.

- Spread top with butter. Brown sandwiches, buttered side down. Spread butter on other side, turn and cook other side until golden brown. Serve hot. Serves 4 to 6.

Mock Millionaire Sandwiches

¾ pound bacon, cooked, crumbled	340 g
1 (4 ounce) can chopped ripe olives, drained	115 g
½ cup chopped pecans	55 g
1½ cups mayonnaise	335 g
White or whole wheat bread, crusts removed	

- In bowl, combine bacon, olives, pecans and mayonnaise; blend well. Spread on white or whole wheat bread. Cut sandwiches into 3 strips. Serves 4.

 Buy large bags of chips or smaller ones on sale instead of boxes of the individual serving sizes. You can quickly put some chips into a baggie and save a lot more money than buying the individual packages.

Salami-on-Rye Sandwiches

24 salami slices
48 slices party rye bread
1 (8 ounce) jar dijon-style mustard 225 g

- Place 1 slice of salami folded in half or quartered to fit on rye bread. Spread with mustard and top with second slice of party rye for quick party sandwiches. Yields 24 sandwiches.

• • • • •

Bratwurst Heroes

1 (6 - 8 count) package bratwurst sausages
Hot dog buns
1 (8 ounce) carton marinara sauce 225 g
1 (8 ounce) jar roasted bell peppers 225 g
6 - 8 slices pepper-Jack cheese

- Heat bratwurst on grill until hot and turn frequently. When brats are just about done, toast buns cut-side down on grill. In saucepan, heat marinara sauce. Place brats on toasted buns and layer bell peppers, marinara sauce and cheese over bratwurst. Serves 6 to 8.

• • • • •

Meatball Subs

1 (18 ounce) package frozen cooked meatballs, thawed
    or homemade meatballs 510 g
1 (28 ounce) jar chunky spaghetti sauce 795 g
6 submarine or hoagie buns
1 (12 ounce) package shredded mozzarella cheese 340 g

- Preheat oven to 450° (230° C).

- In saucepan, combine meatballs and spaghetti sauce and heat until hot. Shave thin layer off top of each roll.

- With fork, remove some of soft interior of bun to make a "trough". Place rolls on large baking pan and spoon about 3 heaping tablespoons (45 ml) cheese in bottom of roll.

- Bake about 5 minutes or until buns are light brown and cheese melts. Spoon about ¼ cup (60 ml) spaghetti sauce and 2 to 3 meatballs in each bun. Top subs with little more sauce and generous topping of cheese. Serve hot. Serves 4 to 6.

• • • • •

Meatball Hoagies

1 small onion, diced	
1 small green bell pepper, diced	
Vegetable oil	
1 (15 ounce) can sloppy Joe sauce	425 g
1 (18 ounce) package frozen cooked meatballs, thawed	510 g
4 hoagie buns	

- Saute onion and pepper in a little oil. Add sauce and meatballs, cook 10 minutes or until thoroughly hot and stir often. Spoon evenly onto hoagie buns. Serves 4.

Philly Meatball Sandwiches

1 tablespoon oil	15 ml
1 cup chopped onions	160 g
1 cup chopped bell peppers	150 g
½ (18 ounce) package frozen cooked meatballs	½ (510 g)
6 hoagie rolls, toasted	
1 (8 ounce) package shredded cheddar cheese	225 g

- In skillet with oil on medium heat, cook and stir onions and bell peppers for 5 minutes. Add meatballs, cover and cook, stirring occasionally, for about 12 minutes or until meatballs are thoroughly hot.

- Spoon mixture into toasted rolls and sprinkle cheese over meatballs. Serve hot. Serves 4 to 6.

TIP: *Depending on the time of the year, it may be less expensive to substitute a package of frozen chopped bell peppers and onions.*

Baked Crab Sandwiches

Butter	
12 slices thin bread, crusts removed	
16 ounces imitation crabmeat, flaked	455 g
1 (8 ounce) package shredded cheddar cheese	225 g
4 eggs, beaten	
3 cups milk	750 ml
½ teaspoon curry powder	2 ml

- Butter 6 slices bread and place butter-side down in sprayed 9 x 13-inch (23 x 33 cm) baking dish. Spread crabmeat over bread and top with remaining 6 slices, butter-side up. Sprinkle with cheese. Mix eggs, milk and curry powder and pour carefully over bread. Cover and refrigerate for 4 hours.

- When ready to bake, preheat oven to 325° (165° C). Bake for 45 minutes. Serves 6.

Basic Breads

Bread is an attractive accompaniment to a meal. It makes the meal complete and fills up hungry appetites.

Twist Sticks

½ cup sour cream	120 g
½ (1 ounce) packet savory herb with garlic soup mix	½ (30 g)
1 (8 ounce) package refrigerated crescent rolls	225 g

- Preheat oven to 375° (190° C).

- Combine sour cream and soup mix. Spread out crescent rolls into 1 long piece of dough and press seams together. Spread mixture evenly onto dough. Cut dough into 1-inch (2.5 cm) strips and twist each strip loosely. Bake for 12 to 15 minutes. Serves 6 to 8.

• • • • •

Poppy Seed Breadsticks

1½ cups shredded Monterey Jack cheese	170 g
¼ cup poppy seeds	35 g
2 tablespoons dry onion soup mix	30 ml
2 (11 ounce) cans refrigerated breadstick dough	2 (310 g)

- Preheat oven to 375° (190° C).

- In large shallow bowl, combine cheese, poppy seeds and soup mix.

- Separate breadstick dough and stretch slightly until each stick is about 12 inches (30 cm) long. Cut dough in pieces 3 to 4 inches (8 to 10 cm) long. Dip strips in cheese mixture and turn to coat all sides. Place on sprayed baking pan and bake about 12 minutes or until breadsticks brown. Serves 6 to 8.

• • • • •

Cheese Bread

1 (16 ounce) package shredded sharp cheddar cheese	455 g
1 cup mayonnaise	225 g
1 (1 ounce) packet ranch dressing mix	30 g
10 (1 inch) slices French bread	10 (2.5 cm)

- Preheat oven to 350° (175°).

- Combine cheese, mayonnaise and dressing mix. Spread on bread slices and heat in oven until brown. Serves 6 to 8.

• • • • •

Chile Bread

1 loaf unsliced Italian bread	
½ cup (1 stick) butter, melted	115 g
1 (4 ounce) can diced green chilies, drained	115 g
¾ cup shredded Monterey Jack cheese	85 g

- Preheat oven to 350° (175° C).

- Slice bread almost through. Combine melted butter, chilies and cheese. Spread between bread slices. Wrap loaf with foil. Bake for 15 minutes. Serves 4 to 6.

• • • • •

Crispy Herb Bread

1½ teaspoons basil	7 ml
1 teaspoon rosemary	5 ml
½ teaspoon thyme	2 ml
1 cup (2 sticks) butter, melted	230 g
1 package hot dog buns	

- Combine all ingredients except buns and let stand several hours at room temperature.

- When ready to bake, preheat oven to 300° (150° C).

- Spread on buns and cut into strips. Bake for 15 to 20 minutes. Serves 6 to 8.

• • • • •

Easy Garlic Bread

1 (16 ounce) loaf French bread	455 g
½ cup (1 stick) butter, softened	115 g
Garlic salt or garlic powder	

- Preheat oven to 425° (220° C).

- Cut bread diagonally into 1-inch (2.5 cm) slices. Spread butter on slices and sprinkle with garlic salt or garlic powder.

- Place slices on baking sheet and bake, turning once, until golden brown on both sides. Serves 8.

• • • • •

Garlic Toast

1 tablespoon garlic powder	15 ml
2 tablespoons dried parsley flakes	30 ml
½ cup (1 stick) butter, melted	115 g
1 cup grated parmesan cheese	100 g
1 (16 ounce) loaf sliced French bread	455 g

- Preheat oven to 225° (110° C).

- Combine garlic powder, parsley, parmesan, butter and cheese and spread on bread slices. Place on cookie sheet and bake for 1 hour. Serves 6 to 8.

• • • • •

Hot Cheesy Bread Slices

1 (8 ounce) package shredded cheddar cheese	225 g
1 cup mayonnaise	225 g
1 (16 ounce) loaf French bread, cut in ½-inch slices	455 g (1.2 cm)

- Preheat oven to 350° (175° C).

- Combine cheese and mayonnaise and mix well. Spread on bread slices. Place on baking sheet and bake for 8 to 10 minutes. Serves 6.

• • • • •

Mozzarella Loaf

1 (16 ounce) loaf French bread	455 g
12 slices mozzarella cheese	
¼ cup grated parmesan cheese	25 g
6 tablespoons (¾ stick) butter, softened	85 g
½ teaspoon garlic salt	2 ml

- Preheat oven to 375° (190° C).

- Cut loaf into 12 thick slices. Place slices of mozzarella cheese between bread slices.

- Combine parmesan cheese, butter and garlic salt. Spread on each side of bread.

- Reshape loaf and press slices firmly together. Brush remaining butter mixture on outside of loaf and wrap in foil. Bake for 8 to 10 minutes. Serves 4 to 6.

• • • • •

Hot Parmesan Bread

½ cup Caesar dressing	125 ml
⅓ cup grated parmesan cheese	35 g
1 (16 ounce) unsliced loaf Italian bread	455 g

- Preheat broiler.

- In small bowl, combine dressing and cheese. Spread 1 teaspoon (5 ml) dressing-cheese mixture on each bread slice. Place bread on baking sheet and broil until golden brown. Serves 4 to 6.

• • • • •

Italian Toast

2 large firm, ripe tomatoes, chopped, drained	
1 cup loosely packed, chopped fresh basil	40 g
¼ cup olive oil	60 ml
1 (16 ounce) loaf Italian bread	455 g

- Mix tomatoes, basil and olive oil in medium bowl. Let stand at room temperature. Add a little salt and pepper.

- Slice bread, arrange on baking sheet and toast under broiler, turning once, until golden brown on both sides. Top hot toast with tomato mixture. Serves 4 to 6.

• • • • •

Pizza Bread

1 pound frozen pizza crust dough	455 g
2 teaspoons olive oil	10 ml
1 tablespoon thyme	15 ml
¾ teaspoon sea salt	4 ml

- Preheat oven to 450° (230° C).

- Press dough onto sprayed cookie sheet. Pierce dough all over with fork. Drizzle oil over dough. Sprinkle with thyme and salt. Bake until golden brown, about 10 minutes. Cut in wedges. Serves 4 to 6.

• • • • •

Guard against impulse-buying. By planning ahead and shopping with a list, you will save money. And, always eat before you shop. When you are hungry, you can easily add an extra $20 or $30 to your bill.

Italian Butter Fingers

2 cups buttermilk biscuit mix	240 g
1 egg	
⅓ cup milk	75 ml
½ cup (1 stick) butter	115 g
2 tablespoons dried parsley flakes	30 ml
1½ teaspoons Italian herb seasoning	7 ml
⅓ cup grated parmesan cheese	35 g

- Preheat oven to 375° (190° C).

- Combine baking mix, egg and just enough milk to make thick dough. Turn dough out onto lightly floured surface and knead lightly. Pat into rectangular shape about 9 x 13 inches (23 x 33 cm).

- Add butter to 10 x 15-inch (25 x 38 cm) pan and melt in hot oven.

- Cut dough into 12 or 14 strips with sharp knife or pizza cutter. Cut each strip in half and place evenly on top of melted butter in pan. Combine parsley flakes, Italian seasoning and parmesan and sprinkle mixture over strips. Bake for 10 to 12 minutes or until golden brown. Serve hot. Serves 4 to 6.

• • • • •

Creamy Butter Bread

1 cup (2 sticks) butter, softened	230 g
2 cups flour	240 g
1 (8 ounce) carton sour cream	225 g

- Preheat oven to 350° (175° C).

- Combine all ingredients and mix well. Drop by teaspoonfuls into sprayed miniature muffin cups. Bake for 20 minutes or until light brown. Serves 4 to 6.

• • • • •

Mayonnaise Rolls

2 cups flour	240 g
1 cup milk	250 ml
¼ cup mayonnaise	55 g

- Preheat oven to 400° (205° C).

- Combine all ingredients, mix well and pour into sprayed muffin cups. Bake for 22 minutes. Serves 4 to 6.

• • • • •

Italian Crescent Rolls

1 (8 ounce) package refrigerated crescent rolls	225 g
¼ cup (½ stick) butter, melted	60 ml
1 teaspoon Italian herb seasoning	4 ml

- Preheat oven to 375° (190° C).

- Unroll crescent rolls and separate into 8 triangles. Brush with melted butter and sprinkle with seasoning. Roll dough according to package directions and place on baking sheet. Bake for 10 minutes or until golden brown. Serves 4 to 6.

• • • • •

Easy Rolls

1 (¼ ounce) package yeast	10 g
¼ cup sugar	50 g
1 egg	
4 cups self-rising flour	500 g
¾ cup oil	175 ml

- Mix yeast, 2 cups (500 ml) lukewarm water and sugar. Set aside for 5 minutes. Add egg and mix with whisk. Add flour and oil. (Batter will be thin.) Pour into container, cover and refrigerate until ready to use.

- When ready to bake, preheat oven to 375° (190° C).

- Spoon batter into sprayed muffin cups about half full. Bake for 7 to 8 minutes. Serves 6 to 10.

• • • • •

No-Peek Popovers

2 eggs	
1 cup milk	250 ml
1 cup flour	120 g

- Combine all ingredients and mix well.

- Pour into 8 sprayed muffin cups, three-fourths full. Place in cold oven, turn oven to 450° (230° C), bake for 30 minutes and do not peek. Serves 4 to 6.

• • • • •

Sour Cream Rolls

1 cup flour	120 g
½ cup (1 stick) butter, melted	115 g
1 (8 ounce) carton sour cream	240 g

- Preheat oven to 350° (175° C).

- Combine flour, butter and sour cream and mix well. Pour into sprayed miniature muffin cups and bake for 15 minutes. Serves 4.

• • • • •

Cheddar Puffs

½ cup (1 stick) butter, softened	115 g
1 cup shredded cheddar cheese	115 g
1¼ cups flour	150 g

- Preheat oven to 375° (190° C).

- Process butter and cheese in blender until they blend smooth. Stir in flour and ¼ teaspoon (1 ml) salt. Knead lightly with hands.

- Roll 1 (5 ml) teaspoon dough into balls, one at a time. Place on baking sheet. Bake for 12 to 15 minutes or until golden brown. Serves 4 to 6.

• • • • •

Cheese Muffins

3¾ cups buttermilk baking mix	450 g
1¼ cups shredded cheddar cheese	140 g
1 egg, beaten	
1¼ cups milk	310 ml
Dash chili powder	

- Preheat oven to 325° (165° C).

- In large bowl, combine all ingredients and beat vigorously by hand. Pour into sprayed or paper-lined muffin cups. Bake for 35 minutes. Serves 4 to 6.

• • • • •

 Plan shopping with refrigerated and frozen items last. *The more you organize your list, the quicker and cheaper your trip to the store will be.*

Salad Muffins

⅓ cup sugar	65 g
⅓ cup oil	75 ml
¾ cup milk	175 ml
2 eggs	
2 cups biscuit mix	240 g

- Preheat oven to 400° (205° C).

- In mixing bowl, combine sugar, oil and milk. Beat in eggs and biscuit mix and mix well. (Mixture will be a little lumpy.)

- Pour into sprayed or paper-lined muffin cups and fill two-thirds full. Bake for about 10 minutes or until light brown. Serves 4 to 6.

• • • • •

Beer Muffins

2 cups biscuit mix	240 g
2 teaspoons sugar	10 ml
⅔ cup beer	150 ml
1 egg, slightly beaten	

- Preheat oven to 400° (205° C).

- Mix biscuit mix and sugar. Add beer and egg. Fill sprayed or paper-lined muffin cups two-thirds full. Bake for 15 minutes or until golden brown. Serves 4 to 6.

• • • • •

Cheddar Biscuits

2 cups biscuit mix	240 g
⅔ cup milk	150 ml
½ cup shredded cheddar cheese	55 g
2 tablespoons butter, melted	30 ml
1 teaspoon garlic powder	5 ml

- Preheat oven to 350° (175° C).

- Mix biscuit mix, milk and cheese to form dough. (If dough is too sticky, add more biscuit mix.) Drop by rounded tablespoonfuls onto sprayed baking sheet and bake for 8 to 10 minutes. Mix butter and garlic powder and brush over warm biscuits. Yields 9 biscuits.

• • • • •

Cheese Puffs

1 (12 count) can refrigerated biscuits
12 cheddar cheese cubes
Vegetable oil

- Separate biscuits and roll out or press out flat. Place cheese cube in center and shape into ball. Drop in boiling oil and deep fry until golden and puffy. Drain on paper towels. Serves 6.

• • • • •

Onion Biscuits

2 cups biscuit mix	240 g
¼ cup milk	60 ml
1 (8 ounce) carton French onion dip	225 g

- Preheat oven to 375° (190° C).

- Combine all ingredients and mix well. Drop dough by tablespoonfuls in mounds onto sprayed baking sheet. Bake for 12 minutes. Serves 4 to 6.

• • • • •

Quick Creamy Biscuits

2½ cups biscuit mix	300 g
1 (8 ounce) carton whipping cream	250 ml
2 tablespoons sugar	

- Preheat oven to 375° (190° C).

- Mix all ingredients and place dough on floured board. Knead several times.

- Pat out to ½-inch (1.2 cm) thickness. Cut with biscuit cutter. Place on sprayed baking pan and bake for 12 to 15 minutes or until light brown. Serves 8.

• • • • •

Practice FIFO in your pantry, freezer and refrigerator.
FIFO stands for "first in, first out". Organize your foods by putting the new things in the back to be sure you use the oldest first.

Cream-Style Corn Sticks

2 cups biscuit mix	240 g
3 fresh green onions, finely chopped	
1 (8 ounce) can cream-style corn	225 g
½ cup (1 stick) butter, melted	115 g

- Preheat oven to 400° (205° C).

- In medium bowl, combine biscuit mix, green onions and cream-style corn and stir well.

- On floured surface, roll out dough and cut into 3 x 1-inch (8 x 2.5 cm) strips. Roll dough in melted butter, place on sprayed baking sheet and bake 15 to 17 minutes. Serves 4 to 6.

• • • • •

Cowboy Corn Cakes

2 cups yellow cornmeal	320 g
½ cup flour	60 g
2 tablespoons oil	30 ml

- Combine cornmeal and flour with 1 teaspoon (10 ml) salt. Stir in 2 cups (500 ml) boiling water and form mixture into 10 to 12 patties. Heat oil in large skillet over medium-high heat. Fry patties for 3 to 5 minutes on each side or until brown. Serves 4 to 6.

• • • • •

Broccoli Cornbread

1 (8 ounce) box cornbread mix	225 g
2 eggs, beaten	
1 (10 ounce) package frozen chopped broccoli,	
thawed, drained	280 g
½ cup minced onion	80 g
½ cup cottage cheese	105 g
¾ cup (1½ sticks) butter, melted	90 g

- Preheat oven to 350° (175° C).

- Combine cornbread mix with eggs. Add broccoli, onion, cottage cheese and melted butter. Stir to blend. Bake in sprayed 8 x 8-inch (20 x 20 cm) pan for 35 minutes. Serves 4 to 6.

• • • • •

Cheddar Cornbread

2 (8 ounce) packages cornbread muffin mix	2 (225 g)
2 eggs, beaten	
½ cup milk	125 ml
½ cup plain yogurt	115 g
1 (15 ounce) can cream-style corn	425 g
½ cup shredded cheddar cheese	55 g

- Preheat oven to 400° (205° C).

- In bowl, combine cornbread mix, eggs, milk and yogurt until they blend. Stir in corn and cheese. Pour into sprayed 9 x 13-inch (23 x 33 cm) baking dish. Bake for 18 to 20 minutes or until light brown. Serves 6 to 8.

• • • • •

Souper-Sausage Cornbread

1 (10 ounce) can cream of celery soup	280 g
2 eggs	
¼ cup milk	60 ml
2 (6 ounce) package corn muffin mix	2 (170 g)
¼ pound pork sausage, cooked, drained, crumbled	115 g

- Preheat oven to 400° (205° C).

- In bowl, combine soup, eggs and milk. Stir in muffin mix just until they blend. Fold in sausage.

- Spoon mixture into sprayed 9 x 13-inch (23 x 33 cm) baking pan. Bake for about 20 minutes or until light brown. Serves 6 to 8.

• • • • •

Hush Puppies

1½ cups cornmeal	240 g
¼ cup flour	30 g
2 teaspoons baking powder	10 ml
1 cup milk	250 ml
1 egg	
½ cup chopped onion	40 g
Oil	

- Stir cornmeal, flour, baking powder and 1¼ teaspoons (6 ml) salt together. Beat milk and egg. Add it and onion to cornmeal mixture. Drop by heaping teaspoons into hot oil. Serves 4 to 6.

• • • • •

Mexican Spoon Bread

1 cup yellow cornmeal	160 g
1 tablespoon sugar	15 ml
½ teaspoon baking soda	2 ml
¾ cup milk	175 ml
⅓ cup oil	75 ml
2 eggs, beaten	
1 (15 ounce) can cream-style corn	425 g
1 (4 ounce) can diced green chilies	115 g
1 (8 ounce) package shredded cheddar cheese, divided	225 g

- Preheat oven to 350° (175° C).

- In mixing bowl, mix cornmeal, sugar, 1 teaspoon (5 ml) salt and baking soda. Stir in milk and oil and mix well. Add eggs and corn and stir.

- Spoon half batter into sprayed 9 x 13-inch (23 x 33 cm) baking pan. Sprinkle half green chilies and half cheese over batter. Repeat layers, ending with cheese. Bake uncovered for 35 to 40 minutes or until light brown. Serve from pan. Serves 4 to 6.

• • • • •

One-Pan Banana Bread

⅓ cup oil	75 ml
1½ cups mashed ripe bananas	345 g
½ teaspoon vanilla	2 ml
3 eggs	
2⅔ cups biscuit mix	320 g
1 cup sugar	200 g
½ cup chopped nuts	85 g

- Preheat oven to 350° (175° C).

- Mix all ingredients and pour into sprayed, floured 9 x 5-inch (23 x 13 cm) loaf pan. Bake for 55 to 65 minutes. Cool 5 minutes and remove from pan. Cool on wire rack. Serves 6 to 8.

• • • • •

 Read advertisements in the newspaper or online. Check out grocery store circulars to find the best values for the week. The best specials can guide your menu selections and where to shop.

Poppy Seed Bread

3¾ cups biscuit mix	450 g
1½ cups shredded cheddar cheese	170 g
1 tablespoon poppy seeds	15 ml
1 egg, beaten	
1½ cups milk	375 ml

- Preheat oven to 350° (175° C).

- Combine all ingredients and beat vigorously for 1 minute. Pour into sprayed, floured loaf pan. Bake for 50 to 60 minutes or until toothpick inserted in center comes out clean. Remove from pan and cool before slicing. Serves 4 to 6.

• • • • •

Zucchini Bread

1 (18 ounce) box spice cake mix	510 g
2 cups shredded zucchini	480 ml
½ cup chopped black walnuts or pecans	120 ml

- Preheat oven to 350° (175° C).

- Prepare cake mix according to package directions.

- Use paper towels to squeeze liquid from zucchini. Stir zucchini and nuts into spice cake mix and mix well.

- Pour into 2 sprayed, floured loaf pans and bake for 50 to 60 minutes. Serves 12 to 16.

• • • • •

Strawberry Bread

3 cups flour	360 g
1 teaspoon baking soda	5 ml
1 tablespoon ground cinnamon	15 ml
2 cups sugar	200 g
3 eggs	
1 cup oil	250 ml
1 (10 ounce) package frozen sliced strawberries, thawed	280 g

- Preheat oven to 350° (175° C).

- Combine flour, baking soda, cinnamon and sugar with ½ teaspoon (2 ml) salt and mix well. Combine eggs, oil and strawberries.

- Add to dry ingredients and mix well. Pour into 2 sprayed, floured loaf pans. Bake for 1 hour. Serves 6 to 8.

Budget-Helper Salads

Fresh and savory, sweet and fruity, salads take many forms and flavors to delight the senses and complement a lunch or supper.

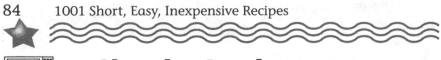

Chunky Applesauce

3 cups chopped Gala apples	375 g
⅓ cup sugar	65 g
½ teaspoon cinnamon	2 ml

- Spread apples in glass dish. Cover with plastic wrap open on 1 side and microwave on HIGH for 1 minute. Stir and microwave for 1 additional minute. Stir in sugar and microwave on HIGH for 2 minutes. Stir and sprinkle with cinnamon. Yields 2 cups.

Cinnamon-Apple Salad

⅔ cup cinnamon Red Hots® candies	150 g
1 (3 ounce) package cherry gelatin	85 g
1½ cups applesauce	385 g

- Heat cinnamon Red Hots® in ⅔ (150 ml) cup boiling water until candy melts. Pour over dry gelatin and stir until it dissolves well. Refrigerate until partially set. Stir in applesauce and pour into glass serving dish. Refrigerate until firm. Serves 2.

Blueberry Salad

2 (3 ounce) boxes grape gelatin	2 (85 g)
1 (20 ounce) can blueberry pie filling	565 g
1 (20 ounce) can crushed pineapple with juice	565 g

- Dissolve gelatin in 1 cup (250 ml) boiling water. Refrigerate until partially set and stir in blueberry pie filling and pineapple with juice. Pour into 9 x 13-inch (23 x 33 cm) glass dish and refrigerate until firm. Serves 6 to 8.

Cherry-Berry Salad

1 (6 ounce) package cherry gelatin	170 g
1 (10 ounce) package frozen strawberries, thawed	280 g
1 (16 ounce) can whole cranberry sauce	455 g

- Dissolve gelatin in 1 cup (250 ml) boiling water and mix well. Stir in strawberries with juice and cranberry sauce and mix well. Pour into 7 x 11-inch (18 x 28 cm) glass dish and refrigerate until set. Serves 6.

TIP: To add a special touch, frost firm gelatin with sour cream.

• • • • •

Cherry-Cranberry Salad

1 (6 ounce) package cherry gelatin   170 g
1 (20 ounce) can cherry pie filling   565 g
1 (16 ounce) can whole cranberry sauce   455 g

- In mixing bowl, combine cherry gelatin and 1½ cups (375 ml) boiling water and mix until gelatin dissolves. Add pie filling and cranberry sauce to gelatin and mix well.

- Pour into 9 x 13-inch (23 x 33 cm) dish. Place salad in freezer for 45 minutes to congeal or refrigerate for 2 to 3 hours. Serves 4 to 6.

Cranberry Mousse

1 (15 ounce) can jellied cranberry sauce   425 g
1 (8 ounce) can crushed pineapple, drained   225 g
1 (8 ounce) carton sour cream   225 g
1 tablespoon mayonnaise   15 ml

- In saucepan, combine cranberry sauce and crushed pineapple. Cook until cranberry sauce liquefies. Fold in sour cream and mayonnaise. Pour into molds or muffin cups and freeze. Serves 4 to 6.

Creamy Cranberry Salad

1 (6 ounce) package cherry gelatin   170 g
1 (8 ounce) carton sour cream   225 g
1 (16 ounce) can whole cranberry sauce 455 g
1 (15 ounce) can crushed pineapple   425 g

- Dissolve gelatin in 1¼ cups (310 ml) boiling water and mix well. Stir in remaining ingredients and pour into 7 x 11-inch (18 x 28 cm) glass baking dish. Refrigerate until firm. Serves 6.

Cran-Apple Salad

1 (6 ounce) package orange gelatin   170 g
2 apples, peeled, chopped
1 (16 ounce) can whole cranberry sauce 455 g

- Prepare gelatin with 1 cup (250 ml) boiling water, stir until it dissolves and cool. Add apples and cranberry sauce, mix well and pour into 7 x 11-inch (18 x 28 cm) glass dish. Cover and refrigerate until firm. Serves 6 to 8.

• • • • •

Frozen Cranberry Salad

1 (16 ounce) can whole cranberry sauce	455 g
1 (8 ounce) carton frozen whipped topping, thawed	250 ml
1 (15 ounce) can crushed pineapple, drained	425 g

- Combine all ingredients and mix well. Spoon into 7 x 11-inch (18 x 28 cm) dish and freeze. Serves 8.

TIP: You can make individual servings by lining a muffin pan with paper cups, fill with salad and freeze.

• • • • •

Grapefruit-Avocado Salad

2 (15 ounce) cans grapefruit sections, drained	2 (425 g)
2 ripe avocados, peeled, sliced	
½ cup slivered almonds, chopped	85 g
½ cup poppy seed salad dressing	125 ml
Lettuce	

- Combine grapefruit, avocados and almonds. Toss with poppy seed dressing. Serve on bed of lettuce. Serves 6 to 8.

• • • • •

Shamrock Salad

1 (6 ounce) package lime gelatin	170 g
1 pint vanilla ice cream	475 ml
2 bananas, sliced, or 2 apples, chopped	

- Mix gelatin with 1½ cups (375 ml) boiling water, cool and stir in ice cream. Refrigerate until partially set and stir in bananas or apples. Spoon into glass serving dish and refrigerate until firm. Serves 8.

• • • • •

Emerald Salad

1 (3 ounce) package lime-flavored gelatin	85 g
¾ cup shredded cucumber	90 g
2 teaspoons grated onion	10 ml
1 cup cottage cheese	215 g
1 cup mayonnaise	225 g
⅓ cup blanched almonds	60 g

- Dissolve gelatin in ¾ cup (175 ml) boiling water. Refrigerate until slightly congealed and then add remaining ingredients. Refrigerate until set. Serves 6.

Lime-Yogurt Salad

1 (6 ounce) package lime gelatin	170 g
1 (8 ounce) carton vanilla yogurt	227 g
1 (8 ounce) can pear slices, drained	225 g

- Stir gelatin into 1½ cups (375 ml) boiling water until it dissolves. Divide gelatin into 2 bowls. Blend yogurt into 1 bowl gelatin. Stir pears into gelatin in other bowl.

- Pour gelatin-yogurt mixture into square 9-inch (23 cm) dish and chill until set. Spoon pear mixture on top of gelatin-yogurt mixture. Refrigerate until firm and cut into squares to serve. Serves 6.

Lime-Gelatin Salad

1 (6 ounce) package lime gelatin	170 g
1 (15 ounce) can crushed pineapple with juice	425 g
1 cup cottage cheese	215 g

- Dissolve gelatin in 1 cup (250 ml) boiling water and refrigerate until partially set.

- Stir in pineapple and cottage cheese and pour into 7 x 11-inch (18 x 28 cm) glass dish. Refrigerate until firm and cut in squares to serve. Serves 6.

Mandarin-Orange Whip

1 (3 ounce) box orange gelatin	85 g
1 (8 ounce) carton frozen whipped topping. thawed	225 g
2 (11 ounce) cans mandarin oranges, drained	2 (310 g)

- Combine dry gelatin and whipped topping and mix well. Stir in drained oranges and spoon into pretty serving dish. Refrigerate for a couple of hours before serving. Serves 6.

TIP: *Fold in 1 (8 ounce/225 g) can well drained crushed pineapple to add a different flavor.*

Triple Orange Salad

1 (6 ounce) package orange gelatin	170 g
1 pint orange sherbet	475 ml
1 (11 ounce) can mandarin oranges, drained	310 g

- Dissolve gelatin in 1½ cups (375 ml) boiling water and cool. Stir in sherbet and then oranges. Refrigerate until firm. Serves 6.

• • • • •

Quick Ambrosia

1 (11 ounce) can mandarin oranges, drained	310 g
1 (15 ounce) can pineapple chunks, drained	425 g
2 tablespoons shredded coconut	30 ml

- Combine oranges and pineapple. Divide among 4 dessert dishes and sprinkle each serving with coconut. Serves 4.

Peach and Cottage Cheese Salad

1 cup cottage cheese	215 g
1 (15 ounce) can peach slices, drained	425 g
Maraschino cherries	

- Place scoop of cottage cheese in center of salad plate and place peach slices around it. Place maraschino cherry on cottage cheese as garnish. Serves 2.

Pear-Cheese Salad

Shredded lettuce	
2 (15 ounce) cans pear halves	2 (425 g)
1 (8 ounce) package shredded cheddar cheese	225 g

- On individual salad plates, place shredded lettuce and top with 2 pear halves. Sprinkle with cheese. Serves 4.

Pistachio Salad

1 (20 ounce) can crushed pineapple with juice	565 g
2 (3 ounce) packages pistachio instant pudding mix	2 (85 g)
¾ cup chopped pecans	85 g
1 (12 ounce) carton frozen whipped topping, thawed	340 g

- Mix pineapple with instant pudding mix and stir until it thickens slightly. Add pecans. Mix well and fold in whipped topping; refrigerate. Serves 4 to 6.

Sunny Day Salad

1 (6 ounce) carton plain yogurt	170 g
1 tablespoon honey	15 ml
1 (8 ounce) can sliced pineapple, drained	225 g

- Mix yogurt with honey. Place 1 slice pineapple on each salad plate. Spoon 1 tablespoon (15 ml) yogurt in middle. Serves 4.

• • • • •

Pineapple Crunch Gelatin

1 (3 ounce) box orange or lime gelatin	85 g
½ cup grated carrots	55 g
1 (8 ounce) can crushed pineapple, drained	225 g

- Stir gelatin in ¾ cup (175 ml) boiling water until dissolved.
  Refrigerate until partially set. Stir in carrots and pineapple and pour
  into serving bowl. Refrigerate until firm. Serves 2.

• • • • •

Tropical Pineapple Boats

1 fresh pineapple	
1 (15 ounce) can tropical fruit salad, drained	425 g
2 tablespoons shredded coconut	30 ml

- Cut fresh whole pineapple in half vertically (leaves and all). Remove
  core and fruit but leave ½-inch thick shell. Cube pineapple core and
  set aside.

- Fill pineapple shells with tropical fruit mixed with cubed pineapple
  and sprinkle coconut over top. Serves 4 to 6.

• • • • •

Raspberry Sherbet Salad

1 (6 ounce) package raspberry gelatin	170 g
1 pint raspberry sherbet	475 ml
1 pint fresh or frozen raspberries	125 g/250 g

- Dissolve gelatin in 1½ cups (375 ml) boiling water, mix well
  and refrigerate until partially set. Fold in sherbet and mix well.
  Refrigerate until partially set. Stir in berries and pour into
  9 x 13-inch (23 x 33 cm) glass dish.   Refrigerate until set and
  cut into squares. Serves 8.

• • • • •

Raspberry-Applesauce Salad

1 cup applesauce	255 g
1 (3 ounce) package raspberry gelatin	85 g
1 (10 ounce) package frozen raspberries, thawed	280 g

- Heat applesauce to a boil. Stir in dry gelatin and mix well. Stir
  in raspberries and pour into mold or bowl. Refrigerate until firm.
  Serves 4.

Raspberry Salad

1 (6 ounce) package raspberry gelatin	170 g
1 (8 ounce) carton frozen whipped topping, thawed	225 g
1 (10 ounce) package frozen unsweetened raspberries, thawed, drained	280 g

- Prepare gelatin with 1½ cups (375 ml) boiling water and mix until dissolved. Cover and refrigerate until partially set.

- Beat gelatin with electric mixer until fluffy and fold in whipped topping and raspberries. Cover and refrigerate until firm. Serves 4 to 6.

• • • • •

Layered Raspberry-Cranberry Salad

1 (6 ounce) package raspberry gelatin	170 g
1 (16 ounce) can whole cranberry sauce	455 g
1 cup sour cream	240 g

- Prepare gelatin with 1½ cups (375 ml) boiling water; stir until completely dissolved. Refrigerate until it is partially set. Stir in cranberries. Pour half mixture into 7 x 11-inch (18 x 28 cm) dish and freeze until firm.

- Spread sour cream over mixture and top with remaining berry-gelatin mixture at room temperature. Refrigerate until firm. Serves 6.

• • • • •

Serendipity Salad

1 (6 ounce) package raspberry gelatin	170 g
1 (15 ounce) can fruit cocktail with juice	425 g
1 (8 ounce) can crushed pineapple with juice	225 g
2 bananas, cut into small chunks	
1 cup miniature marshmallows	45 g

- Dissolve gelatin in 1½ cups (375 ml) boiling water and mix well. Add fruit cocktail and pineapple and chill until gelatin begins to thicken. Add bananas and marshmallows and pour into sherbet dishes.

- Cover with plastic wrap and refrigerate. You could also pour salad into 7 x 11-inch (18 x 28 cm) glass dish and cut into squares to serve. Serves 4 to 6.

• • • • •

Strawberry-Ginger Ale Salad

1 (6 ounce) package strawberry gelatin	170 g
1 cup ginger ale, chilled	250 ml
1 (10 ounce) package frozen strawberries, thawed	280 g

- Dissolve gelatin in 1 cup (250 ml) boiling water. Stir in ginger ale. Refrigerate until partially set.

- Stir in strawberries and mix well. Pour into mold or a 9-inch square dish and refrigerate until firm. Serves 6.

• • • • •

Strawberry Souffle Salad

1 (6 ounce) package strawberry gelatin	170 g
2 cups mashed strawberries	330 g

- Stir gelatin in 1 cup (250 ml) boiling water until it dissolves. Add mashed berries and mix. Refrigerate until mixture becomes thick and whip with electric mixer to very stiff froth. Serve in sherbet dishes or in small bowls. Serves 3.

• • • • •

Instant Strawberry Salad

1 (16 ounce) carton cottage cheese, drained	455 g
1 (6 ounce) package strawberry gelatin	170 g
1 (8 ounce) carton frozen whipped topping, thawed	225 g

- Combine cottage cheese with dry gelatin and mix well. Fold in whipped topping and spoon into pretty glass serving dish. Refrigerate for 2 to 3 hours before serving. Serves 6.

• • • • •

Fruit Salad

1 (14 ounce) can sweetened condensed milk, chilled	395 g
2 tablespoons lemon juice	30 ml
2 (15 ounce) cans fruit cocktail, chilled, well drained	2 (425 g)
1 (20 ounce) can pineapple tidbits, chilled, drained	565 g
1 (8 ounce) carton frozen whipped topping, thawed	225 g

- In large bowl, combine condensed milk and lemon juice. Mix well, add fruit cocktail and pineapple and mix gently. Fold in whipped topping. Serves 6 to 8.

• • • • •

Honey-Fruit Salad

1 (15 ounce) can pineapple chunks with juice	425 g
2 oranges, peeled, sectioned	
1 apple, cored, diced	
1 banana, sliced	
½ cup chopped pecans	55 g
¼ cup honey	85 g
1 tablespoon lemon juice	15 ml

• Combine all ingredients in salad bowl and refrigerate. Serves 4 to 6.

• • • • •

Peachy Fruit Salad

2 (20 ounce) cans peach pie filling	2 (565 g)
1 (20 ounce) can pineapple chunks, drained	565 g
1 (11 ounce) can mandarin oranges, drained	310 g
1 (8 ounce) jar maraschino cherries, halved, drained	225 g
1 cup miniature marshmallows	45 g

• Combine all ingredients in large bowl, fold together gently and refrigerate. (Sliced bananas may be added, if you like.) Serves 4 to 6.

• • • • •

Fantastic Fruit Salad

2 (11 ounce) cans mandarin oranges	2 (310 g)
2 (15 ounce) cans pineapple chunks	2 (425 g)
1 (16 ounce) carton frozen strawberries, thawed	455 g
1 (20 ounce) can peach pie filling	565 g
1 (20 ounce) can apricot pie filling	565 g

• Drain oranges, pineapple and strawberries. Combine all ingredients and gently fold together. Spoon into glass serving bowl. Refrigerate. Serves 6 to 8.

• • • • •

Stained-Glass Fruit Salad

1 (16 ounce) package frozen unsweetened strawberries, thawed, drained	455 g
1 (20 ounce) can pineapple tidbits, drained	565 g
2 (20 ounce) cans peach pie filling	2 (565 g)
3 bananas, sliced	

• Drain strawberries and pineapple. Mix all ingredients, place in pretty bowl and refrigerate overnight. Serves 6 to 8.

Fancy Fruit

2 (20 ounce) cans peach pie filling, chilled	2 (565 g)
1 (15 ounce) can pear slices, halved, chilled	425 g
1 (16 ounce) package frozen sweetened strawberries, thawed	455 g
1 (20 ounce) can pineapple tidbits, drained, chilled	565 g

- Combine all ingredients in pretty bowl and serve. Serves 6 to 8.

• • • • •

Crunchy Fruit Salad

2 red apples with peels, chopped	
⅓ cup sunflower seeds	45 g
½ cup green grapes	75
⅓ cup vanilla yogurt	115 g

- Combine all ingredients and stir to coat fruit. Refrigerate until ready to serve. Serves 4 to 6.

• • • • •

Cottage Fruit Salad

1 (16 ounce) carton small curd cottage cheese	455 g
1 (6 ounce) package orange gelatin	170 g
2 (11 ounce) cans mandarin oranges, drained	2 (310 g)
1 (20 ounce) can chunk pineapple, drained	565 g
1 (8 ounce) carton frozen whipped topping, thawed	225 g

- Sprinkle gelatin over cottage cheese and mix well. Add oranges and pineapple and mix well. Fold in whipped topping and refrigerate. Serves 6 to 8.

• • • • •

Angel Whip Salad

1 (16 ounce) carton frozen whipped topping, thawed	455 g
1 (20 ounce) can cherry pie filling	565 g
1 (14 ounce) can sweetened condensed milk	395 g
1 (8 ounce) can crushed pineapple, drained	225 g
1 (3 ounce) can flaked coconut	85 g
1 cup miniature marshmallows	45 g

- Combine all ingredients and refrigerate. Serves 4 to 6.

• • • • •

Fluffy Fruit Salad

2 (20 ounce) cans pineapple tidbits, drained	2 (565 g)
1 (16 ounce) can whole cranberry sauce	455 g
2 (11 ounce) cans mandarin oranges, drained	2 (310 g)
½ cup chopped pecans	55 g
1 (8 ounce) carton frozen whipped topping, thawed	225 g

- In bowl, combine pineapple, cranberry sauce, oranges and pecans and fold in whipped topping. Serves 6 to 8.

Sunflower Salad

2 apples, cored, chopped	
1 cup halved seedless green grapes	150 g
½ cup chopped celery	50 g
¾ cup chopped pecans	85 g
⅓ cup mayonnaise	75 g

- Combine all ingredients and refrigerate. Serves 4.

Apple Cabbage Salad

1 medium head cabbage, finely chopped	
2 red apples, cored, chopped	
5 tablespoons sugar	65 g
1 (8 ounce) can crushed pineapple with juice	225 g
6 marshmallows, cut in small pieces	
½ cup chopped nuts	85 g
1 tablespoon vinegar	15 ml

- Place cabbage and apples in bowl. Add sugar, pineapple and marshmallows; mix well. Refrigerate for 30 minutes.   Just before serving, \add nuts and vinegar and mix gently. Serves 4 to 6.

TIP: *Serve on crisp piece of lettuce.*

Fruit Cup

1 mango, peeled, chopped	
2 kiwifruit, peeled, chopped	
1 (15 ounce) can pineapple tidbits, drained	425 g
1 tablespoon lime juice	15 ml
Granola cereal	

- Mix fruit and lime juice. Serve sprinkled with granola cereal. Serves 3 to 4.

• • • • •

Tropical Fruit Trio

1 (24 ounce) jar mango wedges, drained, chopped	680 g
2 medium kiwifruit, peeled, thinly sliced	
2 medium bananas, thinly sliced	
1 teaspoon lemon juice	5 ml

- Toss fruit with lemon juice and refrigerate. Serves 6 to 8.

• • • • •

Strawberry-Slaw Salad

1 (10 ounce) package romaine lettuce, torn	280 g
1 cup broccoli slaw	90 g
1 pint large fresh strawberries, quartered	360 g
½ red onion, coarsely chopped	
Raspberry vinaigrette salad dressing	

- In salad bowl, toss all ingredients except dressing. When ready to serve, toss with raspberry vinaigrette salad dressing. Serves 4 to 6.

• • • • •

Calypso Coleslaw

1 (16 ounce) package shredded cabbage	455 g
1 bunch green onions with tops, sliced	
2 cups cubed cheddar or mozzarella cheese	265 g
¼ cup sliced black olives	35 g
1 (15 ounce) can whole kernel corn with peppers, drained	425 g

- Combine all slaw ingredients and add few sprinkles of salt.

Dressing:

1 cup mayonnaise	225 g
2 tablespoons sugar	30 ml
1 tablespoon mustard	15 ml
2 tablespoons vinegar	30 ml

- Combine dressing ingredients and mix well. Toss dressing and slaw, cover and refrigerate. Serves 8.

• • • • •

Make your own salad dressings as an alternative to expensive bottled dressings. Many salad dressing recipes are simple and only a whisk or two away.

Noodle Coleslaw

1 (16 ounce) package coleslaw mix	455 g
1 cup sunflower seeds	130 g
1 green bell pepper, seeded, chopped	
1 bunch green onions, chopped	
2 (3 ounce) packages chicken-flavored ramen noodles	2 (85 g)
1 (16 ounce) bottle Italian salad dressing	500 ml

• Combine coleslaw, sunflower seeds, bell pepper, onions and
  seasoning packets. Break ramen noodles into smaller pieces
  and add to coleslaw mixture. Toss with dressing and refrigerate
  overnight. Serves 4.

Coleslaw Dressing

1 cup mayonnaise	225 g
⅓ cup sugar	65 g
¼ cup vinegar	60 ml

• Combine all ingredients and mix well. Refrigerate. Use dressing for
  coleslaw or waldorf salad. Yields 1¼ cups.

Coleslaw Deluxe

1 (16 ounce) package shredded cabbage	455 g
1 bunch green onions, sliced	
2 cups cubed cheddar cheese	265 g
¼ cup sliced ripe olives	35 g
1 (12 ounce) can Mexicorn®, drained	340 g
1 cup mayonnaise	225 g
3 tablespoons sugar	35 g
2 tablespoons vinegar	30 ml

• Combine cabbage, onions, cheese, olives and Mexicorn® and mix.
  Combine remaining ingredients and toss with slaw. Cover and
  refrigerate. Serves 6 to 8.

Hawaiian Coleslaw

1 (16 ounce) package shredded coleslaw mix	455 g
1 (8 ounce) can crushed pineapple, drained	225 g
1 (8 ounce) bottle coleslaw dressing, chilled	225 g
¼ cup flaked coconut, optional	20 g

• In salad bowl, toss slaw mix, pineapple, dressing and coconut and
  refrigerate. Serves 4 to 6.

• • • • •

Hot Slaw

1 (2 pound) head cabbage	910 g
6 strips bacon	
¼ cup packed brown sugar	55 g
½ teaspoon celery seed	2 ml
½ teaspoon dry mustard	2 ml
¼ cup vinegar	60 ml

- Shred cabbage. Dice bacon and cook until crisp. Remove bacon and save pan drippings. Add sugar, celery seed, mustard, ½ teaspoon (2 ml) salt and vinegar to skillet with drippings. When mixture is hot, pour over cabbage and turn to mix well. Add crumbled bacon and serve. Serves 6 to 8.

Pasta-Turkey Salad Supper

1 (12 ounce) package tri-color spiral pasta	340 g
1 cup fresh broccoli florets	70 g
1 cup fresh cauliflower florets	100 g
2 small yellow squash, sliced	
1 cup halved cherry tomatoes	150 g
1 (8 ounce) bottle cheddar-parmesan ranch dressing	250 ml
1½ pound hickory-smoked turkey breast, cut into strips	680 g

- Cook pasta according to package directions. Drain and rinse in cold water. Place in large salad bowl and add broccoli, cauliflower, squash and tomatoes. Toss with dressing. Place strips of turkey breast in rows over salad. Serve immediately. Serves 6 to 8.

Pasta Salad Bowl

1 (12 ounce) package bow-tie pasta	340 g
1 (16 ounce) package frozen green peas, thawed	455 g
1 seedless cucumber, thinly sliced	
1 pound deli ham, cut in strips	455 g

- Cook pasta according to package directions. Drain and cool under cold running water and drain again. Transfer to serving bowl and add peas, cucumber slices and ham strips.

Dressing:

⅔ cup mayonnaise	150 g
¼ cup cider vinegar	60 ml
1 teaspoon sugar	5 ml
2 teaspoons dried dill weed	10 ml

- In small bowl, combine all dressing ingredients and spoon over salad. Toss to mix and coat well. Refrigerate. Serves 6 to 8.

Macaroni Salad

1 (8 ounce) package macaroni, cooked, drained	225 g
1 (3 ounce) package pepperoni, diced	85 g
1½ cups shredded provolone cheese	170 g
3 green onions with tops, chopped	
1 (15 ounce) can garbanzo beans, drained	425 g
Italian dressing	

- Combine all ingredients except dressing and toss. Use desired amount of dressing and toss. Refrigerate 1 to 2 hours. Serves 4 to 6.

Spinach and Apple Salad

⅓ cup frozen orange juice concentrate, thawed	75 ml
¼ cup mayonnaise	75 g
1 (10 ounce) package fresh spinach	280 g
1 red apple with peel, diced	
5 slices bacon, fried, crumbled	

- Mix orange juice concentrate and mayonnaise. When ready to serve, mix spinach and apple in salad bowl. (Cut apple at the last minute.) Pour orange juice-mayonnaise dressing over salad and top with bacon. Serves 4 to 6.

Spinach, Apple and Walnut Salad

1 (10 ounce) package fresh spinach, torn into pieces	280 g
2 red apples, cored, chopped	
½ cup coarsely chopped walnuts	65 g
½ cup vinaigrette salad dressing	125 ml

- Combine spinach, apples and walnuts in salad bowl and toss with dressing until they mix well. (If desired, add more dressing.) Refrigerate until ready to serve. Serves 4.

Spinach-Orange Salad

1 (10 ounce) package fresh baby spinach	280 g
2 (11 ounce) cans mandarin oranges, drained	2 (310 g)
⅓ cup slivered almonds, toasted	55 g
1 bunch fresh green onions, sliced	
½ cup vinaigrette salad dressing	125 ml

- In salad bowl, combine all salad ingredients and toss with dressing. Serves 4.

● ● ● ● ●

Greek Summer Salad

4 cups fresh spinach, torn into pieces	120 g
1½ cups sliced strawberries	250 g
⅓ cup crumbled feta cheese	50 g
½ cup wild berry vinaigrette	125 ml

* Combine spinach, strawberries and cheese and toss with dressing.
  (If desired, you can add more dressing.) Serves 4.

Spinach-Strawberry Salad

2 (10 ounce) packages baby spinach	2 (280 g)
1 pint fresh strawberries, halved	305 g
1 (8 ounce) bottle poppy seed salad dressing	250 ml
½ cup slivered almonds, toasted	85 g

* In salad bowl, combine spinach and strawberries and toss. When
  ready to serve, toss with salad dressing and sprinkle almonds on top.
  Serves 6 to 8.

Splendid Spinach Salad

8 cups fresh spinach	240 g
¾ cup chopped nuts	95 g
1 cup fresh raspberries or sliced strawberries	125 g/165 g
3 kiwifruit, sliced	

* Toss all ingredients.

Dressing:

2 tablespoons raspberry vinegar (or cider vinegar)	30 ml
2 tablespoons raspberry or strawberry jam	30 ml
⅓ cup oil	75 ml

* Mix dressing ingredients. Pour over salad ingredients and toss.
  Serves 4 to 6.

Raspberry-Spinach Salad

2 (10 ounce) packages baby spinach	2 (280 g)
1 cup fresh raspberries	125 g
½ red onion, sliced in rings	
¼ cup real bacon bits	30 g
1 (8 ounce) bottle raspberry salad dressing	250 ml

* Mix all salad ingredients and toss with dressing. Serves 4 to 6.

● ● ● ● ●

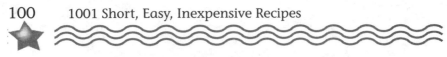

Sunny Spinach Salad

1 (10 ounce) package fresh spinach	280 g
1 medium red onion, thinly sliced	
¾ cup chopped, dried apricots	150 g
⅓ cup sunflower seeds	45 g
Vinaigrette salad dressing	

- Combine ingredients. Serve with vinaigrette dressing. Serves 4 to 6.

● ● ● ● ●

Spinach-Sprout Salad

1 (10 ounce) package baby spinach, chilled	280 g
1 cup fresh bean sprouts, chilled	130 g
8 slices precooked bacon, crumbled	
½ cup lime-basil vinaigrette salad dressing	125 ml
3 eggs, hard-boiled, sliced, chilled	

- In salad bowl, combine spinach, bean sprouts and crumbled bacon and toss with lime-basil vinaigrette salad dressing. Place egg slices on top and refrigerate. Serves 4 to 6.

● ● ● ● ●

Spinach-Pecan Salad

1 (10 ounce) package baby spinach	280 g
2 eggs, hard-boiled, sliced	
½ cup chopped pecans, toasted	55 g
1 (8 ounce) package precooked bacon, crumbled	225 g
¼ cup crumbled blue cheese	45 g
½ cup Italian salad dressing	125 ml

- In salad bowl, combine spinach, sliced eggs, pecans, bacon and blue cheese and toss. Drizzle with Italian salad dressing. Serves 4.

● ● ● ● ●

Spinach-Bacon Salad

2 quarts fresh spinach, torn into pieces	240 g
8 bacon slices, cooked, crumbled	
3 eggs, hard-boiled, chopped	
¾ cup ranch dressing	175 ml

- Combine all salad ingredients. Toss with dressing. Serves 4 to 6.

● ● ● ● ●

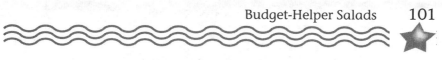

Spinach Salad

½ cup slivered almonds   85 g
1 (10 ounce) package fresh baby spinach   280 g
2 eggs, hard-boiled, sliced
1 red bell pepper, seeded, julienned
Raspberry vinaigrette dressing

- Preheat oven to 275° (135° C).

- Toast almonds on baking sheet for 10 minutes.

- In salad bowl, combine all ingredients except dressing. Just before serving, toss with raspberry-vinaigrette dressing. Serves 4 to 6.

• • • • •

Spinach Salad with Sprouts

1 (10 ounce) package baby spinach   280 g
2 cups fresh bean sprouts   210 g
1 (8 ounce) can sliced water chestnuts, drained   225 g
½ cup mayonnaise   110 g

- Mix all ingredients and toss. Serves 4.

• • • • •

Special Spinach Salad

1 (10 ounce) package fresh spinach   280 g
1 (15 ounce) can bean sprouts, drained   425 g
8 slices bacon, cooked crisp
1 (8 ounce) can sliced water chestnuts, drained   225 g
Vinaigrette salad dressing

- Combine spinach and bean sprouts. When ready to serve, add crumbled bacon and water chestnuts. Toss with vinaigrette salad dressing. Serves 4.

TIP: *Make your own vinaigrette by mixing 3 parts olive oil and 1 part red wine vinegar.*

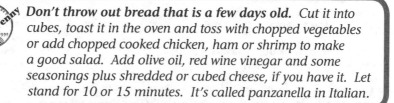

Don't throw out bread that is a few days old. *Cut it into cubes, toast it in the oven and toss with chopped vegetables or add chopped cooked chicken, ham or shrimp to make a good salad. Add olive oil, red wine vinegar and some seasonings plus shredded or cubed cheese, if you have it. Let stand for 10 or 15 minutes. It's called panzanella in Italian.*

Russian Salad

1 (10 ounce) package fresh spinach	280 g
3 eggs, hard-boiled, sliced	
1 bunch green onions, chopped	
1 (8 ounce) package fresh mushrooms, sliced	225 g
½ pound bacon, fried, crumbled	225 g
1½ cups fresh beans sprouts	155 g
Catalina dressing	

- Combine all salad ingredients and toss with desired amount of dressing. Serves 4 to 6.

• • • • •

Tangy Spinach Salad

1 (10 ounce) package baby spinach	280 g
1 cup drained cottage cheese	215 g
1 red bell pepper, seeded, julienned	
½ cup honey-mustard salad dressing	125 ml

- Combine spinach, cottage cheese and bell pepper and toss with dressing. Serves 4 to 6.

• • • • •

Swiss-Spinach Salad

1 (10 ounce) bag baby spinach	280 g
½ red onion, chopped	
1 (8 ounce) package shredded Swiss cheese	225 g
½ cup wild berry vinaigrette dressing	125 ml
½ cup sunflower seeds, toasted	65 g

- In salad bowl, combine spinach, onion and cheese. Toss with wild berry vinaigrette dressing. Sprinkle sunflower seeds over top of salad. Serves 4.

• • • • •

Festive Salad

1 (10 ounce) package mixed salad greens	280 g
1 red apple, cored, diced	
1 green apple, cored, diced	
1 cup shredded parmesan cheese	100 g
½ cup Craisins®	60 g
½ cup slivered almonds, toasted	85 g
½ cup poppy seed dressing	125 ml

- In large salad bowl, toss greens, apples, cheese, Craisins® and almonds. Drizzle dressing over salad and toss. Serves 4.

Berry Delicious Salad

1 (10 ounce) package mixed salad greens	280 g
2 cups fresh blueberries	295 g
⅔ cup crumbled gorgonzola cheese	115 g
⅓ cup chopped pecans, toasted	55 g
⅓ cup raspberry-vinaigrette dressing	75 ml

- In salad bowl combine salad greens, blueberries, cheese and pecans. Toss salad with dressing and refrigerate. Serves 4.

• • • • •

Green and Red Salad

4 cups torn mixed salad greens	215 g
3 fresh green onions with tops, chopped	
2 medium red apples with peel, cored, diced	
1 cup fresh raspberries	125 g
½ cup poppy seed dressing	125 ml

- Toss salad greens, onions and fruit. Drizzle with dressing and toss. Serves 4 to 6.

• • • • •

Green Spring Salad Mix

2 (10 ounce) bags spring-mix salad greens	2 (280 g)
1 bunch fresh green onions, sliced	
1 (8 ounce) bottle creamy Italian salad dressing	250 ml
1 (16 ounce) package seasoned croutons	455 g

- In salad bowl, toss salad, green onions and half dressing. Top with croutons. Serves 4 to 6.

• • • • •

Italian Green Salad

1 (10 ounce) package Italian-blend salad greens	280 g
1 seedless cucumber, sliced	
1 small zucchini, sliced	
Creamy Italian dressing	
⅓ cup sunflower seeds	45 g

- In salad bowl, combine salad greens, cucumber and zucchini. When ready to serve, toss with creamy Italian dressing and sprinkle sunflower seeds on top. Add croutons, if desired. Serves 4.

• • • • •

Spring Salad

1 (10 ounce) package spring-mix salad greens	280 g
2 cups fresh broccoli florets	140 g
1 seedless cucumber, peeled, sliced	
1 (8 ounce) bottle ranch salad dressing	225 g

- Combine greens, broccoli and cucumber and toss with as much dressing as needed. Serves 4 to 6.

• • • • •

Spring Greens

1 (10 ounce) package spring-mix salad greens	280 g
1 seedless cucumber, sliced	
1 bunch red radishes, sliced	
1 orange bell pepper, seeded, chopped	
1 (8 ounce) jar refrigerated honey-mustard salad dressing	250 ml

- In salad bowl, toss greens, cucumber, radishes and bell pepper. Add dressing as needed. Serves 6.

• • • • •

Spruced-Up Green Salad

1 (10 ounce) package spring-mix salad greens	280 g
1 bunch red radishes, sliced	
1 small zucchini with peel, sliced	
1 cup fresh broccoli florets	70 g
1 (8 ounce) bottle honey-mustard vinaigrette salad dressing	250 ml

- In salad bowl, combine salad greens, radishes, zucchini and broccoli florets. Toss with salad dressing. Serves 4.

• • • • •

Mixed Green Salad

1 (10 ounce) package mixed salad greens, chilled	280 g
2 tomatoes, chopped	
1 (8 ounce) bottle creamy ranch salad dressing	250 g
1 (6 ounce) package seasoned croutons	170 g

- Combine salad greens and chopped tomatoes. When ready to serve, toss with just enough dressing to moisten greens. Top with seasoned croutons. Serves 4 to 6.

• • • • •

Nutty Green Salad

6 cups torn mixed salad greens   320 g
1 medium zucchini, sliced
1 (8 ounce) can sliced water chestnuts, drained   225 g
½ cup peanuts   70 g
⅓ cup Italian salad dressing   75 ml

- Toss greens, zucchini, water chestnuts and peanuts. When ready to serve, add salad dressing and toss. Serves 4 to 6.

Spring Mix Special

1 (10 ounce) package spring-mix salad greens   280 g
1 small red onion, sliced
10 cherry tomatoes, halved
2 small zucchini, sliced
Honey-mustard dressing

- In salad bowl, toss greens, red onion, tomatoes and zucchini. Spoon about 2 tablespoons (30 ml) honey-mustard dressing on each serving. Serves 4.

Tossed Italian Green Salad

1 (10 ounce) package Italian-blend mixed greens   280 g
1 seedless cucumber, sliced
1 rib celery, sliced
2 small zucchini, sliced
Creamy Italian salad dressing

- In salad bowl, combine mixed greens, cucumber, celery and zucchini and toss. Dress with creamy Italian or favorite dressing. Serves 4 to 6.

Three-Bean Deluxe Salad

⅓ pound cooked chicken or beef, cut into strips   150 g
1 (15 ounce) can 3-bean salad, chilled, drained   425 g
1 (8 ounce) package cubed mozzarella cheese   225 g
1 (10 ounce) bag mixed salad greens   280 g
Italian salad dressing

- In large salad bowl, lightly toss beef, 3-bean salad and cheese. Pour in just enough dressing to moisten greens. Serves 4.

TIP: This recipe is great with leftover chicken, turkey or fajita meat.

• • • • •

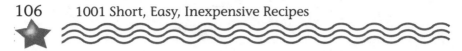

Greens and Avocado Toss

1 (10 ounce) package tossed green salad	280 g
2 avocados, peeled, sliced	
1 seedless cucumber, sliced	
½ cup honey-mustard salad dressing	125 ml

- Combine greens, avocados and cucumber slices and toss with dressing. Serves 4 to 6.

• • • • •

Romaine Salad

1 (10 ounce) package romaine lettuce, torn	280 g
2 cups broccoli florets	140 g
1 (1 pint) carton large fresh strawberries, quartered	360 g
½ red onion, coarsely chopped	
½ cup raspberry-vinaigrette dressing	125 ml

- In salad bowl, toss all ingredients except dressing. When ready to serve, toss with raspberry-vinaigrette salad dressing (not fat-free dressing). Serves 4.

• • • • •

Boston Bibb Lettuce Salad

1 head bibb lettuce, torn into pieces	
1 (11 ounce) can mandarin oranges, drained	310 g
⅓ cup chopped walnuts	45 g
⅓ cup poppy seed dressing	75 ml

- Combine lettuce, oranges and walnuts. Toss with dressing. Serves 4.

• • • • •

Artichoke-Tomato Salad

1 head romaine lettuce, torn into pieces	
1 (14 ounce) can artichoke hearts, drained, chopped	395 g
1 large tomato, cut in wedges	
⅓ cup creamy Italian dressing	75 ml

- Combine and toss all ingredients. Serves 4.

• • • • •

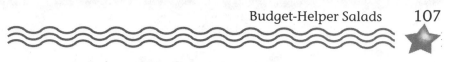

Caesar Salad

2 (8 ounce) packages romaine lettuce	2 (225 g)
1 (8 ounce) package shredded mozzarella cheese	225 g
1 (8 ounce) bottle Caesar salad dressing	250 ml
1 (6 ounce) box seasoned croutons	170 g

- Combine lettuce and cheese and toss with dressing. Sprinkle croutons over salad and serve. Serves 4 to 6.

• • • • •

Crunchy Salad

¼ cup sesame seeds	30 g
½ cup sunflower seeds	65 g
½ cup slivered almonds	85 g
1 head red leaf lettuce	
Creamy Italian dressing	

- Preheat oven to 300° (150° C) .

- Toast sesame seeds, sunflower seeds and almonds for about 10 minutes or until light brown. Tear lettuce into bite-size pieces and add seed-almond mixture. Toss with creamy Italian dressing. Serves 4 to 6.

• • • • •

Fresh Green Salad

1 (10 ounce) package romaine lettuce, chopped	280 g
1 seedless cucumber, sliced	
1 yellow bell pepper, seeded, chopped	
½ cup Craisins®	60 g
1 (8 ounce) bottle balsamic-vinaigrette salad dressing	250 ml

- In salad bowl, combine all ingredients except dressing. Serve with dressing. Serves 4 to 6.

• • • • •

Pepperoni Salad

2 cups lettuce, torn in bite-size pieces	90 g
½ cup pepperoni slices	50 g
½ cup shredded mozzarella cheese	55 g
Italian salad dressing	

- Combine lettuce, pepperoni and cheese and toss. Serve with desired amount Italian salad dressing. Serves 2.

TIP: Add sliced black olives for another flavor.

Seven-Layer Salad

1 small head lettuce, chopped	
1 (8 ounce) can sliced water chestnuts	225 g
1 red onion, chopped	
1 (10 ounce) package frozen peas, thawed	280 g
6 eggs, hard-boiled, sliced	
6 slices bacon, fried crisp, crumbled	
½ cup mayonnaise	110 g
1 (8 ounce) package shredded mozzarella cheese	225 g

- Layer lettuce, water chestnuts, red onion, peas, eggs and bacon in bowl in order listed. Seal with mayonnaise. Top with mozzarella cheese. Refrigerate uncovered for 24 hours. Serves 6.

• • • • •

Sesame-Romaine Salad

1 large head romaine lettuce	
2 tablespoons sesame seeds, toasted	30 ml
6 strips bacon, fried, crumbled	
½ cup shredded Swiss cheese	55 g
⅓ cup creamy Italian salad dressing	75 ml

- Wash and dry lettuce. Tear into bite-size pieces. When ready to serve, sprinkle sesame seeds, bacon and cheese over lettuce and toss with creamy Italian salad dressing. Serves 4 to 6.

• • • • •

Swiss Salad

1 large head romaine lettuce	
1 bunch fresh green onions with tops, chopped	
1 (8 ounce) package shredded Swiss cheese	225 g
½ cup sunflower seeds	65 g
⅔ cup salad oil	150 ml
⅓ cup red wine vinegar	75 ml

- Tear lettuce into bite-size pieces. Add onions, cheese and sunflower seeds and toss. Mix oil and vinegar plus 1 tablespoon (15 ml) salt for dressing and refrigerate. Toss with salad when ready to serve. Serves 4 to 6.

• • • • •

Tossed Zucchini Salad

½ cup oil	125 ml
3 tablespoons vinegar	45 ml
1½ teaspoons sugar	7 ml
2 tomatoes, cut in wedges	
2 cups thinly sliced zucchini	250 g
4 cups torn romaine lettuce	190 g

- Combine oil, vinegar, sugar, ¼ teaspoon (1 ml) salt and dash of pepper in jar with lid. Shake to mix. Refrigerate for 1 to 2 hours. In large bowl, toss tomatoes, zucchini and romaine. Toss salad with desired amount of dressing. Serves 4 to 6.

• • • • •

Frito Salad

1 head iceberg lettuce	
1 onion, chopped	
1 (16 ounce) package shredded cheddar cheese	455 g
3 tomatoes, chopped	
1 (15 ounce) can chili beans, rinsed, drained	425 g
1 (8 ounce) bottle Catalina dressing	250 ml
1 (13 ounce) package Fritos® corn chips, crushed	370 g

- Tear lettuce into bite-size pieces. Add onion, cheese, tomatoes, beans and dressing. Just before serving, toss with corn chips. Serves 4 to 6.

• • • • •

Turkey Salad

1 (10 ounce) package romaine lettuce, torn	280 g
1 (15 ounce) can black beans, rinsed, drained	425 g
1 (8 ounce) package cheddar cheese, cubed	225 g
2 - 3 cups cooked, diced turkey	280 - 420 g
⅓ cup precooked, crumbled bacon	35 g

Dressing:

½ cup mayonnaise	110 g
¾ cup salsa	200 g

- In salad bowl, combine lettuce, beans, cheese and turkey and mix well. Combine mayonnaise, salsa and ¾ teaspoon (4 ml) pepper. Spoon over salad and toss. Serves 4 to 6.

• • • • •

Luscious Papaya-Chicken Salad

This is a good time to use leftover grilled chicken breasts.

1 (10 ounce) package romaine lettuce leaves	280 g
2 ripe papayas, peeled, seeded, cubed	
1 large red bell pepper, seeded, sliced	
¼ cup lime juice	60 ml
¼ cup honey	85 g
2 teaspoons minced garlic	10 ml
3 tablespoons extra-virgin olive oil	45 ml
2 cups cooked, cubed chicken breast	280 g
½ cup chopped pecans, toasted	55 g

- In large salad bowl, combine lettuce, papayas and bell pepper. In small bowl, whisk lime juice, honey, garlic and a little salt. Slowly add olive oil in thin stream and whisk dressing until they blend well. Pour dressing over salad, add cubed chicken and toss. Sprinkle pecans over top of salad. Serves 6.

• • • • •

Ranch Chicken Salad

1 (20 ounce) can pineapple chunks, drained but save juice	565 g
2 cups cooked, cubed chicken	280 g
1 cup sliced celery	100 g
1 (1 ounce) packet dry buttermilk ranch-style dressing mix	30 g
½ cup mayonnaise	110 g

- Drain pineapple and set aside juice. Combine chicken, celery and pineapple in medium bowl. In separate bowl, combine dressing mix, mayonnaise and ¼ cup (60 ml) pineapple juice. Add dressing to chicken mixture and toss to coat. Refrigerate. Serves 4 to 6.

• • • • •

Chicken-Artichoke Salad

4 cups cooked, chopped chicken breasts	560 g
1 (14 ounce) can artichoke hearts, drained, chopped	395 g
½ cup chopped walnuts	65 g
1 cup chopped red bell pepper	150 g
⅔ cup mayonnaise	150 g

- In bowl, combine all ingredients and add a little salt and pepper. Cover and refrigerate until ready to serve. Serves 4 to 6.

• • • • •

Chicken Waldorf Salad

1 pound boneless, skinless chicken breasts	455 g
1 red apple with peel, sliced	
1 green apple with peel, sliced	
1 cup sliced celery	100 g
½ cup chopped walnuts	65 g
2 (6 ounce) cartons orange yogurt	2 (170 g)
½ cup mayonnaise	110 g
1 (6 ounce) package shredded lettuce	170 g

- Place chicken in large saucepan and cover with water. On high heat, cook about 15 minutes. Drain and cool. Cut into 1-inch (2.5 cm) chunks and season with a little salt and pepper.

- Place in large salad bowl. Add apples, celery and walnuts. Stir in yogurt and mayonnaise. Toss to mix well. Serve over shredded lettuce. (May be served room temperature or refrigerated several hours). Serves 6.

• • • • •

Fruited Ham Toss

2 cups sliced red apples	360 g
4 cups mixed salad greens	220 g
1 (6 ounce) package cooked sliced ham	170 g
Ranch-style dressing	

- Combine apples and salad greens. Cut ham into strips and toss with greens and apples. Serve with desired amount of ranch-style dressing. Serves 4.

• • • • •

Supper Salad Supreme

2 (15 ounce) cans great northern beans, rinsed, drained	2 (425 g)
1 pound cooked ham, cubed	455 g
2 bunches fresh broccoli, cut into florets	
1 red bell pepper, seeded, julienned	
1 orange bell pepper, seeded, julienned	
¾ pound Swiss cheese, cubed	340 g
1 cup garlic-vinaigrette salad dressing	250 ml

- In large bowl, combine beans, ham, broccoli florets, bell peppers and Swiss cheese. Toss with salad dressing. Serves 4 to 6.

• • • • •

Crabmeat Salad

1 (8 ounce) package imitation crabmeat	225 g
1 cup chopped apples	125 g
¼ cup mayonnaise	55 g
Lettuce leaves	

- Combine crabmeat, apples and mayonnaise and mix well. Refrigerate. Serve on lettuce leaves. Serves 2.

• • • • •

Shrimp and Spinach Salad

1 (8 ounce) package frozen salad shrimp, drained	225 g
3 cups fresh spinach, torn into pieces	90 g
½ cup chopped celery	50 g
Thousand island dressing	

- Combine shrimp, spinach and celery and toss with dressing. Serves 4.

• • • • •

Tuna-Artichoke Salad

2 (6 ounce) cans tuna	2 (170 g)
1 (14 ounce) can artichoke hearts, drained, chopped	395 g
Mayonnaise	

- Drain tuna and flake. Combine tuna with artichoke hearts and enough mayonnaise to moisten. Mix well. Serves 6.

TIP: Add slivered almonds or substitute cubed chicken breast for tuna.

• • • • •

Three-Bean Salad

1 (15 ounce) can cut green beans, drained	425 g
1 (15 ounce) can cut wax beans, drained	425 g
1 (15 ounce) can kidney beans, drained	425 g
1 (8 ounce) bottle Italian salad dressing	250 ml
1 (4 ounce) jar diced pimentos, drained	115 g

- Combine ingredients and refrigerate. Season to taste. Serves 6 to 8.

TIP: Add chopped onions and cherry tomato halves, if desired.

• • • • •

Rainbow Bean Salad

2 (15 ounce) cans cut green beans, drained	2 (425 g)
1 (15 ounce) can yellow wax beans, drained	425 g
1 small red onion, chopped	
1 orange bell pepper, seeded, julienned	
¾ cup Italian dressing	175 ml

- In container with lid, combine green beans, wax beans, red onion and bell pepper. Pour Italian dressing over vegetables just to cover. Refrigerate several hours. Serves 6 to 8.

• • • • •

Black Bean Salad

2 (15 ounce) cans black beans, rinsed, drained	2 (425 g)
2 (11 ounce) cans Mexicorn®, drained	2 (310 g)
1 green bell pepper, seeded, chopped	
1 small red onion, chopped	
1 (8 ounce) bottle garlic-vinaigrette salad dressing	250 ml

- In bowl with lid, combine all salad ingredients and cover with dressing. Refrigerate several hours before serving. Serves 6 to 8.

• • • • •

Bell Pepper Salad

1 medium red bell pepper, seeded, sliced	
1 medium green bell pepper, seeded, sliced	
1 medium yellow bell pepper, seeded, sliced	
½ cup vinaigrette dressing	125 ml

- Mix peppers in large bowl and toss with dressing. Refrigerate until ready to serve. Serves 4.

• • • • •

Make your own croutons with day-old bread. *Cut bread into cubes and toss in a plastic bag with garlic salt or other seasonings. Then spread the cubed bread in a single layer on a baking or cookie sheet and put into the oven when you turn it off after baking something. Leave in the oven until it has completely cooled. Store your croutons in a tightly sealed container and they will keep for a long time.*

Fresh Broccoli Salad

2 bunches broccoli	
½ pound bacon, fried, crumbled	225 g
½ cup chopped sweet onion	80 g
1 red bell pepper, seeded, chopped	
1 cup shredded sharp cheddar cheese	115 g

Dressing:

1 cup mayonnaise	225 g
2 tablespoons vinegar	30 ml
¼ cup sugar	50 g

- Chop tender portions of broccoli into bite-size florets.   Mix bacon with broccoli, onion, bell pepper and cheese. Combine dressing ingredients and toss salad with dressing just before serving. Serves 4 to 6.

• • • • •

Broccoli-Pepper Salad

5 cups broccoli florets, stemmed	355 g
1 sweet red bell pepper, seeded, julienned	
1 cup diagonally sliced celery	100 g
1 (8 ounce) package cubed Monterey Jack cheese	225 g
½ cup honey-mustard salad dressing	125 ml

- In bowl with lid, combine all salad ingredients and mix well. Toss with honey-mustard salad dressing. Serves 4 to 6.

• • • • •

Broccoli-Noodle Salad

1 cup slivered almonds	170 g
1 cup sunflower seeds	130 g
2 (3 ounce) packages chicken-flavored ramen noodles	2 (85 g)
1 (10 ounce) package broccoli slaw	280 g
1 (8 ounce) bottle Italian salad dressing	250 ml

- Preheat oven to 275° (135° C).

- Toast almonds and sunflower seeds in oven for about 10 minutes. Break up ramen noodles and mix with slaw, almonds, sunflower seeds and seasoning packets.

- Toss with Italian salad dressing and refrigerate several hours before serving. Serves 8 to 10.

• • • • •

Broccoli-Green Bean Salad

1 large bunch broccoli, cut into florets
2 (15 ounce) cans cut green beans, drained   2 (425 g)
1 bunch fresh green onions, chopped
2 (6 ounce) jars marinated artichoke hearts, chopped, drained   2 (170 g)
1½ cups ranch dressing   375 ml

- Combine broccoli, green beans, onions and artichokes and mix
  well. Add dressing and toss. Refrigerate 24 hours before serving.
  Serves 6 to 8.

• • • • •

Broccoli-Cauliflower Salad

1 small head cauliflower
3 bunches broccoli
1 cup mayonnaise   225 g
1 tablespoon vinegar   15 ml
1 tablespoon sugar   15 ml
1 bunch green onions, chopped
1 (8 ounce) package shredded mozzarella cheese   225 g

- Cut cauliflower and broccoli into florets. Combine mayonnaise,
  vinegar and sugar. Combine cauliflower, broccoli, mayonnaise
  mixture, onions and cheese. Add a little salt, toss and refrigerate.
  Serves 8 to 10.

• • • • •

Broccoli Salad

5 cups broccoli florets, stemmed, chilled   355 g
1 red bell pepper, seeded, julienned, chilled
1 cup diagonally sliced celery, chilled   100 g
1 (8 ounce) package shredded Monterey Jack cheese   225 g
1 zucchini, sliced
1 cup creamy Italian salad dressing   250 ml

- In salad bowl, combine all salad ingredients and toss with creamy
  Italian salad dressing. Refrigerate for several hours or freeze
  for about 15 minutes (no longer). Salad is best served cold.
  Serves 4 to 6.

• • • • •

If celery gets limp, place it in a tall container filled with cold
water. Refrigerate and the celery will become crisp again.

Raisin-Broccoli Salad

1 bunch fresh broccoli, cut in bite-size florets	
½ purple onion, sliced, separated into rings	
½ cup golden raisins	75 g
1 cup slivered almonds, toasted	170 g
Bacon bits	

- In large bowl, combine broccoli, onion, raisins and almonds.

Dressing:

1 cup mayonnaise	225 g
¼ cup sugar	50 g
2 tablespoons vinegar	30 ml

- In separate bowl, combine all dressing ingredients plus 1 teaspoon (5 ml) salt and ½ teaspoon (2 ml) pepper; pour over vegetables and toss well. Refrigerate for several hours before serving. Sprinkle bacon bits over salad just before serving. Serves 4 to 6.

• • • • •

Carrot-Raisin Salad

1 (16 ounce) package shredded carrots	455 g
1 cup raisins	160 g
½ cup mayonnaise	110 g

- Combine all ingredients, mix well and refrigerate. Serves 6.

• • • • •

Carrot Salad

3 cups finely grated carrots	330 g
1 (8 ounce) can crushed pineapple, drained	225 g
¼ cup flaked coconut	20 g
1 tablespoon sugar	15 ml
⅓ cup mayonnaise	75 g

- Combine carrots, pineapple and coconut. Combine sugar and mayonnaise; add to salad and mix well. Refrigerate. Serves 4 to 6.

 Make your own salad dressings. This is quick, easy, just as good as and cheaper than expensive bottled dressings. An easy vinaigrette is a mix of 3 to 4 parts olive oil with 1 part vinegar or lemon juice. Flavor the vinegar with tarragon or rosemary.

Cauliflower-Bacon Salad

1 large head cauliflower, cut into florets
2 green bell peppers, seeded, chopped
1½ cups cubed mozzarella cheese   200 g
12 – 14 slices bacon, cooked, crumbled
1 bunch fresh green onions, sliced

Dressing:

1 cup mayonnaise   225 g
1 tablespoon sugar   15 ml
1 tablespoon lemon juice   15 ml

- In plastic bowl with lid, combine cauliflower, bell peppers, cheese, bacon and green onions. In small bowl, combine mayonnaise, sugar, lemon juice and 1 teaspoon (5 ml) salt and stir to blend well.

- Spoon dressing over salad and toss to coat. Cover and refrigerate several hours before serving. Serves 6.

• • • • •

Italian Cauliflower Salad

1 head cauliflower, broken in florets
1 (8 ounce) bottle Italian salad dressing   250 ml
1 (4 ounce) can sliced mushrooms, drained   115 g
1 onion, chopped
1 (15 ounce) can green peas, drained   425 g

- Mix all ingredients and refrigerate overnight. Serves 6 to 8.

• • • • •

Marinated Corn Salad

3 (15 ounce) cans whole kernel corn, drained   3 (425 g)
1 green bell pepper, seeded, chopped
¾ cup chopped celery   75 g
1 (8 ounce) bottle Italian salad dressing   250 ml

- In bowl with lid, combine corn, bell pepper and celery. Pour salad dressing over vegetables. Refrigerate several hours before serving. Serves 4 to 6.

TIP: *For a special little zip, add several dashes hot sauce or walnuts for a little crunch.*

• • • • •

Corny Salad

3 (11 ounce) cans Mexicorn®, drained, chilled	3 (310 g)
1 (15 ounce) can green peas, drained, chilled	425 g
2 yellow bell peppers, seeded, chopped, chilled	
1 (8 ounce) bottle Italian dressing, chilled	250 ml

- In serving bowl with lid, combine corn, peas and peppers and pour dressing over vegetables. Refrigerate. When serving, use slotted spoon. Serves 4 to 6.

• • • • •

Sunshine Salad

3 (11 ounce) cans Mexicorn®, drained chilled	3 (310 g)
1 (15 ounce) can green peas, drained, chilled	425 g
1 (15 ounce) can wax beans, drained, rinsed, chilled	425 g
1 (8 ounce) bottle Italian dressing, chilled	250 ml

- In bowl with lid, combine corn, peas and beans. Add Italian dressing and toss. Refrigerate. Serves 8 to 10.

• • • • •

Redneck Salad

2 (15 ounce) cans whole kernel corn, drained	2 (425 g)
2 (15 ounce) cans black-eyed peas, drained	2 (425 g)
1 tomato, diced	
1 red onion, sliced	
1 (16 ounce) bottle zesty Italian dressing	500 ml

- Combine corn and peas in bowl. Add tomato and onion. Pour about half dressing over mixture (add more as needed) and refrigerate for 4 to 5 hours before serving. Serves 6.

• • • • •

Cucumber Salad

4 cucumbers, peeled, sliced	
1 medium onion, sliced into rings	
1½ cups mayonnaise	335 g
½ cup sugar	100 g
½ cup vinegar	125 ml

- Cover cucumbers and onions with dressing and refrigerate overnight in covered plastic bowl. Sprinkle a little salt over salad. Serves 4 to 6.

• • • • •

Green and White Salad

1 (16 ounce) package frozen green peas, thawed	455 g
1 head cauliflower, cut into bite-size pieces	
1 (8 ounce) carton sour cream	225 g
1 (1 ounce) packet dry ranch salad dressing	30 g

- In large bowl, combine peas and cauliflower. Combine sour cream and salad dressing. Toss with vegetables. Refrigerate. Serves 6 to 8.

• • • • •

English Pea Salad

1 (16 ounce) bag frozen green peas, thawed	455 g
1 bunch fresh green onions, chopped	
½ cup chopped celery	50 g
½ cup sweet pickle relish	125 g
Mayonnaise	

- Mix peas, onions, celery and relish. Add enough mayonnaise to hold salad together. Refrigerate. Serves 6 to 8.

• • • • •

Crunchy Pea Salad

1 (16 ounce) package frozen green peas, thawed	455 g
½ head cauliflower, cut into small florets	
1 cup chopped celery	50 g
1 (8 ounce) can sliced water chestnuts, drained	225 g
1½ cups mayonnaise	335 g
¼ cup Italian dressing	60 ml
1 cup chopped pecans	110 g

- Combine peas, cauliflower, celery, water chestnuts and about 1 teaspoon (5 ml) salt in large bowl. Mix mayonnaise and Italian dressing. Combine with salad, cover and refrigerate. When ready to serve, add pecans and toss well. Serves 6 to 8.

• • • • •

Take advantage of store brands. *Many store brands are manufactured by the same companies who make name brand products. They are very similar, if not the same, but cost less.*

Pea-Nut Salad

1 (16 ounce) package frozen baby peas, thawed, drained	455 g
¾ cup chopped celery, chilled	75 g
¼ cup chopped red bell pepper, chilled	35 g
1 cup peanut pieces, chilled	170 g
½ cup mayonnaise	110 g

- Combine peas, celery, bell pepper and peanuts. Toss. Add mayonnaise and mix well. Refrigerate. Serves 4 to 6.

• • • • •

Layered Potato Salad

12 medium red potatoes with peels	
1 cup sour cream	240 g
1 cup mayonnaise	225 g
½ teaspoon prepared horseradish	2 ml
1 cup chopped green onions	50 g/95 g

- Boil potatoes and cool.

- Mix sour cream, mayonnaise, horseradish and dash of salt in bowl.

- Slice potatoes and place half in 9 x 13-inch (23 x 33 cm) baking pan. Pour half of sour cream-mayonnaise mixture over potatoes. Sprinkle with half green onions. Repeat layers. Refrigerate. Serves 4 to 6.

• • • • •

Sour Cream Potato Salad

6 medium potatoes	
¼ cup oil	60 ml
¾ cup sour cream	180 g
½ cup mayonnaise	110 g
2 eggs, hard-boiled, chopped	

- Peel potatoes and cut into uniform cubes. Cook in boiling, salted water until done. Drain. Chill potatoes in refrigerator.

- Stir oil into chilled potatoes. Add sour cream, mayonnaise, eggs and a little salt and pepper and mix well. Serves 6 to 8.

• • • • •

Potato Salad Extra

1 (24 ounce) carton deli potato salad	680 g
3 fresh green onions, chopped	
1 (4 ounce) jar diced pimentos, drained	115 g
1 (10 ounce) jar stuffed green olives, chopped	280 g

- In serving bowl, combine potato salad, onions, pimentos and olives. Serves 6 to 8.

● ● ● ● ●

Tomato-Asparagus Salad

1 pound fresh asparagus spears	910 g
1 head romaine lettuce	
2 fresh tomatoes, sliced	
Italian salad dressing	

- Cook fresh asparagus in boiling water for 5 to 6 minutes or until tender and drain. Refrigerate until cold.

- Line 4 salad plates with romaine lettuce leaves. Arrange chilled asparagus spears and tomato slices over lettuce. Drizzle with a little Italian salad dressing. Serves 4 to 6.

● ● ● ● ●

Stuffed Tomatoes

4 tomatoes	
1 (12 ounce) carton cottage cheese, drained	340 g
1 small onion, chopped	

- Cut off top of tomatoes, scoop out pulp and drain. Combine cottage cheese and onion; mix well. Fill tomato cavity with cottage cheese mixture. Serves 4.

TIP: *Stuff tomatoes with tuna salad instead of cottage cheese as a variation.*

● ● ● ● ●

 Compare products and prices. *Fresh foods are always tempting, but sometimes frozen or canned are better buys with the same flavor.*

Gazpacho Salad

1 (3 ounce) package lemon gelatin	85 g
1 tablespoon vinegar	15 ml
¼ teaspoon garlic salt	1 ml
1 (15 ounce) can stewed tomatoes	425 g
1 (4 ounce) can diced green chilies	115 g
1 cup peeled, chopped cucumbers	120 g

- Dissolve gelatin in 1 cup (250 ml) boiling water. Add remaining ingredients plus ¼ teaspoon (1 ml) salt and pour into shallow salad bowl. Refrigerate. Serves 4 to 6.

• • • • •

Save money by doing it yourself. *Chop your own vegetables and wash your own lettuce. Make your own marinara and other tomato-based sauces by adding seasonings and sauteed chopped veggies to plain tomato sauce rather than buying the expensive brands. Stay away from sodium-heavy prepackaged rice and pasta mixes; you can easily season your own versions.*

Super-Saver Soups & Stews

*Nothing warms the body and
the soul like good soup.
Soups are not only full of flavor,
they are very filling and fit the budget.*

Cold Strawberry Soup

2¼ cups fresh strawberries	410 g
⅓ cup sugar	65 g
½ cup sour cream	120 g
½ cup whipping cream	125 ml
½ cup light red wine	125 ml

- Place strawberries and sugar in blender and puree. Pour into mixing bowl, stir in sour cream and cream and blend well. Add 1¼ cups (310 ml) water and wine. Stir well and refrigerate. Serves 4.

• • • • •

Quick Chilled Strawberry Soup

2 (10 ounce) packages frozen strawberries in syrup	2 (280 g)
½ cup cranberries	50 g
2 (8 ounce) cartons strawberry yogurt	2 (225 g)

- Combine all ingredients in blender and blend until smooth. Refrigerate for 1 to 2 hours before serving. Serves 6.

• • • • •

Tropical Fruit Soup

1 (15 ounce) can crushed pineapple with juice	425 g
1 (15 ounce) can cream of coconut	445 ml
1½ cups sour cream	360 g
1 (15 ounce) can fruit cocktail with juice	425 g
Sliced bananas and/or sliced strawberries	
Slivered almonds, toasted	

- Combine pineapple, cream of coconut, sour cream and fruit cocktail with 1 cup (250 ml) water in blender for 15 to 20 seconds. Refrigerate overnight.

- To serve, add sliced bananas and/or strawberries. Top with toasted almonds. Serves 6.

• • • • •

Fruits and vegetables are at their best prices at the peak of harvest. You'll be getting the best quality for the lowest cost. When fresh items are out of season, you'll be paying for transportation from far away places, plus the quality may not be as good because of increased time from farm to market.

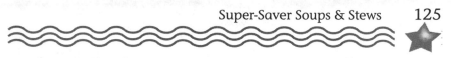

Avocado-Cream Soup

4 ripe avocados, peeled, diced, divided
1½ cups whipping cream, divided   375 ml
2 (14 ounce) cans chicken broth   2 (395 g)
Paprika

- In blender, process half avocados and half cream. Repeat with remaining avocados and cream.

- Bring chicken broth to a boil in saucepan, reduce heat and stir in avocado puree. Add 1 teaspoon (5 ml) salt and refrigerate until thoroughly chilled. Serve in individual bowls and sprinkle a little paprika on top. Serves 4 to 6.

• • • • •

Quick Borscht

1 (15 ounce) jar tiny whole red beets   425 g
1 (14 ounce) can beef broth   395 g
¼ cup sour cream   60 g

- Drain and set aside beet liquid. Chop beets. Combine beets, liquid and broth in saucepan and heat slowly for 10 minutes.

- Refrigerate and serve chilled with dollop of sour cream over top. Serves 4.

• • • • •

Senate Bean Soup

2 cups dried navy beans   290 g
½ pound ham hocks   225 g

- Cover beans with water and soak overnight. Drain and pour beans in 6 cups (1.4 L) water and cook with ham hocks for 2 to 3 hours or until tender. Remove ham hocks, cut up meat and return meat to soup. Heat until hot. Season with a little salt and pepper. Serves 4.

• • • • •

 Make a quick homemade soup *by freezing leftover meat and vegetables from a meal. When you're ready, just mix meat and veggies with broth or tomato juice, season and heat.*

Hearty Bean and Ham Soup

¼ cup (½ stick) butter	55 g
1 (15 ounce) can sliced carrots, drained	425 g
1 cup chopped celery	100 g
2 - 3 cups cooked, diced ham	280 - 420 g
2 (15 ounce) cans navy beans with liquid	2 (425 g)
2 (15 ounce) cans jalapeno pinto beans with liquid	2 (425 g)
2 (14 ounce) cans chicken broth	2 (395 g)
2 teaspoons chili powder	10 ml

- In soup pot with butter, cook carrots and celery about 8 minutes until tender-crisp.

- Add diced ham, beans, broth, chili powder, and a little salt and pepper. Bring to a boil, stirring constantly, for 3 minutes. Reduce heat and simmer for 15 minutes. Serves 6 to 8.

• • • • •

Lentil and Bean Curry Soup

1 (14 ounce) can chicken broth	395 g
1 (7 ounce) package lentil pilaf mix	200 g
1 tablespoon curry powder	15 ml
1 (8 ounce) can green peas	225 g
1 (15 ounce) can diced tomatoes	425 g
1 (15 ounce) can great northern beans, drained	425 g

- Combine 3 cups (750 ml) water, broth, lentil mix and seasoning packet, and curry powder. Bring to boil. Reduce heat and simmer, covered, for 30 minutes. Add peas. Cook uncovered for 5 minutes. Stir in tomatoes and beans. Heat. Serves 4 to 6.

• • • • •

Black-Eyed Pea Chowder

1 pound turkey bacon	455 g
1 tablespoon butter	15 ml
1½ cups chopped onion	240 g
2 (15 ounce) cans black-eyed peas	2 (425 g)
1 (10 ounce) can beef broth	280 g
1 (15 ounce) can whole kernel corn with liquid	425 g
2 (15 ounce) cans Mexican stewed tomatoes	2 (425 g)

- In skillet, brown turkey bacon. Chop into bite-size pieces and set aside. In large heavy pan, melt butter and saute onion until tender.

- Add turkey bacon and all remaining ingredients. Bring to a boil, reduce heat and simmer for 30 minutes. Serves 6 to 8.

Broccoli-Wild Rice Soup

1 (6 ounce) package chicken-flavored wild rice mix	170 g
1 (10 ounce) package frozen chopped broccoli, thawed	280 g
2 teaspoons dried minced onion flakes	10 ml
1 (10 ounce) can cream of chicken soup	280 g
1 (8 ounce) package cream cheese, cubed	225 g

- In large saucepan, combine rice mix, seasoning packet and 6 cups (1.4 L) water. Bring to a boil, reduce heat, cover and simmer for 10 minutes, stirring once.

- Stir in broccoli and onion flakes and simmer for 5 additional minutes. Stir in soup and cream cheese. Cook and stir until cheese melts. Serves 6 to 8.

• • • • •

Incredible Broccoli-Cheese Soup

1 (10 ounce) package frozen chopped broccoli	280 g
3 tablespoons butter	45 ml
¼ medium onion, finely chopped	
¼ cup flour	30 g
1 (16 ounce) carton half-and-half cream	500 ml
1 (14 ounce) can chicken broth	395 g
1 (8 ounce) package cubed mild Mexican Velveeta® cheese	225 g

- Punch several holes in broccoli package and microwave for 5 minutes. Turn package and microwave additional 4 minutes. Leave in microwave for 3 minutes.

- In large saucepan, melt butter and saute onion, but do not brown. Add flour, stir and gradually add cream, chicken broth, ½ teaspoon (2 ml) salt and ¼ teaspoon (1 ml) pepper.

- Stir constantly and heat until mixture is slightly thick. Do NOT let mixture come to boil. Add cheese, stir and heat until cheese melts. Add cooked broccoli. Serve piping hot. Serves 6 to 8.

• • • • •

Soups and stews don't cost much. It's easy to make soup stocks from meat scraps and bones boiled with vegetables such as carrots, celery and onions. These are simmered slowly in water in a soup pot until all the flavor is in the stock. Discard the bones, meat and vegetables and you have the start of a delicious soup.

Broccoli-Noodle Soup

1 (12 ounce) package egg noodles	340 g
1 (16 ounce) package, frozen, chopped broccoli	455 g
1 (1 pint) carton half-and-half cream	500 ml
1 (14 ounce) can chicken broth	395 g
1 (16 ounce) box Velveeta® cheese, cubed	455 g

- Cook noodles and broccoli according to package directions. Set aside. Combine half-and-half cream, broth and cheese. Heat on low and stir until cheese melts. Add noodles and broccoli and simmer until mixture heats thoroughly. Serves 6 to 8.

• • • • •

Cabbage and Potato Soup

4 cups coarsely shredded cabbage	280 g
2 medium potatoes, peeled, chopped	
1 cup chopped onion	160 g
2 (15 ounce) cans diced tomatoes with liquid	2 (425 g)
3 tablespoons lemon juice	45 ml
2 tablespoons plus 2 teaspoons sugar	30 ml/10 ml

- In large pot, combine cabbage, potatoes, onion and 3 cups (750 ml) water. Cover and cook on medium heat for 15 minutes. Add remaining ingredients.

- Bring to a boil. Cover and reduce heat to low. Simmer for 45 minutes to 1 hour or until potatoes are tender. Serves 6 to 8.

• • • • •

Corn Soup

2 (15 ounce) cans whole kernel corn with liquid	2 (425 g)
3 tablespoons chunky salsa	45 ml
2 tablespoons peach preserves	30 ml

- Combine all ingredients with 1 cup (250 ml) water and mix well. Bring to a boil, reduce heat and simmer 5 minutes. Serves 4.

• • • • •

Buy lemons in quantity when on sale and freeze the juice and zest. Freeze the juice in 1 tablespoon amount in ice cube trays. Once frozen, put the cubes in a resealable plastic bag and use as needed.

Microwave Mushroom Soup

1 (10 ounce) can cream of mushroom soup	280 g
1 (10 ounce) can beef broth	280 g
1 (4 ounce) can sliced mushrooms	115 g

- Combine mushroom soup and broth in 2-quart (2 L) bowl and mix well. Microwave on HIGH for 1 minute and stir. Add sliced mushrooms and mix.

- Microwave on MEDIUM for 1 additional minute or until hot. Stir before serving. Serves 2.

Favorite Onion Soup

½ pound white onions, sliced, separated into rings	225 g
½ cup (1 stick) butter	55 g
3 tablespoons flour	45 ml
2 (14 ounce) cans chicken broth	2 (395 g)
2 (14 ounce) cans beef broth	2 (395 g)
1 cup shredded Swiss cheese	110 g
8 slices French bread	

- Preheat broiler.

- In large saucepan, saute onions in butter until onions are transparent, but not brown. When tender, turn heat to simmer, sprinkle with flour and stir vigorously. Stir in broths. Heat thoroughly and divide among 8 ovenproof bowls.

- Mix cheese with 1 tablespoon (15 ml) water to form a smooth paste and spread over bread. Float slice of bread on top of each serving. Place all bowls on oven rack 4 inches (10 cm) from broiler. Broil until cheese melts. Serves 8.

Speedy Pea Soup

1 (15 ounce) can green peas with liquid	425 g
1 cup half-and-half cream	250 ml
¼ medium onion, chopped	
3 tablespoons butter	45 ml
Croutons	

- Heat green peas and cream. Pour into blender. Add onion, butter, ¼ teaspoon (1 ml) salt and dash of pepper. Blend until smooth, about 1 minute. Pour from container into saucepan and heat thoroughly, but do not boil. Pour into soup bowls and garnish with croutons. Serves 4 to 6.

• • • • •

Potato Soup

1 large baking potato, peeled, cubed	
1 (14 ounce) can chicken broth	395 g
1 cup shredded Velveeta® cheese	115 g
1 (8 ounce) carton whipping cream	250 ml

- Boil potato, drain and mash with fork. Add broth, cheese and cream to mashed potatoes in saucepan, heat and stir often until hot. Serves 4.

• • • • •

Heidelberg Soup

2 (10 ounce) cans potato soup	2 (280 g)
6 slices salami, cubed	
10 green onions, chopped	

- Dilute soup according to label directions. Saute cubed salami and onions in sprayed skillet and add to soup. Heat thoroughly and serve hot. Serves 4.

• • • • •

Homemade Tomato Soup

3 (15 ounce) cans whole tomatoes with liquid	3 (425 g)
1 (14 ounce) can chicken broth	395 g
1 tablespoon sugar	15 ml
1 tablespoon minced garlic	15 ml
¾ cup whipping cream	175 ml

- With blender, puree tomatoes (in batches) and pour into large saucepan. Add chicken broth, sugar, garlic and a little salt and bring to boiling. Reduce heat and stir in whipping cream.

- Cook, stirring constantly, for 2 to 3 minutes or until soup is hot. Do not boil. Serves 4 to 6.

• • • • •

South-of-the-Border Tomato Soup

1 (18 ounce) can spicy tomato cocktail juice	510 g
⅓ cup minced onion	55 g
2 avocados, peeled, seeded, diced, divided	

- Heat tomato juice and onion for 5 minutes or until very hot. Stir in three-fourths of diced avocado and heat. Pour into bowls and sprinkle remaining diced avocado on top of soup and serve immediately. Serves 2.

El Paso Tomato Soup

1 (10 ounce) can tomato soup	280 g
1 (14 ounce) can stewed tomatoes with onion	395 g
1 (10 ounce) can diced tomatoes and green chilies	280 g

- Mix all ingredients plus 1 soup can water in saucepan. Heat to boiling, stirring often. Reduce heat and simmer for 5 minutes. Serves 3.

• • • • •

Cheesy French Onion Soup

1 (10 ounce) can fiesta nacho cheese soup	280 g
2 (10 ounce) cans French onion soup	2 (280 g)
Croutons	
Grated parmesan cheese	

- In saucepan, combine soups and 2 soup cans water and heat thoroughly. Top each serving with croutons and sprinkle with cheese. Serves 4 to 6.

• • • • •

Tomato-Basil Soup

1 (15 ounce) can diced tomatoes with liquid	425 g
12 - 14 fresh basil leaves	
4 cups tomato juice	945 ml
1 (8 ounce) carton whipping cream	250 ml
¼ cup (½ stick) butter	55 g

- Place tomatoes with liquid in saucepan and simmer for 30 minutes. Puree tomatoes with liquid and basil leaves in blender. Return to saucepan and add tomato juice, cream, butter, and ¼ teaspoon (1 ml) each of salt and pepper. Heat thoroughly, but do not boil. Serves 4 to 6.

• • • • •

Spicy Tomato Soup

2 (10 ounce) cans tomato soup	2 (280 g)
1 (15 ounce) can Mexican stewed tomatoes	425 g
Sour cream	
½ pound bacon, fried, drained, crumbled	225 g

- In saucepan, combine soup and stewed tomatoes and heat. Place dollop of sour cream on each serving and sprinkle crumbled bacon over sour cream. Serves 4.

Snappy Spicy Tomato Soup

2 (10 ounce) cans tomato soup	2 (280 g)
1 (10 ounce) can tomato bisque soup	280 g
1 (10 ounce) can diced tomatoes and green chilies	280 g
½ cup sour cream	120 g

- In saucepan over medium heat, combine soups, tomatoes and green chilies, and ¾ cup (175 ml) water and heat until hot. When ready to serve (make sure soup is still very hot), stir in sour cream and pour into cups. Serves 4.

• • • • •

Cheesy Vegetable Soup

1 (16 ounce) bag frozen mixed vegetables	455 g
3 (14 ounce) cans chicken broth	3 (395 g)
1 (8 ounce) package shredded Velveeta® cheese	225 g
1 (10 ounce) can diced tomatoes and green chilies	280 g

- Cook vegetables in broth. Add cheese and stir until cheese melts. Add tomatoes and green chilies. Heat thoroughly. Serves 4 to 6.

• • • • •

Warm-Your-Soul Soup

3 (14 ounce) cans chicken broth	3 (395 g)
2 (15 ounce) cans Italian stewed tomatoes	2 (425 g)
1 onion, chopped	
1 rib celery, chopped	
1 (8 ounce) package fettuccine	225 g

- In large soup pot, combine broth, tomatoes, onion, celery and 2 cups (500 ml) water. Bring to a boil, reduce heat and simmer until onion and celery are tender-crisp. Cook fettuccine according to package directions. Stir into broth mixture with a little salt and pepper. Cook until thoroughly hot. Serves 6.

• • • • •

Cut loss; don't toss. *Bits of leftovers can easily go into soups, stews, stir-fry, sandwiches, etc., later in the week.*

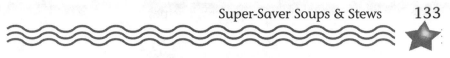

Tortellini Soup

3 (14 ounce) cans chicken broth	3 (395 g)
2 (9 ounce) packages refrigerated cheese tortellini	2 (255 g)
1 (15 ounce) can cannellini beans, rinsed, drained	425 g
1 (4 ounce) jar diced pimentos	115 g
1 teaspoon dried basil	5 ml
1 tablespoon balsamic vinegar	15 ml

- In large saucepan, bring broth to boiling. Add tortellini and cook about 6 minutes or until tender. Stir in beans, pimentos, basil, vinegar and a little salt and pepper. Simmer for 8 to 10 minutes. Serves 4 to 6.

• • • • •

Vegetarian Chili

2 (15 ounce) cans stewed tomatoes	2 (425 g)
1 (15 ounce) can kidney beans, rinsed, drained	425 g
1 (15 ounce) can pinto beans with liquid	425 g
1 (10 ounce) package frozen chopped bell peppers and onions	280 g
1 tablespoon chili powder	15 ml
1 (8 ounce) package elbow macaroni	225 g
¼ cup (½ stick) butter, sliced	55 g
1 (8 ounce) package shredded cheddar cheese	

- Combine tomatoes, beans, bell peppers and onions, chili powder, and 1 cup (250 ml) water in slow cooker. Cover and cook on LOW for 4 to 5 hours or HIGH for 2 hours.

- Cook macaroni according to package directions, drain and stir butter into hot pasta. Fold into chili. Before serving, sprinkle with cheese. Serves 6.

• • • • •

Chili

1 pound lean ground beef	455 g
2 teaspoons garlic powder	10 ml
2 tablespoons chili powder	30 ml
1 tablespoon flour	15 ml
1 (8 ounce) can tomato sauce	225 g

- Brown hamburger meat with garlic powder. Drain excess fat. Add chili powder, flour and 1 teaspoon (5 ml) salt. Stir and mix well.

- Add tomato sauce and 1 cup (250 ml) water. Heat to boiling, reduce heat and simmer 20 minutes. Stir often. Serves 3 to 4.

• • • • •

Chili Soup

3 (15 ounce) cans chili with beans	3 (425 g)
1 (15 ounce) can whole kernel corn	425 g
1 (14 ounce) can beef broth	395 g
2 (15 ounce) cans Mexican stewed tomatoes	2 (425 g)
2 teaspoons ground cumin	10 ml
2 teaspoons chili powder	10 ml

- Combine all ingredients in saucepan. Bring to a boil, reduce heat and simmer for 15 minutes. Serves 4 to 6.

• • • • •

Beefy Vegetable Soup

1 pound lean ground beef	455 g
1 (46 ounce) can cocktail vegetable juice	1.4 L
1 (1 ounce) packet onion soup mix	30 g
1 (3 ounce) package beef-flavored ramen noodles	85 g
1 (16 ounce) package frozen mixed vegetables	455 g

- In large soup pot over medium heat, cook beef until no longer pink. Drain. Stir in cocktail juice, soup mix, contents of noodle seasoning packet and mixed vegetables.

- Heat mixture to boiling, reduce heat and simmer uncovered for 6 minutes or until vegetables are tender-crisp. Return to boiling, stir in noodles and cook for 3 minutes. Serves 4 to 6.

• • • • •

Mexican Vegetable Beef Soup

1 pound ground beef	455 g
2 (10 ounce) cans vegetable soup	2 (280 g)
1 (14 ounce) can beef broth	395 g
1 (10 ounce) can diced tomatoes and green chilies with liquid	280 g

- In skillet, brown ground beef and drain. Stir in soups, broth, tomatoes and green chilies with liquid, and 2 cups (500 ml) water. Heat on high heat until hot, stirring often. Reduce heat to low and simmer for 30 minutes. Serves 4 to 6.

Buy meats on sale and cut up any leftovers for soups and stews. *Freeze stock or soup for later use in ice cube trays. After the cubes are frozen, place the cubes in freezer containers or plastic bags.*

Santa Fe Stew

1½ pounds ground beef	680 g
1 (1 ounce) packet taco seasoning	30 g
1 (1 ounce) packet ranch-style dressing mix	30 g
1 (15 ounce) can whole kernel corn with liquid	425 g
1 (15 ounce) can kidney beans with liquid	425 g
2 (15 ounce) cans pinto beans with liquid	2 (425 g)
2 (15 ounce) cans stewed tomatoes with liquid	425 g
1 (10 ounce) can diced tomatoes and green chilies	280 g

- Cook beef until brown. Drain well if necessary. Add both packages of seasoning and mix well. Add corn, beans, stewed tomatoes, and tomatoes and green chilies and mix well. Simmer for 25 minutes. If you want it really hot, use 2 cans diced tomatoes and green chilies. Serves 6.

• • • • •

Minute Stew

1 pound extra lean ground beef	455 g
2 (15 ounce) cans stewed tomatoes and onions with liquid	2 (425 g)
1 (8 ounce) can whole kernel corn, drained	225 g
1 (14 ounce) can beef broth	395 g

- Brown ground meat in skillet and drain. Add tomatoes, corn and broth to meat in skillet and mix well. Heat on high, stirring often, until stew comes to boil. Lower heat and simmer for 20 minutes and stir often. Serves 4 to 6.

• • • • •

Easy Oven Soup

1 (1 ounce) packet dry onion soup mix	30 g
1 (10 ounce) can cream of mushroom soup	280 g
1 cup red wine	250 ml
1 (16 ounce) package frozen stew meat	455 g

- Preheat oven to 300° (150° C).

- In large heavy pan, mix soup mix, soup, wine, 1 cup (250 ml) water and a little pepper. Stir in meat. Cover and bake for 3 to 4 hours. Serves 4.

• • • • •

Steakhouse Stew

1 pound beef stew meat	455 g
1 (15 ounce) can stewed tomatoes	425 g
1 (10 ounce) can French onion soup	280 g
1 (10 ounce) can tomato soup	280 g
1 (16 ounce) package frozen stew vegetables, thawed	455 g

- In skillet with a little oil, cook stew meat until juices evaporate. Transfer to soup pot. Add 1 cup (250 ml) water, tomatoes, soups and vegetables and heat to boiling.

- Reduce heat to low and cook on medium for about 15 minutes or until vegetables and beef are tender. Serves 4.

• • • • •

No-Peek Stew

2 pounds beef stew meat, fat trimmed	910 g
1 (10 ounce) can cream of mushroom soup	280 g
1 (1 ounce) packet dry onion soup mix	30 g
Cooked rice or noodles	

- Preheat oven to 325° (165° C).

- In roasting pan, combine all ingredients and mix well. Stir in 1 cup (250 ml) water, cover and bake for 2 hours 30 minutes. Do not peek! Serve over rice or noodles. Serves 4.

• • • • •

Mushroom Soup

1 (10 ounce) can cream of mushroom soup	280 g
1 (14 ounce) can beef broth	395 g
1 (2.2 ounce) can dried beef, chopped	60 g

- Combine all ingredients with ¾ cup (175 ml) water in medium saucepan. Mix well and heat thoroughly. Serves 3 to 4.

• • • • •

While you may enjoy the convenience of purchasing stew meat already cut up, a chuck roast on sale may be a better buy. Part of the roast can be used as a roast and the rest cut up in 1-inch stewing cubes.

Chicken-Noodle Soup Supper

1 (3 ounce) package chicken-flavored ramen noodles, broken	85 g
1 (10 ounce) package frozen green peas, thawed	280 g
1 tablespoon butter	15 ml
1 (4 ounce) jar sliced mushrooms, drained	115 g
3 cups cooked, cubed chicken	420 g

- In large saucepan, heat 2¼ cups (560 ml) water to boiling. Add ramen noodles, contents of seasoning packet, peas and butter. Heat to boiling, reduce heat to medium and cook for about 5 minutes.

- Stir in mushrooms and chicken and continue cooking over low heat until all ingredients are hot. Serves 6.

• • • • •

Chicken-Vegetable Chili

1 (16 ounce) package frozen chopped bell peppers and onions	455 g
Oil	
2 tablespoons minced garlic	30 ml
2 tablespoons chili powder	30 ml
1 tablespoon ground cumin	15 ml
2 pounds boneless, skinless chicken breast halves, cut into small pieces	910 g
2 (14 ounce) cans chicken broth	2 (395 g)
3 (15 ounce) cans pinto beans with jalapenos, divided	3 (425 g)

- Cook bell peppers and onions with a little oil in skillet for about 5 minutes, stirring occasionally. Add garlic, chili powder, cumin, chicken, broth and a little salt. While stirring, bring to a boil.

- Cover and simmer for 15 minutes. Place 1 can beans in shallow bowl and mash with fork. Add mashed beans and remaining 2 cans beans to pot. Bring to a boil, reduce heat and simmer for 10 minutes. Serves 6 to 8.

• • • • •

When cutting up a whole chicken, save the odds and ends such as the giblets, neck, tail, wingtips and freeze. When you have several packets of these bits of chicken, use them to make chicken stock.

A Different Chili

Oil	
2 onions, coarsely chopped	
3 (15 ounce) cans great northern beans, drained, divided	3 (425 g)
2 (14 ounce) cans chicken broth	2 (395 g)
2 tablespoons minced garlic	30 ml
1 (7 ounce) can diced green chilies	200 g
1 tablespoon ground cumin	15 ml
3 cups cooked, diced chicken breasts	420 g
1 (8 ounce) package shredded Monterey Jack cheese	225 g

- In large heavy pot with a little oil, cook onions for about 5 minutes, but do not brown. Place 1 can beans in shallow bowl and mash with fork. Add mashed beans, 2 remaining cans beans, broth, garlic, green chilies and cumin. Bring to boil and reduce heat. Cover and simmer 30 minutes.

- Add diced chicken, stir to blend well and heat until chili is thoroughly hot. Top each serving with 3 tablespoons (45 ml) Jack cheese. Serves 4 to 6.

• • • • •

Zesty Chicken-Cream Soup

1 (10 ounce) can cream of celery soup	280 g
1 (10 ounce) can cream of mushroom soup	280 g
1 (10 ounce) can cream of chicken soup	280 g
2 (14 ounce) cans chicken broth	2 (395 g)
2 soup cans milk	
2 teaspoons garlic powder	1 ml
1 (16 ounce) package cubed Mexican Velveeta® cheese	455 g
4 boneless, skinless chicken breasts, cooked, diced	

- In soup pot or large roasting pan, combine all ingredients and heat while stirring constantly; do not boil. Reduce heat to medium-low and cook until cheese melts. Serve piping hot. Serves 6 to 8.

• • • • •

Speedy Taco Soup

2 (14 ounce) cans chicken broth	2 (396 g)
1 (12 ounce) can chunk chicken breast with liquid	340 g
1 (16 ounce) jar mild thick-and-chunky salsa	455 g
2 (15 ounce) cans pinto beans with liquid	2 (425 g)
1 (15 ounce) can whole kernel corn, drained	425 g

- In large saucepan, combine broth, chicken with liquid, salsa, beans and corn. Heat to boiling, reduce heat and simmer for 15 minutes. Serves 4 to 6.

Cheesy Chicken Soup

1 (10 ounce) can fiesta nacho cheese soup	280 g
1 (10 ounce) can cream of chicken soup	280 g
2 (14 ounce) cans chicken broth	2 (395 g)
1 cup half-and-half cream	250 ml
2 (12 ounce) cans white chicken breast with liquid	2 (340 g)

- In saucepan over medium heat, combine all ingredients and stir until soup is hot. Serves 4 to 6.

• • • • •

Six-Can Chicken Soup

2 (14 ounce) cans chicken broth	2 (395 g)
1 (10 ounce) can cream of chicken soup	280 g
1 (12 ounce) can chicken breast	340 g
1 (15 ounce) can chili beans	425 g
1 (10 ounce) can diced tomatoes and green chilies	280 g
1 (16 ounce) bag tortilla chips	455 g
1 (8 ounce) package shredded Velveeta® cheese	225 g
Sour cream	

- In saucepan combine broth, soup, chicken, beans, and tomatoes and green chilies; simmer for 30 minutes. Serve over a few crushed tortilla chips and top with cheese and sour cream. Serves 5 to 6.

• • • • •

Spicy Turkey Soup

3 - 4 cups cooked, chopped turkey	420 - 560 g
2 (14 ounce) cans chicken broth	2 (395 g)
2 (10 ounce) cans diced tomatoes and green chilies	2 (280 g)
1 (15 ounce) can whole kernel corn	425 g
1 large onion, chopped	
1 (10 ounce) can tomato soup	280 g
2 teaspoons garlic powder	10 ml
3 tablespoons cornstarch	45 ml

- In large roasting pan, combine turkey, broth, tomatoes and green chilies, corn, onion, soup, and garlic powder. Mix cornstarch with 3 tablespoons (45 ml) water and add to soup mixture.

- Bring mixture to a boil, reduce heat and simmer for 2 hours. Stir occasionally. Serves 4 to 6.

• • • • •

Hearty 15-Minute Turkey Soup

1 (14 ounce) can chicken broth	395 g
3 (15 ounce) cans navy beans, rinsed, drained	3 (425 g)
1 (28 ounce) can diced tomatoes with liquid	795 g
2 - 3 cups cooked, cubed white turkey meat	280 - 420 g
2 teaspoons minced garlic	10 ml
¼ teaspoon cayenne pepper	1 ml
⅓ cup grated parmesan cheese	35 g

- Mix all ingredients except cheese and heat. Garnish with parmesan cheese. Serves 6 to 8.

• • • • •

Pinto Bean Soup

2 (1 pound) packages dry pinto beans	2 (455 g)
1 smoked ham hock or 2 cups chopped ham	280 g

- Wash beans, cover with cold water and soak overnight. Drain, cover beans with water and bring to a boil. Add ham, reduce heat and simmer slowly 3 to 4 hours. (You may need to add more water.)

- When beans are tender, remove 2 to 3 cups beans and smash with potato masher. Return to pot and season with a little salt and pepper. Serves 4 to 6.

• • • • •

Sausage and Corn Chowder

½ pound hot Italian sausage	225 g
2 (15 ounce) cans Mexicorn® with liquid	2 (425 g)
2 (14 ounce) cans chicken broth	2 (395 g)
1 rib celery, sliced	
½ cup chopped onion	80 g

- Remove casing from sausage, place sausage in skillet and crumble. Cook over medium heat until meat is done.

- Stir in corn, chicken broth, celery, onions, and a little salt and pepper. Mix well and bring to a boil. Lower heat and simmer for 20 minutes or until hot. Serves 4.

• • • • •

Spaghetti Soup

1 (8 ounce) package thin spaghetti, broken into fourths	225 g
1 (18 ounce) package frozen cooked meatballs, thawed	510 g
1 (28 ounce) jar spaghetti sauce	795 g
1 (15 ounce) can Mexican stewed tomatoes	425 g

• In soup pot with 3 quarts (3 L) boiling water and a little salt, cook spaghetti for about 6 minutes (no need to drain). When spaghetti is done, add meatballs, spaghetti sauce and stewed tomatoes and cook until mixture is hot. Serves 4 to 6.

• • • • •

Easy Meaty Minestrone

2 (20 ounce) cans minestrone soup	2 (565 g)
1 (15 ounce) can pinto beans with liquid	425 g
1 (18 ounce) package frozen cooked Italian meatballs, thawed	510 g
1 (5 ounce) package grated parmesan cheese	145 g

• In large saucepan, combine soup, beans, meatballs and ½ cup (125 ml) water. Bring to a boil, reduce heat to low and simmer for about 15 minutes. Sprinkle each serving with parmesan cheese. Serves 4 to 6.

• • • • •

Three-Can Clam Chowder

1 (10 ounce) can New England clam chowder	280 g
1 (10 ounce) can cream of celery soup	280 g
1 (10 ounce) can cream of potato soup	280 g
1 cup milk	250 ml

• Combine all ingredients in saucepan and mix well. Heat thoroughly. Serves 4.

• • • • •

Every time you bake or boil a chicken, you have chicken stock. Pour the grease off the top and pour the stock into a jar or freezer container. Freeze the homemade stock instead of paying more for canned chicken stock or broth.

Crab-Corn Chowder

1 (1 ounce) packet leek soup mix	30 g
2 cups milk	500 ml
1 (8 ounce) can whole kernel corn	225 g
½ (8 ounce) package cubed Velveeta® cheese	½ (225 g)
1 (7 ounce) package imitation crabmeat, flaked	200 g

- In large saucepan, combine soup mix and milk and cook over medium heat, stirring constantly, until soup thickens. While still on medium heat, add corn and cheese, stirring just until cheese melts. Stir in crab and bring to a boil. Reduce heat and simmer 10 minutes. Serves 4 to 6.

• • • • •

Look for quality cookware and utensils at garage and yard sales and even at flea markets. Some people will sell things in good condition just because they wanted cookware in a different color. Sales of this nature can be a great opportunity to pick up cast iron pots and skillets – even though you may have to scour rust and reseason them.

Bag-of-Tricks Sides

Vegetables and other side dishes fill out a menu – as well as a family. Tasty and attractive, they add vitamins and other nutrients.

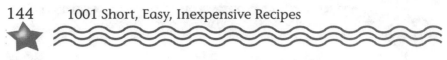

Sauteed Apples

4 - 6 apples, peeled, cored, sliced
1 cup flour   120 g
3 tablespoons butter, melted   45 ml
Sugar
Cinnamon

- Roll apples in flour and saute in melted butter until golden brown.
  Sprinkle with sugar or cinnamon Serve with ham or roast pork.
  Yields 2 to 3 cups.

Artichoke-Spinach Casserole

1 (16 ounce) can artichoke hearts, drained   455 g
2 (16 ounce) packages frozen chopped spinach, cooked,
        drained well   2 (455 g)
2 (3 ounce) packages cream cheese, cubed   2 (85 g)
¼ cup (½ stick) butter, melted, divided   55 g
½ cup breadcrumbs   60 g

- Preheat oven to 350° (175° C).

- Arrange artichoke hearts in sprayed 9 x 13-inch (23 x 33 cm) baking
  dish. Blend cooked spinach and cheese with half of melted butter
  and a little salt and pepper. Pour on top of artichokes. Refrigerate
  at least 45 minutes.

- Blend crumbs with remaining butter and add to top before baking.
  Bake for 25 minutes. Serves 6 to 8.

Asparagus Salad

2 (15 ounce) cans asparagus spears, drained   2 (425 g)
1 cup shredded Swiss cheese   110 g
3 fresh green onions with tops, chopped

- Place asparagus on serving plate and sprinkle cheese and onions on
  top. Serve at room temperature. Serves 4 to 6.

Tarragon Asparagus

1 pound fresh asparagus spears   455 g
1 tablespoon tarragon   15 ml
Butter spray

- Wash asparagus and break off at tender point. Steam over boiling
  water for 6 minutes or until barely tender. Remove from heat and
  drain. Spray with butter spray and sprinkle with tarragon and
  ¼ teaspoon (1 ml) pepper. Serves 2 to 4.

Deluxe Asparagus

1 (15 ounce) can cut asparagus	425 g
2 eggs, beaten	
¾ cup shredded Mexican 4-cheese blend	85 g

- Preheat oven to 350° (175° C).

- Drain asparagus and set aside ¼ cup (60 ml) liquid.

- In mixing bowl, combine eggs and set aside asparagus liquid and mix well. Arrange asparagus in a 9-inch sprayed baking dish and pour egg mixture over asparagus. Sprinkle cheese over top and bake for 30 minutes. Serves 2 to 4.

• • • • •

Buffet Asparagus Casserole

2 (15 ounce) cans asparagus, drained	2(425 g)
1 (15 ounce) can green peas, drained	425 g
½ cup shredded cheddar cheese	60 g
1 (10 ounce) can cream of mushroom soup	280 g
1 cup seasoned breadcrumbs	120 g

- Preheat oven to 350° (175° C).

- Layer vegetables and cheese in sprayed 7 x 11-inch (18 x 28 cm) baking dish. Spread soup over vegetables. Sprinkle breadcrumbs over casserole and bake for 30 minutes or until bubbly. Serves 4 to 6.

• • • • •

Asparagus Bake

3 (15 ounce) cans cut asparagus, drained	3 (425 g)
3 eggs, hard-boiled, sliced	
⅓ cup milk	75 ml
1½ cups shredded cheddar cheese	170 g
1¼ cups cheese cracker crumbs	75 g

- Preheat oven to 350° (175° C).

- Place asparagus in sprayed 7 x 11-inch (18 x 28 cm) baking dish, layer hard-boiled eggs on top and pour milk over casserole. Sprinkle cheese on top and add cracker crumbs. Bake uncovered for 30 minutes. Serves 4 to 6.

• • • • •

Asparagus Amandine

1 (10 ounce) can cream of chicken soup	280 g
3 eggs, hard-boiled, sliced	
1 cup cubed American cheese	130 g
1 (10 ounce) package frozen cut asparagus, cooked	280 g
1 cup sliced almonds	170 g
½ cup crushed croutons	60 g

- Preheat oven to 350° (175° C).

- Combine soup, eggs, cheese and asparagus. Pour mixture into sprayed baking dish. Cover with almonds and crushed croutons. Bake for 30 to 40 minutes or until bubbly and slightly brown on top. Serves 4.

• • • • •

Speedy Baked Beans

3 (15 ounce) cans pork and beans	3 (425 g)
½ cup chili sauce	135 g
⅓ cup packed brown sugar	75 g

- Preheat oven to 325° (165° C).

- Mix beans, chili sauce and sugar. Bake uncovered in sprayed baking dish for 1 hour. Serves 6 to 8.

TIP: For added flavor, place 3 or 4 strips of bacon and fresh chopped onion on top of beans before baking.

• • • • •

Country Baked Beans

4 (15 ounce) cans baked beans, drained	4 (425 g)
1 (12 ounce) bottle chili sauce	340 g
1 large onion, chopped	
½ pound bacon, cooked, crumbled	225 g
2 cups packed brown sugar	440 g

- Preheat oven to 325° (165° C).

- In unsprayed 3-quart (3 L) baking dish, combine all ingredients and stir until they blend. Bake uncovered for 55 minutes or until hot throughout. Serves 6 to 8.

The best money-saving tip for canned goods is to buy store brands on sale. Stock up when the prices are right.

Baked Beans Creole

3 slices bacon, diced	
½ cup minced onion	80 g
2 (15 ounce) cans baked beans	2 (425 g)
1 (15 ounce) can stewed tomatoes	425 g
1 teaspoon sugar	5 ml

- Preheat oven to 425° (220° C).

- Fry bacon until crisp. Remove from pan.

- Brown onions in bacon grease and combine with bacon. Arrange beans and bacon-onion mixture in alternate layers in sprayed 3-quart (3 L) baking dish. Mix tomatoes and sugar and pour over all.

- Bake for about 30 minutes. Serves 4 to 6.

• • • • •

Ranch-Style Beans

1 (16 ounce) package dried pinto beans	455 g
1 large onion, diced	
1 tablespoon oil	15 ml
2 cloves garlic	
2 teaspoons chili powder	10 ml
1 (15 ounce) can diced tomatoes	425 g

- Rinse beans well. Cover beans with 7 cups (1.7 L) water and let stand for 6 to 8 hours or overnight.

- Bring beans and water to a boil. Add oil, onion, garlic, chili powder and 2 teaspoons (10 ml) salt. Cover, simmer for 1 hour 30 minutes and stir occasionally. Add tomatoes and cook for 1 additional hour or until beans are tender. Serves 4 to 5.

• • • • •

Refried Beans and Cheese

1 (15 ounce) can refried beans	425 g
⅓ cup shredded cheddar cheese	40 g
1 - 2 tablespoons chopped green onions	15 - 30 ml

- Spoon beans into microwave-safe dish and microwave on HIGH for 2 minutes. Sprinkle cheese over top of beans and microwave until cheese melts. Before serving, sprinkle chopped green onions over beans. Serve as a vegetable or as a dip with tortilla chips. Serves 2 to 3.

Baked Refried Beans

1 (15 ounce) can refried beans	425 g
⅓ cup chunky salsa	90 g
½ teaspoon cayenne pepper	2 ml
1 (8 ounce) package shredded cheddar cheese	225 g

- Preheat oven to 350° (175° C).

- Place refried beans in sprayed 9-inch (23 cm) baking dish and stir in salsa and cayenne pepper. Bake uncovered for 10 minutes. Sprinkle cheese over top of beans and bake for additional 4 to 5 minutes. Serves 4 to 6.

Good Luck Black-Eyed Peas

*Eating black-eyed peas on New Year's Day
brings good luck in the New Year!*

1 (15 ounce) can black-eyed peas, drained	425 g
8 slices pepperoni, chopped	
2 tablespoons chopped onion	30 ml

- Combine peas, pepperoni and onion and mix well. Heat thoroughly. Serves 2 to 4.

Magic Black-Eyed Peas

1 (15 ounce) can black-eyed peas, drained	425 g
3 green onions with tops, chopped	
½ cup chopped green bell peppers	75 g
⅓ cup chopped celery	35 g
⅓ cup Italian dressing	75 ml

- Combine all ingredients with a little pepper and refrigerate. Serves 3 to 4.

Broccoli Casserole

1 (10 ounce) package frozen broccoli florets, thawed	280 g
1 (10 ounce) can cream of celery soup	280 g
½ cup shredded cheddar cheese	55 g

- Preheat oven to 350° (175° C).

- Cook broccoli according to package directions and drain. Spread in sprayed baking dish. Cover with celery soup and bake for 20 to 25 minutes or until hot. Sprinkle with cheese and return to oven for 5 minutes. Serves 2 to 3.

Lemon Broccoli

1 (10 ounce) package frozen broccoli	280 g
2 tablespoons butter	30 ml
1½ tablespoons lemon juice	22 ml

- Prepare broccoli according to package directions and drain. Melt butter and remove from heat. Stir in lemon juice and mix well. Pour mixture over broccoli. Serves 2 to 3.

Cheddar-Broccoli Bake

1 (10 ounce) can cheddar cheese soup	280 g
½ cup milk	125 ml
1 (16 ounce) bag frozen broccoli florets, cooked, drained	455 g
1 (3 ounce) can fried onions	85 g

- Preheat oven to 350° (175° C).

- Combine soup, milk and broccoli. Spoon into sprayed 2-quart (2 L) baking dish and sprinkle with fried onions. Bake 25 minutes or until onions are golden. Serves 4 to 6.

 # Crunchy Broccoli

2 (10 ounce) packages frozen broccoli florets	2 (280 g)
1 (8 ounce) can sliced water chestnuts, drained, chopped	225 g
½ cup (1 stick) butter, melted	115 g
1 (1 ounce) packet dry onion soup mix	30 g

- Place broccoli in microwave-safe dish, cover and microwave on HIGH for 5 minutes. Turn dish and cook for additional 4 minutes. Add water chestnuts. Combine melted butter and soup mix and blend well. Toss with cooked broccoli. Serves 4 to 6

■ ■ ■ ■ ■

 # Orange Broccoli

1½ pounds fresh broccoli	680 g
¼ cup (½ stick) butter, melted	55 g
3 tablespoons orange juice	45 ml

- Trim broccoli and discard some stems. Microwave broccoli for 5 minutes. Turn and microwave for additional 4 minutes.

- Combine butter and orange juice in small bowl and pour over broccoli. Serves 3 to 4.

● ● ● ● ●

Creamy Vegetable Casserole

1 (16 ounce) package frozen broccoli, carrots and cauliflower	455 g
1 (10 ounce) can cream of mushroom soup	280 g
1 (8 ounce) carton garden-vegetable cream cheese	225 g
1 cup seasoned croutons	120 g

- Preheat oven to 375° (190° C).

- Cook vegetables according to package directions, drain and place in large bowl. Place soup and cream cheese in saucepan and heat, stirring constantly, just enough to mix easily.

- Pour soup mixture into vegetable mixture, stir well and pour into sprayed 2-quart (2 L) baking dish. Sprinkle with croutons and bake uncovered for 25 minutes or until bubbly. Serves 4.

• • • • •

Herb-Seasoned Vegetables

1 (14 ounce) can seasoned chicken broth with Italian herbs	395 g
½ teaspoon garlic powder	2 ml
1 (16 ounce) package frozen vegetables (broccoli, cauliflower, etc.)	455 g
½ cup grated parmesan cheese	50 g

- Heat broth, garlic and vegetables in saucepan and bring to a boil. Lower heat, cover and cook for 5 minutes or until tender-crisp. Drain. Place in serving dish and sprinkle parmesan cheese over vegetables. Serves 4 to 6.

• • • • •

Vegetable Medley

1 (10 ounce) can celery soup	280 g
¼ cup milk	60 ml
¼ cup (½ stick) butter	55 g
2 cups broccoli florets	140 g
2 cups cauliflower florets	200 g
1 (15 ounce) can whole kernel corn	425 g
1 (8 ounce) package shredded cheddar cheese	115 g

- In saucepan over medium heat, combine soup, milk and butter. Heat just to boiling and stir often. Stir in broccoli, cauliflower and corn; return to boiling.

- Reduce heat to low, cover and cook 20 minutes or until vegetables are tender; stir occasionally. Stir in cheese and heat until cheese melts. Serves 6.

Marinated Brussels Sprouts Medley

2 (10 ounce) packages frozen Brussels sprouts, thawed	2 (280 g)
1 cup Italian dressing	250 ml
1 cup chopped green bell pepper	150 g
½ cup chopped onion	80 g

- Cook Brussels sprouts according to package directions and drain. Mix Italian dressing, bell pepper and onion. Pour over Brussels sprouts and refrigerate for at least 24 hours. Drain to serve. Serves 4 to 6.

• • • • •

Cabbage Casserole

1 head cabbage, cut, cooked, drained	
1 (10 ounce) can cream of chicken soup	280 g
1 cup shredded cheddar cheese	115 g

- Preheat oven to 350° (175° C).

- In sprayed baking dish, place layers of half cabbage, half soup and half cheese. Repeat layers and bake for 30 minutes. Serves 4.

• • • • •

Orange Carrots

1 tablespoon butter	15 ml
2 tablespoons orange marmalade	30 ml
1 (15 ounce) can sliced carrots, drained	425 g

- Combine butter and marmalade in saucepan and heat until mixture melts. Stir often. Add carrots. Stir and heat until hot and glazed. Serves 2 to 3.

• • • • •

Ritzy Carrot Casserole

2 (15 ounce) cans diced carrots, drained	2 (425 g)
1 (10 ounce) can cream of chicken soup	280 g
1 tube round, buttery crackers, crushed	

- Preheat oven to 300° (150° C).

- Heat carrots and pour into sprayed baking dish. Spoon soup over carrots and sprinkle cracker crumbs over top. Bake for 30 minutes or until golden brown. Serves 6.

Carrots and Mashed Potatoes

4 potatoes, peeled, cubed
1 large carrot, peeled, coarsely chopped
⅓ cup milk   75 ml
1 teaspoon dried dill weed   5 ml
½ cup (1 stick) butter   110 g

- Place potatoes and carrots in water. Boil for 25 minutes. Drain.
  Return to pot and mash. Stir in milk, dill and butter. Season with a
  little salt and pepper. Serves 4. to 6.

● ● ● ● ●

Cauliflower and Green Peas

1 (16 ounce) package frozen cauliflower, thawed   455 g
1 cup chopped celery   100 g
¼ cup (½ stick) butter   55 g
1 (15 ounce) can green peas, drained   425 g

- Cook cauliflower according to package directions and drain. Saute
  celery in butter and stir in peas and cauliflower. Heat thoroughly.
  Serves 4 to 6.

● ● ● ● ●

Cauliflower Medley

1 head cauliflower, cut into florets
1 (15 ounce) can Italian stewed tomatoes   425 g
1 bell pepper, seeded, chopped
1 onion, chopped
¼ cup (½ stick) butter   55 g
1 cup shredded cheddar cheese   115 g

- Preheat oven to 350° (175° C). In large saucepan, place cauliflower,
  stewed tomatoes, bell pepper, onion and butter with about
  2 tablespoons (30 ml) water and some salt and pepper.

- Cook in covered saucepan on medium heat until cauliflower is done,
  about 10 minutes. (Do not let cauliflower get mushy.)

- Place in sprayed 2-quart (2 L) baking dish and sprinkle cheese on
  top. Bake just until cheese melts. Serves 4.

Line the vegetable drawers of the refrigerator with a
couple of layers of paper towels to keep fruit and vegetables
fresh longer.

Company Cauliflower

1 head cauliflower, divided
1 cup sour cream, divided   240 g
1 cup shredded cheddar cheese, divided   115 g

- Preheat oven to 325° (165°C).

- Rinse cauliflower and separate into florets. Cook in 2-quart (2 L)
  covered saucepan in 1-inch boiling, salted water for 8 to 10 minutes
  or until tender; drain well. Place half cauliflower in sprayed
  baking dish.

- Spread half sour cream over cauliflower.   Sprinkle with half cheese
  and repeat layers. Bake for 20 minutes or until hot and cheese
  melts. Serves 4.

• • • • •

Stuffed Celery

4 ribs celery
1 (8 ounce) package cream cheese, softened   225 g
2 tablespoons mayonnaise   30 ml
16 pimento-stuffed green olives, sliced

- Cut celery into 2-inch (5 cm) lengths. With mixer, beat cream cheese
  and mayonnaise until fluffy. Spread cream cheese mixture on celery
  and dot with green olive slices. Refrigerate. Serves 8.

TIP: *To save a little money, sprinkle with paprika instead of using
     green olives.*

• • • • •

Calico Corn

2 ribs celery, sliced
2 tablespoons butter   30 ml
3 (11 ounce) cans Mexicorn®, drained   3 (310 g)
1 (10 ounce) can fiesta nacho cheese soup   280 g
1 cup coarsely crushed buttery crackers   60 g

- Preheat oven to 375° (190° C).

- Saute celery in butter. Add corn and soup to celery and heat just
  enough to mix well. Pour into sprayed 7 x 11-inch (18 x 28 cm)
  baking dish. Sprinkle crushed crackers over casserole and bake
  uncovered for 20 to 25 minutes or until crumbs brown lightly.
  Serves 4 to 6.

• • • • •

Fantastic Fried Corn

You won't believe how good it is.

2 (16 ounce) packages frozen whole kernel corn	2 (455 g)
½ cup (1 stick) butter	115 g
1 cup whipping cream	250 ml
1 tablespoon sugar	15 ml

- Place corn in large skillet, turn on medium heat and add butter, whipping cream, sugar and 1 teaspoon (5 ml) salt.

- Stirring constantly, cook on medium heat for about 12 to 15 minutes or until most of whipping cream and butter absorbs into corn. Serves 6 to 8.

• • • • •

Mexican Corn

1 (16 ounce) package frozen corn	455 g
2 tablespoons butter	30 ml
½ cup thick-and-chunky salsa	130 g
1 (2 ounce) can sliced ripe olives, drained	55 g

- Cook corn according to package directions and stir in butter, salsa and olives. Cook until hot and drain. Serves 4.

• • • • •

Italian Corn

1 (16 ounce) package frozen whole kernel corn	455 g
2 slices bacon, cooked, diced	
1 small onion, chopped	
1 (15 ounce) can Italian stewed tomatoes	425 g

- Place all ingredients in 2-quart (2 L) pan and cook until most of liquid in tomatoes cooks out. Serves 4 to 6.

• • • • •

Creamed Corn

2 (10 ounce) packages frozen whole kernel corn	2 (280 g)
1 (8 ounce) package cream cheese, softened	225 g
Lemon pepper	

- Cook corn according to package directions and drain. Add cream cheese to hot corn, stirring until cream cheese melts and is thoroughly heated.   Season with a little lemon pepper and 1 teaspoon (5 ml) salt. Serves 6 to 8.

Super Corn Casserole

1 (15 ounce) can whole kernel corn, drained	425 g
1 (15 ounce) can cream-style corn	425 g
½ cup (1 stick) butter, melted	115 g
1 (8 ounce) carton sour cream	225 g
1 (6 ounce) package jalapeno cornbread mix	170 g

- Preheat oven to 350° (175° C).

- Mix all ingredients and pour into sprayed 9 x 13-inch (23 x 33 cm) baking dish. Bake uncovered for 35 minutes. Serves 6 to 8.

Wild West Corn

3 (15 ounce) cans whole kernel corn, drained	3 (425 g)
1 (10 ounce) can diced tomatoes and green chilies, drained	280 g
1 (8 ounce) package shredded Monterey Jack cheese	225 g
1 cup cheese cracker crumbs	60 g

- Preheat oven to 350° (175° C).

- In large bowl, combine corn, tomatoes and green chilies, and cheese and mix well. Pour into sprayed 2½-quart (2.5 L) baking dish. Sprinkle cracker crumbs over casserole. Bake uncovered for 25 minutes. Serves 4 to 6.

Corn with Brussels Sprouts

1 (1 pint) carton fresh brussels sprouts	175 g
1 (15 ounce) can whole kernel corn, drained	425 g
¼ cup (½ stick) butter	55 g
1 teaspoon seasoned salt	5 ml

- Wash and prepare brussels sprouts for cooking. Cook brussels sprouts in ½ cup (125 ml) water for about 10 minutes or until tender. Add corn, butter, seasoned salt and dash of pepper; heat thoroughly. Serves 4 to 6.

Corn Puff Delight

1 (8 ounce) package corn muffin mix	225 g
1 (15 ounce) can cream-style corn	425 g
½ cup sour cream	120 g
3 eggs, slightly beaten	

- Preheat oven to 350° (175° C).

- Combine all ingredients and pour into sprayed 2-quart (2 L) baking dish. Bake uncovered for about 35 minutes. Serves 4.

Corn and Green Chilies Casserole

2 (10 ounce) packages frozen corn	2 (280 g)
2 tablespoons butter	30 ml
1 (8 ounce) package cream cheese	225 g
1 tablespoon sugar	15 ml
1 (4 ounce) can diced green chilies	115 g

Preheat oven to 350° (175° C).

- Cook corn according to package directions and drain. Place butter in saucepan over low heat and add cream cheese. Stir until they melt.

- Stir in corn, sugar and green chilies. Spoon into sprayed 2-quart (2 L) baking dish. Cover and bake for 15 minutes. Remove from oven and sprinkle crackers over casserole. Return to oven for 10 to 15 minutes. Serves 4 to 6.

• • • • •

Corn and Green Bean Casserole

1 (15 ounce) can French green beans with liquid	425 g
1 (8 ounce) can whole kernel corn, drained	225 g
½ cup broken pecans	55 g
⅔ cup shredded cheddar cheese	75 g
1½ cups cracker crumbs	90 g
½ cup (1 stick) butter, melted	115 g

- Preheat oven to 350° (175° C).

- Drain beans and set aside ½ cup (125 ml) liquid. In sprayed 9-inch (23 cm) square baking dish, place in layers half beans, half corn and half pecans. Pour set aside bean liquid over top. Repeat layers of beans, corn and pecans.

- Sprinkle with cheese and crumbs. Pour butter over all. Bake for 30 minutes. Serves 4 to 6.

• • • • •

Baked Corn-on-the-Cob

6 ears fresh corn	
6 tablespoons (¾ stick) butter	85 g
1 teaspoon lemon pepper	5 ml

- Preheat oven to 325° (165° C).

- Husk corn and remove silk. Wash and dry with paper towels. Spread butter on corn, sprinkle with lemon pepper and wrap each ear in foil. Bake for 3 minutes. Serves 3 to 6.

Easy Corn-on-the-Cob

Fresh corn on the cob in husks
Butter

- Remove husks and silks and clean the biggest husk pieces. Wrap corn in husks and place 1-inch (2.5 cm) apart in microwave dish. Cook on HIGH power. Turn corn over 1 time while cooking.

  1 ear   2 to 3 minutes

  2 ears   4 to 6 minutes

  4 ears   8 to 10 minutes

- Season each ear of corn with butter. Serves 1, 2 or 4.

• • • • •

Cranberry-Orange Relish

1 (16 ounce) can whole cranberries	**455 g**
⅔ cup orange marmalade	**215 g**
⅓ cup chopped walnuts	**45 g**

- Combine all ingredients and mix well. Cover and refrigerate for 2 to 3 hours before serving. Serve with pork or ham. Yields 1 pint.

• • • • •

Yummy Cucumbers

2 seedless cucumbers	
1 (8 ounce) carton sour cream	**225 g**
3 tablespoons wine vinegar	**45 ml**
1 tablespoon sugar	**15 ml**
1 small onion, chopped	

- Peel and cut cucumbers into thick slices. Mix cucumbers and 1 tablespoon (15 ml) salt in bowl. Cover with 2 cups (500 ml) cold water. Let stand for 1 hour.

- Drain cucumbers. Mix sour cream, vinegar, sugar, onion and 1 teaspoon (5 ml) salt. Stir mixture into cucumbers. Cover and refrigerate several hours before serving. Serves 4 to 6.

• • • • •

Marinated Cucumbers

⅓ cup vinegar	75 ml
2 tablespoons sugar	30 ml
1 teaspoon dried dill weed	5 ml
3 cucumbers, peeled, sliced	

- Combine vinegar, sugar, 1 teaspoon (5 ml) salt and dill weed. Pour over cucumbers. Refrigerate 1 hour before serving. Serves 6 to 8.

• • • • •

Seasoned Cucumber Slices

2 seedless cucumbers, peeled, sliced	
1 (8 ounce) carton sour cream	225 g
2 tablespoons lemon juice	30 ml
2 tablespoons sugar	30 ml

- Combine all ingredients and a little salt; toss and refrigerate. Serves 4 to 6.

• • • • •

Eggplant Fritters

1 medium eggplant	
1 egg, beaten	
3 tablespoons flour	45 ml
½ teaspoon baking powder	2 ml
Oil	

- Peel and slice eggplant; steam until tender and drain. Mash eggplant until smooth. Add egg, flour, ½ teaspoon (2 ml) salt and baking powder and mix well. Form into patties and deep fry in hot oil. Serves 4.

• • • • •

Chipper Green Bean Casserole

2 (15 ounce) cans green beans, drained	2 (425 g)
1 (10 ounce) can cream of celery soup	280 g
1 cup crushed potato chips	55 g

- Preheat oven to 350° (175° C).

- Combine green beans and soup and pour into sprayed 2-quart (2 L) baking dish. Top with crushed potato chips and bake for 25 to 30 minutes. Serves 6.

• • • • •

Sassy Green Beans

1 (15 ounce) can cut green beans with liquid	425 g
1 teaspoon olive oil	5 ml
1 tablespoon dry onion soup mix	15 ml

- Combine all ingredients in saucepan. Mix and heat thoroughly. Serves 3 to 4.

• • • • •

Nutty Green Beans

1 (16 ounce) package frozen green beans	455 g
¼ cup (½ stick) butter	55 g
¾ cup slivered almonds	125 g
¼ teaspoon garlic powder	1 ml

- Cook beans according to package directions and drain.

- Melt butter in skillet over medium heat; add almonds and cook for about 10 minutes, stirring frequently, until golden.

- Add green beans, garlic powder and a little salt to almonds; mix well and serve hot. Serves 4 to 6.

• • • • •

Green Beans and Ham

¼ cup chopped onion	40 g
1 tablespoon butter	15 ml
2 (15 ounce) cans green beans, drained	2 (425 g)
½ cup chopped cooked ham	70 g
1 (2 ounce) can diced pimento	55 g

- Saute onion in butter. Combine onion and remaining ingredients in saucepan on high heat and bring to a boil. Reduce heat, cover and simmer for 15 minutes. Stir as needed. Serve hot. Serves 6 to 8.

• • • • •

 Remember, canned vegetables are processed at the peak of harvest. Veggies like beets, corn, green beans, peas and tomatoes are great in cans. Many are available in "no salt" and "reduced sodium" at the same cost.

Green Beans and Bacon

6 slices bacon
2 pounds fresh green beans or 2 (15 ounce) cans
    green beans   910 g/2 (425 g)
1 cup chopped onion   160 g

- Fry bacon until crisp and drain on paper towels.

- If you cook fresh green beans, add 1 tablespoon (15 ml) water, cover and cook for 3 minutes. Uncover and cook for additional 10 minutes. If you cook canned green beans, 4 minutes of cooking time is enough.

- Cook onion in bacon drippings until translucent. Stir onion and ½ teaspoon (2 ml) salt into beans and cook for 1 minute.

- Crumble bacon and add just before serving. Serves 6.

• • • • •

Garlic Green Beans

3 (15 ounce) cans whole green beans, drained   3 (425 g)
⅔ cup oil   150 ml
⅓ cup vinegar   75 ml
½ cup sugar   100 g
2 tablespoons minced garlic   30 ml

- Place green beans in container with lid. Mix oil, vinegar, sugar and garlic. Pour over beans and sprinkle with a little salt and pepper. Cover and refrigerate overnight. Serves 6.

• • • • •

Elegant Green Beans

1 pound fresh green beans   455 g
1 onion, thinly sliced, separated into rings
6 tablespoons olive oil   90 ml
1 tablespoon sugar   15 ml
1 tablespoon white vinegar   15 ml
1 tablespoon lemon juice   15 ml

- Steam beans with onion 10 minutes or until crisp and tender. Drain and place in medium bowl. Mix all other ingredients with 1 teaspoon (5 ml) salt and ½ teaspoon (2 ml) pepper and pour over beans. Cover and refrigerate several hours. Serves 4 to 6.

• • • • •

Classic Green Bean Casserole

2 (15 ounce) cans green beans, drained	2 (425 g)
1 (10 ounce) can cream of mushroom soup	280 g
1 (3 ounce) can french-fried onions, divided	85 g

- Preheat oven to 350° (175° C).

- Combine beans, soup and half of fried onions and mix well. Pour into sprayed baking dish and bake for 25 minutes. Top with remaining fried onions and bake for additional 10 minutes. Serves 6.

• • • • •

Sesame Seed Green Beans

2 tablespoons olive oil	30 ml
1 teaspoon minced garlic	5 ml
¼ cup sesame seeds	30 g
1 (8 ounce) can French-style green beans, drained	225 g

- Heat oil in skillet. Add garlic, sesame seeds and beans. Mix gently and toss beans until hot. Serves 4.

• • • • •

Basil Green Beans

1 (10 ounce) package frozen French-style green beans	280 g
2 tablespoons butter	30 ml
½ teaspoon dried basil	2 ml

- Combine all ingredients in saucepan, cover and bring to a boil. Reduce heat, simmer until all liquid is gone and stir as needed. Serves 3.

• • • • •

Almond Green Beans

⅓ cup slivered almonds	55 g
¼ cup (½ stick) butter	55 g
1 teaspoon garlic salt	5 ml
2 tablespoons lemon juice	30 ml
1 (16 ounce) package frozen green beans, thawed	455 g

- In saucepan, saute almonds in butter. Add garlic salt and lemon juice and cook until almonds turn golden brown. Add green beans to almond-butter mixture and add ⅓ cup (75 ml) water. Cook for about 10 minutes until beans are tender-crisp. Serves 4 to 6.

Creamy Green Beans

¾ cup milk	175 ml
1 (8 ounce) package cream cheese	225 g
½ teaspoon garlic powder	2 ml
½ cup grated parmesan cheese	50 g
2 (15 ounce) cans green beans	2 (425 g)

- In saucepan, combine milk, cream cheese, garlic powder and parmesan cheese and heat until cheeses melt. Heat green beans in pan, drain and cover with cream cheese mixture. Toss to coat evenly and serve hot.   Serves 4 to 6.

• • • • •

Cheesy Green Bean Casserole

2 (15 ounce) cans cut green beans, drained	2 (425 g)
1 (10 ounce) can cream of mushroom soup	280 g
1 cup shredded cheddar cheese	115 g
1 (3 ounce) can fried onions	85 g

- Preheat oven to 375° (190° C).

- Combine green beans, soup and cheese and spoon into sprayed 7 x 11-inch (18 x 28 cm) baking dish. Top with fried onions and bake for 20 minutes. Serves 4 to 6.

• • • • •

Not-Your-Banquet Beans

3 (15 ounce) cans cut green beans, drained	3 (425 g)
1 (8 ounce) can sliced water chestnuts, drained, chopped	225 g
½ cup slivered almonds	85 g
1 (12 ounce) package cubed Mexican Velveeta® cheese	340 g
1½ cups cracker crumbs	90 g
¼ cup (½ stick) butter, melted	55 g

- Preheat oven to 350° (175° C).

- Place green beans in sprayed 9 x 13-inch (23 x 33 cm) baking dish and cover with water chestnuts and almonds. Spread cheese over casserole.

- Place casserole in microwave and heat just long enough for cheese to begin to melt. (Watch closely). Combine cracker crumbs and butter and sprinkle over casserole. Bake uncovered for 30 minutes. Serves 6 to 8.

• • • • •

Hominy Casserole

2 (15 ounce) cans yellow hominy, drained   2 (425 g)
1 small onion, chopped
1 cup shredded cheddar cheese   115 g

- Preheat oven to 350° (175° C). Place alternate layers of half hominy, half onion and half cheese in sprayed baking dish. Repeat layers and bake for 30 minutes. Serves 6.

• • • • •

Fried Okra and Tomatoes

1 (10 ounce) package frozen cut okra, thawed, drained   280 g
½ cup cornmeal   80 g
3 slices bacon, cut into pieces
1½ medium tomatoes, chopped
1 teaspoon minced fresh hot red chili pepper   5 ml

- Shake okra in plastic bag with cornmeal mixed with ¾ teaspoon (4 ml) salt. Fry bacon in skillet until crisp, remove and set aside. Add okra to bacon drippings and saute. Add tomatoes, chili pepper and bacon. Cook for 15 minutes or until tomatoes are soft; add a little salt. Serves 4 to 6.

• • • • •

Scalloped Onions

6 onions, peeled, sliced
1 (8 ounce) package shredded Velveeta® cheese   225 g
3 cups crushed potato chips   170 g

- Preheat oven to 350° (175° C).

- Boil onions until limp and transparent. In sprayed baking dish, layer half onions, half cheese and half potato chips. Repeat layers and bake for 20 minutes. Serves 4 to 6.

• • • • •

Vidalia Onions

4 Vidalia® onions or sweet onions
4 teaspoons butter   20 ml
4 teaspoons chicken bouillon granules   20 ml

- Peel onions and use spoon to "hollow out" onion tops. Spoon butter and bouillon into each cavity and place on microwave-safe dish. Microwave on HIGH for about 2 minutes or until fork-tender. Serves 4.

Red Hot Onions

3 large purple onions
2 tablespoons hot sauce   30 ml
3 tablespoons olive oil   45 ml
3 tablespoons red wine vinegar   45 ml

- Cut onions into thin slices. Pour 1 cup (250 ml) boiling water over onions, let stand for 1 minute and drain. Combine hot sauce, oil and vinegar and pour over onion rings in bowl with lid. Cover and refrigerate for at least 3 hours. Drain to serve. Serves 4 to 6.

• • • • •

Fried Onion Rings

2 onions, sliced, separated into rings
1 cup pancake mix   130 g
Enough water or milk to make batter
Oil

- Combine pancake mix and water (or milk). Dip onion rings into batter and fry in deep oil until golden brown. Drain on paper towels. Serves 4 to 6.

• • • • •

Minted Peas

1 (15 ounce) can green peas with liquid   425 g
1 tablespoon butter   15 ml
⅓ cup mint jelly   105 g

- Cook peas liquid until it has reduced to ¼ cup (60 ml). Stir in peas, butter and mint jelly and heat thoroughly. Serves 2 to 3.

• • • • •

English Pea Casserole

1 (15 ounce) can green peas, drained   425 g
1 (10 ounce) can cream of mushroom soup   280 g
2 strips bacon, diced
1 small onion, chopped

- Preheat oven to 350° (175° C).

- Place peas in sprayed 9-inch (23 cm) square baking pan and add soup. Cook bacon and onion in skillet. Pour over peas and soup. Bake for 25 minutes. Serves 4.

Cheesy Green Peas

1 (15 ounce) can green peas with liquid	425 g
3 tablespoons chopped onion	15 ml
1 (8 ounce) jar jalapeno Cheez Whiz®	225 g

- Combine peas, onions and cheese and mix well. Heat thoroughly in microwave for 3 to 4 minutes or bake at 325° (165° C) for 15 minutes. Serves 2 to 3.

• • • • •

Green Peas Deluxe

2 (10 ounce) packages frozen green peas, thawed	2 (280 g)
1 (8 ounce) can sliced water chestnuts, drained, chopped	225 g
1 (10 ounce) can golden cream of mushroom soup	280 g

- Preheat oven to 350° (165° C). Prepare green peas according to package directions and drain. Stir in water chestnuts and soup. Pour into sprayed baking dish and bake for 25 minutes or heat thoroughly in saucepan. Serves 6.

• • • • •

Vegetable Casserole

1 onion, chopped	
1 tablespoon butter	15 ml
2 (15 ounce) cans peas and carrots, drained	2 (425 g)
1 (15 ounce) can green beans, drained	425 g
1 (8 ounce) package cubed Velveeta® cheese	225 g

- Preheat oven to 350° (175° C).

- Saute onion in butter and combine with remaining ingredients. Pour into sprayed 2-quart (2 L) baking dish and bake for 25 to 30 minutes. Serves 6 to 8.

• • • • •

Buy onions on sale and either chop or cut into a rings. Spread the chopped onions or rings on a baking sheet and freeze. Once frozen, pour into a large sealable plastic bag. Remove just the quantity you need when cooking. (The freezer will smell like onions for a short time, but this will dissipate and not add an onion taste to other items in the freezer.)

Show-Stopper Vegetables

2 (10 ounce) packages frozen peas	2 (280 g)
2 (10 ounce) packages frozen French-style green beans	2 (280 g)
1 (10 ounce) package frozen lima beans	280 g
1 (8 ounce) carton whipping cream	250 ml
1½ cups mayonnaise	335 g
½ cup grated parmesan cheese	50 g

- Preheat oven to 350° (175° C).

- Cook vegetables separately according to package directions. Drain and mix vegetables plus 1 teaspoon (5 ml) salt in large bowl.

- Combine whipping cream and mayonnaise. Fold mixture into vegetables and spoon into sprayed 3-quart (3 L) baking dish. Sprinkle with parmesan cheese. Bake for 15 to 20 minutes or until thoroughly hot. Serves 6.

• • • • •

Parmesan Peas

2 (10 ounce) packages frozen green peas	2 (280 g)
3 tablespoons butter, melted	45 ml
1 tablespoon lemon juice	15 ml
⅓ cup grated parmesan cheese	35 g

- Microwave peas, butter and lemon juice in 2 tablespoons (30 ml) water for 6 minutes rotating once. Leave in oven several minutes. Sprinkle with parmesan cheese. Serve hot. Serves 4 to 6.

• • • • •

Green Pea Casserole

2 (10 ounce) packages frozen green peas	280 g
1 cup shredded cheddar cheese	115 g
1 (10 ounce) can golden mushroom soup	280 g

- Preheat oven to 350° (175° C).

- Cook peas according to package directions and drain. Combine peas, cheese and soup and spoon into a 7 x 11-inch (18 x 28 cm) sprayed baking dish. Bake for 30 to 35 minutes. Serves 4 to 6.

TIP: Try topping with 1 cup (55 g) coarsely crushed potato chips.

• • • • •

Pineapple-Cheese Casserole

1 cup sugar	200 g
5 tablespoons flour	40 g
2 (20 ounce) cans unsweetened pineapple chunks, drained	2 (565 g)
1½ cups shredded cheddar cheese	170 g
1 stack round, buttery crackers, crushed	
½ cup (1 stick) butter, melted	115 g

- Preheat oven to 350° (175° C).

- Combine sugar and flour. Layer ingredients in sprayed 9 x 13-inch (23 x 33 cm) baking dish in following order: pineapple, sugar-flour mixture, cheese and cracker crumbs. Drizzle butter over casserole. Bake for 25 minutes or until bubbly. Serves 4 to 6.

• • • • •

 # Glazed Pineapple Slices

1 (20 ounce) can pineapple slices, drained	565 g
2 tablespoons butter, melted	30 ml
3 tablespoons brown sugar	45 ml

- Arrange pineapple slices in large microwaveable dish. Brush with butter and sprinkle with brown sugar. Microwave on HIGH for 1 to 2 minutes or until butter and sugar bubble. Serve hot with ham or pork. Serves 4.

• • • • •

Party Potatoes

1 (8 ounce) package cream cheese with chives, softened	225 g
3 cups leftover mashed potatoes	630 g

- Preheat oven to 350° (175° C).

- Add cream cheese to potatoes.   Pour into sprayed 7 x 11-inch (18 x 28 cm) baking dish. Cover and bake for 30 minutes. Serves 4 to 6.

TIP: *You can also use 1 (22 ounce) carton (625 g) refrigerated mashed potatoes or prepare instant mashed potatoes.*

When considering whether to buy fresh, frozen or canned goods, look at the cost per serving.

Cheesy Potatoes

4 - 5 cups prepared instant mashed potatoes	840 g - 1 kg
1 (10 ounce) can cream of chicken soup	280 g
2 green onions, chopped	
1 cup shredded cheese	240 ml

- Preheat oven to 350° (175° C).

- Mix ingredients with a little salt and pepper and spoon into sprayed 2-quart (2 L) baking dish. Bake until cheese melts. Serves 4 to 6.

Chive-Potato Souffle

3 eggs, separated	
2 cups hot prepared instant mashed potatoes	420 g
½ cup sour cream	120 g
2 heaping tablespoons chopped chives	30 ml

- Preheat oven to 350° (175° C).

- Beat egg whites until stiff and set aside. Beat yolks until smooth and add to potatoes. Fold beaten egg whites, sour cream, chives and 1 teaspoon (5 ml) salt into potato-egg yolk mixture. Pour into sprayed 2-quart (2 L) baking dish. Bake for 45 minutes. Serves 4 to 6.

Ranch Mashed Potatoes

4 cups prepared instant mashed potatoes	840 g
1 (1 ounce) packet ranch dressing mix	30 g
¼ cup (½ stick) butter	55 g

- Combine all ingredients in saucepan. Heat and stir on low until potatoes are thoroughly hot. Serves 6 to 8.

Philly Potatoes

4½ cups hot prepared instant mashed potatoes	945 g
2 tablespoons dried chives	30 ml
1 (8 ounce) package cream cheese, softened	225 g
1 egg, slightly beaten	

- Preheat oven to 350° (175° C).

- Mix all ingredients and blend well. Place in sprayed 3-quart (3 L) baking dish. Cover and bake 30 minutes. Uncover and bake for additional 15 minutes. Serves 6.

• • • • •

Potato Souffle

2⅔ cups dry instant mashed potatoes	160 g
2 eggs, beaten	
1 cup shredded cheddar cheese	115 g
1 (3 ounce) can fried onions	85 g

- Preheat oven to 350° (175° C).

- Prepare mashed potatoes according to package directions. Fold in beaten eggs and cheese and stir well.

- Spoon into sprayed 2-quart (2 L) baking dish. Sprinkle with fried onions. Bake uncovered for 20 to 25 minutes. Serves 4 to 6.

• • • • •

Potato Pancakes

3 pounds white potatoes, peeled, grated	1.4 kg
1 onion, finely minced	
3 eggs, beaten	
½ cup seasoned breadcrumbs	60 g
Oil	

- In large bowl, combine potatoes, onion, eggs, breadcrumbs, and a little salt and pepper and mix well. In skillet, drop by spoonfuls in hot oil and brown on both sides. Serves 4 to 6.

• • • • •

Creamy Mashed Potatoes

6 large potatoes	
1 (8 ounce) carton sour cream	225 g
1 (8 ounce) package cream cheese, softened	225 g

- Preheat oven to 325° (165° C).

- Peel, cut and boil potatoes. Drain. Add sour cream, cream cheese, ½ teaspoon (2 ml) pepper and 1 teaspoon (5 ml) salt. Whip until cream cheese melts. Pour into sprayed 3-quart (3 L) baking dish. Cover and bake for 20 minutes. Serves 4 to 6.

• • • • •

Let old bread get bone dry and process to crumbs in a blender or food processor. Freeze for future use.

Scalloped Potatoes

6 medium potatoes, divided	
½ cup (1 stick) butter, divided	115 g
1 tablespoon flour	15 ml
1 (8 ounce) package shredded cheddar cheese, divided	225 g
¾ cup milk	175 ml

- Preheat oven to 350° (175° C).

- Peel and slice half of potatoes. Place in 3-quart (3 L) sprayed baking dish. Slice half of butter over potatoes and sprinkle with flour. Cover with half cheese and repeat layers of potatoes, butter and cheese. Pour milk over all. Cover and bake for 1 hour. Serves 6 to 8.

• • • • •

Terrific Taters

5 - 6 medium potatoes, peeled, sliced	
1 (8 ounce) carton sour cream	225 g
1 (1 ounce) packet ranch-style salad dressing mix	30 g
1½ cups shredded cheddar cheese	170 g
3 slices bacon, fried, crumbled	

- Preheat oven to 350° (175° C).

- Boil potatoes until tender and drain. Place potatoes in 2-quart (2 L) baking dish. Combine sour cream, salad dressing mix and a little pepper. Toss with potatoes to coat well. Sprinkle with cheese. Bake for 20 minutes. Sprinkle bacon on top. Serves 4 to 6.

• • • • •

Onion Roasted Potatoes

2 pounds potatoes	910 g
1 (1 ounce) packet dry onion soup mix	30 g
⅓ cup olive oil	75 ml

- Preheat oven to 400° (205° C).

- Wash and peel potatoes and cut into chunks. Pour all ingredients into large plastic, resealable bag. Close bag and shake until potatoes coat well.

- Place potatoes in sprayed 9 x 13-inch (23 x 33 cm) baking pan and bake for 40 minutes or until tender and golden brown. Stir occasionally. Serves 4 to 6.

• • • • •

Potato Casserole

5 potatoes, peeled, sliced
1 (10 ounce) can golden cream of mushroom soup   280 g
½ cup milk   125 ml
1 cup shredded cheddar cheese   115 g

- Preheat oven to 400° (205° C).

- Place sliced potatoes in sprayed 2-quart (2 L) baking dish.

- Dilute soup with milk or water and mix well. Pour over potatoes and bake covered for 45 minutes. Top with cheese and bake uncovered for additional 15 minutes. Serves 6.

Nacho Potato Wedges

3 medium potatoes, cut in wedges
¼ cup (½ stick) butter   55 g
1 cup cubed Velveeta® cheese   140 g
1 cup sliced jalapeno peppers   90 g

- Preheat oven to 400° (205° C).

- Bake potatoes for 30 minutes or until tender.

- Melt butter and cheese in microwave for 1 minute on HIGH. Stir and cook until cheese melts and mixture is smooth. Pour over potatoes and dot each potato wedge with one or two jalapeno slices. Serves 4.

Prairie Schooners

4 large potatoes, baked
1 (15 ounce) can chili beans   425 g
1 cup sour cream   240 g
½ cup (1 stick butter), softened   115 g
1 cup shredded cheddar cheese   115 g
1 onion, chopped

- Preheat oven to 425° (220° C).

- Slice top one-third of baked potato lengthwise. Scoop out potato leaving ¼-inch (6 mm) around potato skin. Mash potato until free of lumps.

- Drain beans thoroughly and reserve liquid. Mash beans.

- Whip sour cream, butter, mashed potatoes, mashed beans, and a little salt and pepper. Add bean liquid as needed to moisten. Spoon mixture into potato shells. Top each potato with cheese, onion and salt and pepper to taste. Bake for 10 to 20 minutes. Serves 4.

Twice-Baked Potatoes

4 medium baking potatoes, baked
½ cup bacon bits   40 g
½ cup (1 stick) butter   115 g
½ cup sour cream   120 g
1 cup shredded cheddar cheese   115 g

- Preheat oven to 325° (165° C).

- Cut baked potatoes in half lengthwise. Scoop out flesh carefully. Place skins on baking sheet. In mixing bowl, mash potatoes and add bacon, butter and sour cream. Mix well. Spoon mixture into skins and top with cheese. Bake for 15 minutes. Serves 4.

• • • • •

 # Creamy Baked Potatoes

4 baking potatoes
½ cup (1 stick) butter, softened   115 g
½ cup sour cream   120 g
1 (8 ounce) package shredded cheddar cheese   225 g

- Wash potatoes and prick with fork. Wrap in paper towels and microwave on HIGH for about 8 to 10 minutes and turn once.

- Split potatoes, scoop flesh in bowl, but leave ½-inch (1.2 cm) on skins. Mash potatoes, mix with butter, sour cream and cheese and place mixture in potato shells. Serves 4.

TIP: To keep potatoes warm, place in 275° (135° C) oven.

• • • • •

Vegetable-Stuffed Potatoes

2 (10 ounce) cans fiesta nacho cheese soup   2 (280 g)
1 (16 ounce) package frozen mixed stew vegetables,
    cooked, drained   455 g
8 baking potatoes, washed

- In large saucepan, heat fiesta nacho cheese soup, add cooked vegetables and mix well. Prick potatoes with fork and cook in microwave until insides are tender.

- Slightly mash flesh in each potato and spoon hearty amount of soup-vegetable mixture onto each split potato. If necessary, warm filled potatoes in microwave for 1 to 2 minutes. Serves 8.

• • • • •

Done Right Potatoes

8 medium baking potatoes	
½ cup (1 stick) butter, softened	115 g
1 (10 ounce) can fiesta nacho cheese soup	280 g
1 cup finely chopped ham	140 g
Paprika	

- Preheat oven to 350° (175° C).

- Bake potatoes for 1 hour or until done. Cut potatoes in half lengthwise, scoop out flesh and leave thin shell.

- Increase oven to 425° (220° C).

- Use mixer to whip potato flesh with butter and 1 teaspoon (5 ml) salt. Gradually add soup and ham and beat until light and fluffy. Spoon mixture into potato shells and sprinkle with paprika. Bake for 15 minutes. Serves 8.

• • • • •

 # Broccoli-Ham-Topped Potatoes

5 - 6 large potatoes	
2 cups cooked deli ham, diced	280 g
1 (10 ounce) can cream of broccoli soup	280 g
1 (8 ounce) package shredded cheddar cheese	225 g

- Cook potatoes in microwave until done. Cut potatoes down center and fluff insides with fork. In saucepan over low heat, combine remaining ingredients, heat and stir until they blend well.

- Spoon generous amounts of ham-soup mixture into potatoes and reheat in microwave for 2 to 3 minutes, if necessary. Serves 5 to 6.

• • • • •

 Frozen vegetables are better than canned vegetables because they are quick-frozen just minutes after they come out of the fields. It's easy to open the packages and cook a portion instead of having to use all of it at once. Frozen vegetables last up to four months without loosing nutrients.

Crab-Stuffed Baked Potatoes

4 large baking potatoes	
¼ cup (½ stick) butter	115 g
½ cup whipping cream	125 ml
1 bunch fresh green onions, chopped	
1 (8 ounce) can imitation crabmeat, flaked	225 g
¾ cup shredded cheddar cheese	85 g

- Preheat oven to 375° (190° C).

- Bake potatoes for 1 hour or until well done. Halve each potato lengthwise, scoop out flesh and leave skins intact. In large bowl, mash potatoes with butter.

- Add whipping cream, ¾ teaspoon (4 ml) salt, ½ teaspoon (2 ml) pepper and green onions to potatoes. Stir in crabmeat. Fill potato skins with mixture. Sprinkle with cheese. Bake at 350° (175° C) for 15 minutes. Serves 4.

• • • • •

Potatoes Supreme

1 (32 ounce) package frozen hash-brown potatoes, thawed	910 g
1 onion, chopped	
2 (10 ounce) cans cream of chicken soup	2 (280 g)
1 (8 ounce) carton sour cream	225 g

- Preheat oven to 350° (175° C).

- In large bowl, combine potatoes, onion, soup and sour cream. Pour into sprayed 9 x 13-inch (23 x 33 cm) baking dish. Cover and bake for 1 hour. Serves 6 to 8.

• • • • •

French-Fry Cheese Melt

1 (24 ounce) package french-fried potatoes	680 g
1 (12 ounce) package shredded cheddar cheese	340 g

- Place fries on sprayed large baking sheet and bake according to package directions. Salt and pepper fries and bunch into individual servings. Sprinkle cheese on top. Return to oven and bake until cheese melts. Serves 4 to 6.

• • • • •

Baked Onion French Fries

1 (1 ounce) packet dry onion soup mix	30 g
3 teaspoons canola oil	15 ml
1 (24 ounce) package french-fried potatoes	680 g

- In large bowl, combine soup mix and oil. Add potatoes and stir until coated with soup mixture. Bake according to package directions and stir as needed. Serves 6 to 8.

Rosemary-Roasted Potatoes

2 pounds new red potatoes	910 g
3 tablespoons olive oil	45 ml
2 tablespoons dried rosemary	30 ml

- Preheat oven to 350° (175° C).

- Wash potatoes and peel narrow strip around centers. Place potatoes in sprayed 9 x 13-inch (23 x 33 cm) pan. Drizzle with olive oil and sprinkle with rosemary. Stir to coat. Bake uncovered for 1 hour 15 minutes or until skins are crispy and potatoes are fork tender. Serves 6 to 8.

Roasted New Potatoes

2 tablespoons butter	30 ml
1 teaspoon marjoram	5 ml
4 medium new potatoes, quartered	
3 small onions, quartered	

- Preheat oven to 375° (190° C).

- Melt butter in 2-quart (2 L) baking dish and stir in marjoram. Add potatoes and onions and toss in melted mixture until they coat. Cover and bake for 1 hour. Serves 4.

Boiled New Potatoes

3 pounds small new potatoes	1.4 kg
¾ cup (1½ sticks) butter, melted	170 g
6 tablespoons minced parsley	25 g

- Cook potatoes in 5 cups (1.2 L) boiling water until tender and drain. Sprinkle with melted butter and minced parsley and serve hot. Serves 8.

• • • • •

Baked New Potatoes

1 pound new potatoes with peels	455 g
1 large onion, coarsely chopped	
1 clove garlic, minced	
½ cup (1 stick) butter	115 g

- Preheat oven to 350° (175° C).

- Boil new potatoes. Drain and quarter. In large skillet, saute onion and garlic with butter until onion is translucent. Add 1 teaspoon (5 ml) salt. Add potatoes and toss to coat. Place in sprayed 9 x 13-inch (23 x 33 cm) baking dish. Bake, basting occasionally, for 25 to 30 minutes or until potatoes are fork tender. Serves 4 to 6.

• • • • •

Red Potato Medley

2 tablespoons butter	30 ml
3 cups cubed new (red) potatoes	450 g
1½ cups diagonally sliced carrots	185 g
¾ cup chopped onion	120 g
1 garlic clove, minced	

- In large skillet over medium heat, melt butter, add potatoes and carrots and toss to coat. Add remaining ingredients with ¼ teaspoon (1 ml) each of salt and pepper. Mix well and reduce heat to medium-low.

- Cover and cook for 15 to 20 minutes or until vegetables are tender. Stir every 5 minutes. Serves 4 to 6.

• • • • •

Dilled New Potatoes

24 small new (red) potatoes, peeled, halved	
¼ cup (½ stick) butter, melted	55 g
¼ cup fresh dill weed, chopped	3 g

- Boil potatoes until tender and drain. Combine dill weed and butter and toss with potatoes. Serve hot. Serves 6 to 8.

TIP: *It's easy to grow fresh herbs in the summer and it can be a great money-saver.*

• • • • •

Blue Cheese Potatoes

10 - 15 small new (red) potatoes with peels
1 cup mayonnaise   225 g
¼ cup whipping cream, slightly whipped   60 ml
¼ cup crumbled blue cheese   35 g

- Boil potatoes until tender. Combine mayonnaise, cream and cheese.
  Fold dressing into potatoes. Serves 6.

• • • • •

Quick Potatoes

2 tablespoons butter   30 ml
½ onion, finely minced
½ green bell pepper, seeded, diced
2 (15 ounce) cans sliced new potatoes, drained   2 (425 g)

- Preheat oven to 350° (175° C).

- Melt butter in skillet. Add onion and bell pepper. Cook over
  medium heat until tender. Add potatoes and continue to saute for
  5 minutes. Add a little pepper. Place in sprayed 9-inch (23 cm) pie
  pan and bake for 15 minutes. Serves 6 to 8.

• • • • •

 # Orange Sweet Potatoes

1 (18 ounce) can sweet potatoes, drained   510 g
¼ teaspoon salt   1 ml
⅓ cup orange marmalade   105 g

- Place sweet potatoes in microwaveable casserole dish and sprinkle
  with a little salt. Cover and microwave on HIGH for 4 minutes and
  stir. Spoon marmalade over potatoes, cover and microwave for
  additional 1 or 2 minutes. Stir before serving. Serves 4.

• • • • •

 Buy and prepare foods in quantity. *Take advantage of
bulk-buying. Buy large amounts and freeze in individual
servings when they are on sale. Roast several chickens, bone
what's left to freeze and use in recipes. Many vegetables can
be blanched and frozen with no loss of taste or appearance.*

Glazed Sweet Potatoes

4 sweet potatoes
½ cup packed brown sugar   110 g
¼ cup (½ stick) butter, melted   55 g

- Pierce sweet potatoes several times with fork. Microwave on HIGH
  for 10 minutes or until fork-tender and cool. Peel and slice potatoes
  and place in sprayed microwaveable baking dish.

- Sprinkle brown sugar over potatoes and top with butter. Cover
  and microwave on HIGH for 4 minutes, then stir. Microwave for
  1 or 2 additional minutes and let stand covered for 3 minutes before
  serving. Serves 4.

• • • • •

Sweet Potato Delight

3 cups mashed cooked sweet potatoes   985 g
6 tablespoons (¾ stick) butter   85 g
2 eggs, beaten
¼ cup sugar   50 g

- Preheat oven to 350° (175° C).

- Combine sweet potatoes, butter, eggs and sugar. Pour into sprayed
  9-inch (23 cm) square baking pan.

Topping:

⅓ cup flour   40 g
1 cup packed brown sugar   220 g
½ cup chopped pecans   55 g
6 tablespoons (¾ stick) butter   85 g

- Combine topping ingredients and spread over sweet potato mixture.
  Bake for 30 minutes. Serves 4 to 6.

• • • • •

Ethnic markets frequently have a wider variety of fresh produce furnished by local growers at a lower cost than chain grocery stores.

Sugared Sweet Potatoes

1 (28 ounce) can sweet potatoes with liquid	795 g
¼ cup (½ stick) butter, melted	55 g
1 cup packed brown sugar	200 g
2 eggs, beaten	
½ cup chopped nuts	85 g

- In mixing bowl, beat yams, butter, brown sugar, eggs and cinnamon until fluffy. Cover with paper towel and microwave on HIGH for 5 minutes. Turn once during cooking. Top with nuts. Serves 4 to 6.

• • • • •

Whipped Sweet Potatoes

2 (15 ounce) cans sweet potatoes	2 (425 g)
¼ cup (½ stick) butter, melted	55 g
¼ cup orange juice	60 ml
1 cup miniature marshmallows	45 g

- Preheat oven to 350° (175 C).

- Combine sweet potatoes, butter, orange juice and ½ teaspoon (2 ml) salt in mixing bowl. Beat until fluffy. Fold in marshmallows. Spoon into sprayed 2-quart (2 L) baking dish. Bake uncovered for 25 minutes. Serves 6 to 8.

• • • • •

Snow Peas

1½ pounds fresh snow peas	680 g
1 tablespoon lemon juice	15 ml
3 tablespoons butter	45 ml

- Cook peas in steamer for 3 to 4 minutes. Season with lemon juice, butter and a little salt. Serves 4 to 6.

• • • • •

Buy when plentiful. Even though we can get most fruits and vegetables year-round, they are at their best prices and quality at the peak of harvest when they are most plentiful. If there is a farmer's market nearby, it is well worth the trip to buy fresh produce, often directly from the growers.

Sauteed Snow Peas

1 tablespoon butter	15 ml
¾ pound fresh mushrooms, sliced	340 g
1 (8 ounce) can sliced water chestnuts, drained	225 g
¾ pound fresh snow peas	340 g

- Melt butter over medium heat in skillet. Saute mushrooms and water chestnuts. Add snow peas and saute until peas turn bright green. Serves 6.

• • • • •

Easy Creamed Spinach

1 (10 ounce) package frozen chopped spinach, thawed	280 g
1 (10 ounce) can cream of mushroom soup	280 g
½ teaspoon nutmeg	2 ml

- Cook spinach according to package directions and drain well. Combine spinach and soup and mix well. Simmer for 10 to 15 minutes and stir occasionally. Sprinkle with nutmeg. Serves 6.

• • • • •

Creamed Spinach Bake

2 (10 ounce) packages frozen chopped spinach	2 (280 g)
2 (3 ounce) packages cream cheese, softened	2 (85 g)
3 tablespoons butter	45 ml
1 cup seasoned breadcrumbs	120 g

- Preheat oven to 350° (175° C). Cook spinach according to package directions and drain. Combine cream cheese and butter with spinach. Heat until cream cheese and butter melt and mix well with spinach.

- Pour into sprayed baking dish and sprinkle a little salt over spinach. Cover with breadcrumbs and bake for 15 to 20 minutes. Serves 6 to 8.

Don't throw out old bread. *Use it to make breadcrumbs or delicious bread pudding. Make breadcrumbs by placing slices of bread on a cookie sheet and baking at 400° (205° C). When golden on one side, turn over until golden on the other side. Put in a sealable plastic bag and crush for breadcrumbs. You may want to add seasonings to the crumbs such as garlic salt or other flavors.*

Favorite Spinach

2 (10 ounce) packages frozen chopped spinach, thawed, well drained*	2 (280 g)
1 (1 ounce) packet dry onion soup mix	30 g
1 (8 ounce) carton sour cream	225 g
⅔ cup shredded Monterey Jack cheese	75 g

- Preheat oven to 350° (175° C). Combine spinach, onion soup mix and sour cream. Pour into sprayed 2-quart (2 L) baking dish. Bake for 20 minutes. Take out of oven, sprinkle cheese over top and return casserole to oven for 5 minutes. Serves 6 to 8.

TIP: Squeeze spinach between paper towels to completely remove excess moisture.

• • • • •

Cheesy Spinach

1 (16 ounce) package frozen chopped spinach	455 g
3 eggs, beaten	
½ cup flour	60 g
1 (16 ounce) carton small curd cottage cheese	455 g
1 (8 ounce) package shredded cheddar cheese	225 g

- Preheat oven to 350° (175° C).

- Cook spinach and drain well. Stir in eggs, flour and cottage cheese. Fold in cheddar cheese. Pour into sprayed 1½-quart (1.5 L) baking dish. Bake uncovered for 35 minutes. Serves 4 to 6.

• • • • •

Seasoned Squash and Onions

8 yellow squash, sliced	
2 onions, chopped	
¼ cup (½ stick) butter	55 g
1 cup shredded American cheese	115 g

- Cook squash and onion in small amount of water until tender and drain. Add butter and cheese, toss and serve hot. Serves 4 to 6.

• • • • •

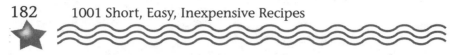

Squash Casserole

6 - 8 small squash, cooked, mashed	
2 beef bouillon cubes	
2 tablespoons butter	30 ml
1 egg, well beaten	
1 (8 ounce) carton sour cream	225 g
½ cup breadcrumbs	60 g

- Preheat oven to 350° (175° C).

- Mix all ingredients plus a little salt and pepper and place in sprayed baking dish. Bake for 25 minutes or until set. Serves 4 to 6.

• • • • •

Grilled Mixed Vegetables

1 yellow squash, washed, cubed	
1 green bell pepper, seeded, quartered	
1 small onion, quartered	
1 (8 ounce) bottle Italian dressing	227 g

- Mix vegetables and spread on aluminum foil. Sprinkle dressing over all. Close foil tightly to make flat package and place on grill rack. Grill for 10 to 15 minutes or until vegetables are tender-crisp. Serves 4.

TIP: You could also add sliced zucchini and mushrooms.

• • • • •

Chile-Cheese Squash

1 pound yellow squash, cubed	455 g
⅔ cup mayonnaise	150
1 (4 ounce) can diced green chilies, drained	115 g
⅔ cup shredded cheddar cheese	75 g
⅔ cup breadcrumbs	80 g

- Cook squash in salted water just until tender-crisp and drain. Return to saucepan, stir in mayonnaise, chilies, cheese and breadcrumbs. Serve hot. Serves 4 to 6.

To make your money stretch, store fresh fruits and vegetables correctly. Don't put tomatoes in the refrigerator unless they are overly ripe. Put them in a paper bag for a couple of days. Don't leave one spoiled item with the good ones because it will ruin all of them more quickly.

Baked Acorn Squash

3 acorn squash	
¾ cup (1½ sticks) butter, divided	170 g
6 tablespoons brown sugar, divided	75 g

- Preheat oven to 350° (175° C).

- Cut each squash in half and remove seeds and pulp. Place
  1 tablespoon (15 ml) butter and 1 tablespoon (15 ml) brown sugar
  in each half. Place squash in large shallow pan with ¼ cup water in
  bottom of pan and bake for 1 hour. Serves 3 to 4.

• • • • •

Mama's Fried Green Tomatoes

2 green tomatoes, sliced	
½ cup flour or cornmeal	60 g/80 g
Vegetable oil	

- Dip tomato slices in flour or cornmeal mixed with a little salt and
  pepper. Fry in oil. Serves 4 to 6.

• • • • •

Snow-Capped Tomatoes

2 tomatoes, halved	
2 cups cottage cheese	430 g

- Place heaping spoonfuls of cottage cheese on tomatoes. Sprinkle
  with salt and pepper. Serves 4.

• • • • •

Broccoli-Stuffed Tomatoes

4 medium tomatoes	
1 (10 ounce) package frozen chopped broccoli	280 g
1 (6 ounce) roll garlic cheese, softened	170 g
½ teaspoon garlic salt	2 ml

- Preheat oven to 350° (175° C).

- Cut tomato tops off and scoop out pulp. Cook frozen broccoli in
  microwave according to package directions and drain well.

- Combine broccoli, cheese and garlic salt. Heat just until cheese
  melts, stuff broccoli mixture into tomatoes and place on sprayed
  baking sheet. Bake for about 10 minutes. Serves 4.

Baked Tomatoes

2 (15 ounce) cans diced tomatoes, drained	2 (425 g)
1½ cups breadcrumbs, toasted, divided	180 g
¼ cup sugar	50 g
½ onion, chopped	
¼ cup (½ stick) butter, melted	55 g

- Preheat oven to 325° (165° C).

- Combine tomatoes, 1 cup (120 g) breadcrumbs, sugar, onion and butter. Pour into sprayed baking dish and cover with remaining breadcrumbs. Bake for 25 to 30 minutes or until crumbs are light brown. Serves 4 to 6.

• • • • •

Savory Tomatoes, Beans and Squash

1 large onion, sliced	
1 clove garlic, minced	
1 teaspoon Italian seasoning	5 ml
2 tablespoons oil	30 ml
2 (15 ounce) cans green beans with liquid	2 (425 g)
1 (15 ounce) can diced tomatoes	425 g
2 cups sliced zucchini	225 g

- Cook onion, garlic and Italian seasoning in oil in large skillet for 3 minutes. Add 1 teaspoon (5 ml) salt and ¼ teaspoon (1 ml) pepper. Add remaining ingredients, cover and simmer for 20 minutes or until zucchini is tender. Serves 6 to 8.

• • • • •

Sauteed Zucchini and Tomatoes

Butter	
1 large zucchini, julienned	
1 large tomato, chopped	
⅓ cup grated parmesan cheese	35 g

- Melt small amount of butter in large skillet. Saute zucchini until it is soft but not brown. Add chopped tomato and a little salt and pepper. Stir until they are hot. Remove from heat, add parmesan cheese and stir well. Serves 4.

• • • • •

Fried Zucchini

3 large zucchini, grated
3 eggs
⅓ (12 ounce) box round buttery crackers, crushed   ⅓ (340 g)
½ cup grated parmesan cheese   50 g
Vegetable oil

- Combine zucchini, eggs and cracker crumbs and mix well. Add
  cheese and a little salt and pepper. Drop by spoonfuls into skillet
  with a little oil. Fry for about 15 minutes and brown each side.
  Serves 4.

Zucchini Patties

1½ cups grated zucchini   190 g
1 egg, beaten
2 tablespoons flour   30 ml
⅓ cup finely minced onion   55 g
3 tablespoons vegetable oil   45 g

- Mix all ingredients except oil. Heat skillet with oil. Drop zucchini
  mixture by tablespoonfuls into skillet at medium-high heat. Brown
  both sides. Remove and drain on paper towels. Serves 4.

Zucchini Rounds

½ cup baking mix   60 g
2 beaten eggs
2 cups unpeeled, grated zucchini   250 g
Oil

- Combine baking mix and eggs and mix well. Stir in grated zucchini
  and fry as you would pancakes. Drop spoonfuls of batter onto hot
  greased griddle. Drain and serve hot. Serves 4 to 6.

Everyday Deviled Eggs

6 eggs, hard-boiled
2 tablespoons sweet pickle relish   30 ml
3 tablespoons mayonnaise   45 ml
½ teaspoon dry mustard   2 ml
Paprika

- Peel eggs and cut in half lengthwise. Take yolks out and mash
  with fork. Add relish, mayonnaise and mustard to yolks and mix
  well. Place yolk mixture back into egg white halves. Sprinkle with
  paprika. Serves 4 to 6.

• • • • •

Red Beans and Rice

1 pound dry red beans	455 g
1 meaty ham bone or ham hocks	
2 onions, chopped	
1 teaspoon garlic powder	5 ml
Hot sauce	
Cooked rice	

- Combine all ingredients, except rice, with 8 cups (1.9 L) water and a little salt and pepper. Place in large heavy pan. Bring to a boil. Lower heat, simmer and stir occasionally for 4 hours.

- When soft enough, mash some beans against side of pot to thicken sauce. Serve over hot cooked rice. Serves 4 to 6.

• • • • •

Black-Eyed Pea Rice

1 cup rice	185 g
1 onion, chopped	
3 tablespoons butter	45 ml
2 (15 ounce) cans black-eyed peas	2 (425 g)

- Cook rice in 2 cups (500 ml) boiling, salted water according to package directions.

- Saute onion in butter. Add black-eyed peas and heat thoroughly. Serve peas over rice. Serves 2 to 4.

TIP: Add 1 cup (140 g) cooked, chopped ham to make a heartier dish.

• • • • •

Broccoli-Rice Casserole

1 (10 ounce) box frozen chopped broccoli, thawed	280 g
1 cup cooked rice	160 g
1 (8 ounce) jar Cheese Whiz®	225 g

- Preheat oven to 350° (175° C).

- Cook broccoli according to package directions and drain. Combine broccoli, rice and Cheez Whiz® and mix well. Pour into sprayed 9-inch baking dish and bake for 20 to 30 minutes. Serves 4.

• • • • •

Brown Rice

2 (14 ounce) cans chicken broth	2 (395 g)
1 cup brown rice	185 g
1 teaspoon dried parsley	5 ml

- Bring broth to a boil over high heat in heavy saucepan. Stir in rice, cover and reduce heat to low so rice simmers. Cook for 50 minutes or until tender and broth is absorbed. Uncover and let rice stand for 3 minutes. Fluff with fork. Sprinkle with parsley. Serves 4.

TIP: Add ½ cup (80 g) chopped onion and ½ cup (50 g) chopped celery. Cook with rice.

• • • • •

Carrot-Rice Casserole

¼ cup (½ stick) butter	55 g
1 (16 ounce) package shredded carrots	455 g
1 medium onion, chopped	
1⅓ cups shredded cheddar cheese	150 g
2 cups cooked rice	315 g
2 eggs, beaten	

- Preheat oven to 350° (175° C).

- Melt butter in 10-inch (25 cm) skillet. Add carrots and onions and saute. Stir in cheese, rice, eggs and a little salt. Spoon into sprayed 2-quart (2 L) baking dish. Bake for 18 to 20 minutes. Serves 6 to 8.

• • • • •

Chile-Rice Bake

1 cup instant rice	95 g
1 (1 pint) carton sour cream	455 g
1 (7 ounce) can diced green chilies	200 g
1 (8 ounce) package shredded Monterey Jack cheese	225 g

- Preheat oven to 325° (165° C).

- Cook rice according to package directions. Add remaining ingredients plus ½ teaspoon (2 ml) salt. Place mixture in sprayed 7 x 11-inch (18 x 28 cm) baking dish. Bake covered for 15 to 20 minutes or until hot. Serves 4 to 6.

• • • • •

Dinner Rice

2 cups cooked rice	**315 g**
1 onion, chopped	
¼ cup (½ stick) butter, melted	**55 g**
1 (8 ounce) package shredded Mexican Velveeta® cheese	**225 g**

- Preheat oven to 325° (165° C).

- Combine all ingredients and mix well. Spoon mixture into sprayed 2-quart (2 L) baking dish. Bake covered for 30 minutes. Serves 4.

• • • • •

Rice and Spinach

1 cup instant rice	**95 g**
1 (10 ounce) package frozen chopped spinach	**280 g**
¾ cup shredded cheddar cheese, divided	**85 g**
1 onion, finely chopped	
3 tablespoons butter	**45 ml**

- Preheat oven to 350° (175° C).

- Cook rice in large saucepan according to package directions. Cook spinach according to package directions. Set aside 3 tablespoons (45 ml) cheese for topping.

- Add spinach, onion, butter, remaining cheese and ¼ teaspoon (1 ml) salt to rice. (If rice mixture seems a little dry, add several tablespoons water.) Pour into sprayed 2-quart (2 L) baking dish and bake for 25 minutes. Sprinkle with set aside cheese. Serves 4.

• • • • •

Mexican Fiesta Rice

1 (6 ounce) package Mexican fiesta rice	**170 g**
2 tablespoons butter	**30 ml**
1 cup chopped celery	**100 g**
1 (8 ounce) package shredded Mexican Velveeta® cheese	**225 g**

- Cook rice according to package directions. Add butter and celery and simmer 5 minutes. Stir occasionally. Place in serving dish and cover with cheese. Serves 4 to 6.

• • • • •

Mushroom Rice

1 (6 ounce) package chicken rice and pasta	170 g
1 (4 ounce) can sliced mushrooms, drained	115 g
⅓ cup slivered almonds	55 g
1 (8 ounce) carton sour cream	225 g

- Preheat oven to 350° (175° C).

- Prepare rice according to package directions. Fold in mushrooms, almonds and sour cream. Place in sprayed 3-quart (3 L) baking dish. Bake covered for 25 to 30 minutes. Serves 4 to 6.

● ● ● ● ●

Onion-Rice Casserole

1 (10 ounce) can French onion soup	280 g
1 cup rice	185 g
½ cup chopped celery	50 g

- Combine soup, rice, celery and 1 cup (250 ml) water. Mix well and cook in covered saucepan over medium heat for 25 to 30 minutes or until rice is tender. Fluff with fork. Serves 4.

● ● ● ● ●

Pecan Rice Pilaf

½ cup pecan halves	55 g
3 tablespoons butter, melted	45 ml
1 (7 ounce) package wild rice	200 g

- Saute pecan halves in melted butter. Prepare wild rice according to package directions and stir pecans into rice. Serve hot with chicken or pork. Serves 4 to 6.

● ● ● ● ●

Red Rice

1 meaty ham hock	
2 cups instant rice	190 g
1 (15 ounce) can diced tomatoes with liquid	425 g
1 (10 ounce) can tomato soup	280 g

- Cover ham hock with 3 cups (750 ml) water and simmer for 40 minutes or until meat is easy to remove from bone. Drain in colander and save broth. Combine broth and rice.

- Cook until water absorbs and rice is tender. Add ham bits, tomatoes and soup and cook until excess moisture is gone. Serves 4.

Rice and Peas

1½ cups instant rice   145 g
½ (10 ounce) package frozen green peas, thawed   ½ (280 g)
1 tablespoon butter   15 ml

- Cook rice according to package directions. Add green peas and butter. Heat on low until rice gets hot again. Serves 4.

• • • • •

Rice Pilaf

This rice is great with chicken!

2 cups cooked rice   315 g
⅓ cup raisins or chopped dates   55 g
¼ cup slivered almonds, toasted   40 g

- Combine all ingredients and mix well. Serves 4.

• • • • •

Veggie Rice

3 cups cooked brown rice   585 g
1 (15 ounce) can green peas, drained   425 g
1 tablespoon dried parsley   15 ml
¼ cup (½ stick) butter, melted   55 g

- Combine all ingredients in saucepan on medium heat. Stir until mixture heats thoroughly. Serves 3.

• • • • •

Wild Rice Amandine

1 (6.7 ounce) package long grain-wild rice   200 g
3 tablespoons butter   45 ml
⅓ cup sliced almonds   55 g

- Prepare rice according to package directions. Heat butter and saute almonds. Stir buttered almonds into hot rice. Serves 4.

• • • • •

Baked Macaroni and Cheese

1 (8 ounce) package macaroni	225 g
2⅓ cups milk	575 ml
1 (8 ounce) package cubed Velveeta® cheese	225 g

- Preheat oven to 350° (175° C).

- Cook macaroni according to package directions until tender. Drain. Stir in milk and cheese and mix well. Pour into sprayed baking dish and bake covered for 45 minutes or until set. Serves 6.

• • • • •

Layered Macaroni and Cheese

1 (16 ounce) package macaroni, divided	455 g
1 (12 ounce) package shredded cheddar cheese, divided	340 g
1 (15) ounce) can stewed tomatoes, drained (set aside liquid)	425 g

- Preheat oven to 350° (175° C). Cook macaroni according to package directions. In sprayed 2-quart (2 L) baking dish, make layers of half macaroni, half cheese and half tomatoes.

- Repeat layers. Pour set aside tomato liquid over top and bake covered for 1 hour. Serves 6.

• • • • •

Seasoned Pasta

2 (14 ounce) cans chicken broth with Italian herbs	2 (395 g)
3 cups corkscrew pasta	225 g
½ - 1 cup grated parmesan cheese	50 - 100 g

- In saucepan, heat broth until it boils. Stir in pasta. Reduce heat, simmer on medium until pasta is fork-tender; stir often. Pour into serving bowl and sprinkle with grated parmesan cheese. Serves 6.

• • • • •

Bread that's a few days old is great when seasoned and moistened to use as a stuffing.

Favorite Pasta

1 (8 ounce) package spinach linguine	225 g
1 cup whipping cream	250 ml
1 cup chicken broth	250 ml
½ cup grated parmesan cheese	50 g
½ cup frozen English peas	70 g

- Cook linguine according to package directions, drain and keep warm. Combine whipping cream and chicken broth in saucepan and bring to boil. Reduce heat and simmer for 25 minutes or until it thickens and reduces to 1 cup (250 ml).

- Remove from heat. Add cheese and peas and stir until cheese melts. Toss with linguine and serve immediately. Serves 4 to 6.

Cheese Sauce for Veggies

This is a great way to get kids to eat their veggies.

1 (10 ounce) can cream of mushroom soup	280 g
1 (8 ounce) carton sour cream	225 g
1 cup shredded cheddar cheese	115 g

- In saucepan, combine all ingredients and mix well. Heat on medium until hot, but do not boil. Serve over vegetables. Yields 2½ cups.

Easy Dressing

1 (6 ounce) box cornbread stuffing mix	170 g
1 onion, chopped	
1 (14 ounce) can chicken broth	395 g

- Preheat oven to 325° (165° C).

- Combine stuffing mix, onion and broth and mix well. Pour into sprayed 7 x 11-inch (18 x 28 cm) baking dish and bake for 30 minutes. Serves 4 to 6.

Sausage Dressing

1 (6 ounce) box herb stuffing mix	170 g
1 pound bulk pork sausage	455 g
1 cup chopped onion	160 g

- Preheat oven to 325° (165° C). Prepare stuffing according to package directions. Brown and drain sausage. Remove sausage from skillet and saute onion in drippings. Combine dressing, sausage and onions and mix well. Pour mixture into 2-quart sprayed baking dish and bake for 30 minutes. Serves 6 to 8.

Centsible Chicken

So versatile, chicken can be prepared in an almost endless number of ways so that meals are not the same seven recipes every week.

Alfredo Chicken

Vegetable oil
5 - 6 boneless, skinless chicken breast halves
1 (16 ounce) package frozen broccoli florets, thawed   455 g
1 green bell pepper, seeded, chopped
1 (16 ounce) jar alfredo sauce   455 g

- Preheat oven to 375° (190° C).

- In large skillet with a little oil, brown and cook chicken breasts until juices run clear. Transfer to sprayed 9 x 13-inch (23 x 33 cm) baking dish.

- Microwave broccoli according to package directions and drain. Spoon broccoli and bell pepper over chicken. In small saucepan, heat alfredo sauce with ¼ cup (60 ml) water. Pour over chicken and vegetables. Cover and bake for 15 to 20 minutes. Serves 5 to 6.

SPECIAL NOTE Chicken breast halves are used throughout Chicken Main Dishes, but any piece of chicken will work with these recipes.

Apple Jack Chicken

4 boneless, skinless chicken breasts
2 apples, cored, thinly sliced
4 slices Monterey Jack cheese

- Preheat oven to 350° (175° C).

- Place chicken in sprayed 9 x 13-inch (23 x 33 cm) pan and bake for 40 minutes.

- Turn chicken over and place apple slices over each breast. Bake for additional 10 minutes.

- Top each piece with slice of cheese. Bake for additional 10 minutes or until cheese melts and chicken is tender. Serves 4.

Apricot Chicken

4 boneless, skinless chicken breast halves
1 cup apricot nectar   250 ml
1 (1 ounce) packet dry onion soup mix   30 g

- Preheat oven to 325° (165° C). Arrange chicken breasts in sprayed 9 x 13-inch (23 x 33 cm) baking pan and pour apricot nectar over chicken.

- Sprinkle with soup mix, cover and bake for 1 hour. Remove cover and bake for additional 15 minutes. Serves 4.

Apricot-Glazed Chicken

½ cup teriyaki baste-and-glaze sauce   145 g
½ teaspoon dried ginger   2 ml
1 cup apricot preserves   320 g
4 boneless, skinless chicken breast halves, thawed

- In small bowl, combine teriyaki glaze, ginger and apricot preserves. Mix well and set aside. Salt and pepper chicken breast halves and place on grill over medium heat.

- Grill 18 to 22 minutes (depending on size of chicken breasts) or until chicken is fork-tender. Turn chicken once on grill. When chicken has 5 to 10 minutes remaining in cooking time, brush liberally with teriyaki-apricot mixture. Serves 4.

Artichoke Chicken

4 boneless, skinless chicken breast halves
1 (6.5 ounce) jar marinated artichoke hearts, drained   170 g
4 slices Swiss cheese

- Preheat oven to 325° (165° C). Between 2 pieces wax paper, flatten chicken to uniform thickness.

- Brown chicken breasts on both sides in sprayed skillet and arrange chicken in single layer in sprayed 9 x 13-inch (23 x 33 cm) pan. Coarsely chop artichoke hearts and spread over chicken with a little salt and pepper. Cover and bake 30 to 35 minutes. Remove from oven and lay Swiss cheese over each breast and bake for an additional 5 minutes. Serves 4.

Bacon-Wrapped Chicken

4 boneless, skinless chicken breast halves
1 (8 ounce) carton whipped cream cheese with onion
  and chives, softened   225 g
Butter
4 strips bacon

- Preheat oven to 375° (190° C). Flatten chicken to ½-inch (1.2 cm) thickness. Spread one-fourth cream cheese over each half. Dot with butter and a little salt and roll. Wrap each roll with bacon strip.

- Place seam-side down in sprayed 9 x 13-inch (23 x 33 cm) baking dish. Bake uncovered for 40 to 45 minutes or until juices run clear.

- To brown, broil 6 inches (15 cm) from heat for about 3 minutes or until bacon is crisp. Serves 4.

• • • • •

Baked Breaded Chicken

4 boneless, skinless chicken breast halves
½ cup mayonnaise   110 g
1¼ cups Italian-seasoned dry breadcrumbs   160 g

- Preheat oven to 375° (190° C).

- Brush both sides of chicken with mayonnaise and roll in crumbs until well coated. Place in sprayed baking pan and bake for 45 minutes or until there is no pink in chicken and juices runs clear when pierced with fork. Serves 4.

• • • • •

Baked Chicken Breasts

4 boneless, skinless chicken breast halves
2 (10 ounce) cans cream of chicken soup   2 (280 g)
1 cup shredded Swiss cheese   110 g
2 cups herb-seasoned stuffing mix   100 g
½ cup (1 stick) butter, melted   115 g

- Preheat oven to 350° (175° C). Arrange chicken breasts in sprayed 9 x 13-inch (23 x 33 cm) baking dish. Combine soup with ¼ cup (60 ml) water in small bowl. Pour over chicken breasts and sprinkle with cheese and stuffing mix. Drizzle butter over top of casserole. Bake for 1 hour to 1 hour 15 minutes. Serves 4.

• • • • •

Baked Chicken
and Rice Casserole

1 (6 ounce) box long grain-wild rice mix   170 g
4 - 6 boneless, skinless chicken breast halves
1 (10 ounce) can cream of mushroom soup   280 g

- Preheat oven to 325° (165° C).

- In a sprayed 9 x 13-inch (23 x 33 cm) baking dish, combine rice, seasoning packet and 2 cups (500 ml) hot water. Place chicken over rice and bake covered for 1 hour 30 minutes.

- Dilute mushroom soup with ½ cup (125 ml) water and mix well. Pour over chicken. Bake uncovered for 20 minutes or until soup bubbles and chicken is brown. Serves 4 to 6.

TIP: If cooking only 4 chicken breasts, use a 7 x 11-inch (18 x 28 cm) baking dish.

Baked Mexican Chicken

4 - 6 boneless, skinless chicken breast halves
1 teaspoon taco seasoning mix   5 ml
1 (10 ounce) can enchilada sauce   280 g
Corn tortillas

- Preheat oven to 350° (175° C). Place chicken in sprayed baking dish.
  Sprinkle taco seasoning mix over chicken. Pour enchilada sauce over
  chicken and bake for 1 hour or until tender. Serve with warmed corn
  tortillas. Serves 4 to 6.

• • • • •

Barbecued Skillet Chicken

4 boneless, skinless chicken breast halves
1 (12 ounce) can 7UP®   355 ml
1 (8 ounce) bottle barbecue sauce   225 g

- Place chicken in sprayed skillet. Combine 7UP® and barbecue sauce
  and pour over chicken. Bring to boil and simmer for 1 hour or until
  tender. Serves 4.

• • • • •

Yummy
Barbecued-Grilled Chicken

4 boneless, skinless chicken breast halves
      or 1 chicken, quartered
3 cups ketchup   815 g
½ cup packed brown sugar   110 g
¼ cup Worcestershire sauce   60 ml
2 tablespoons vinegar   30 ml
1 teaspoon hot sauce   5 ml

- Wash chicken breasts and dry with paper towels. In saucepan,
  combine ketchup, brown sugar, Worcestershire sauce, vinegar,
  1 teaspoon (5 ml) salt, ½ teaspoon (2 ml) pepper and hot sauce.
  Bring sauce to boil, reduce heat to low and cook for 15 minutes.

- Fire up grill and smoke over mesquite wood, if possible. Cook
  chicken for 8 to 10 minutes per side. Baste chicken frequently with
  barbecue sauce and turn periodically. Serves 4.

• • • • •

Broccoli-Cheese Chicken

Vegetable oil
4 boneless, skinless chicken breast halves
1 (10 ounce) can broccoli-cheese soup   280 g
1 (16 ounce) package frozen broccoli florets   455 g
½ cup milk   125 ml
Cooked rice

- In skillet with a little oil, cook chicken 15 minutes or until brown on both sides, remove and set aside. In same skillet, combine soup, broccoli, milk and a little pepper and heat to boiling. Return chicken to skillet and reduce heat to low.

- Cover and cook for 25 minutes or until chicken is no longer pink and broccoli is tender. Serve over rice. Serves 4.

• • • • •

Broiled Chicken Cordon Bleu

4 boneless, skinless chicken breast halves
4 slices cheddar or Swiss cheese, divided
4 slices ham or Canadian bacon, fully cooked, divided

- Preheat broiler. Broil chicken breasts 4 inches (10 cm) from heat for 4 minutes. Turn chicken over and broil for 4 or 5 minutes or until tender.

- Cut cheese slices in half, place half slice on top of each chicken breast and top with ham or Canadian bacon slice. Broil for 30 seconds and top with remaining half slices cheese. Broil until cheese melts. Serves 4.

• • • • •

Cajun Oven-Fried Chicken

1 teaspoon Creole seasoning   5 ml
1 cup crushed corn flakes   40 g
4 boneless, skinless chicken breast halves
¼ cup buttermilk*   60 ml

- Preheat oven to 375° (190° C).

- Combine Creole seasoning and corn flake crumbs. Brush chicken with buttermilk and roll in crumb mixture. Place chicken in sprayed 9 x 13-inch (23 x 33 cm) baking dish and bake for 1 hour. Serves 4.

TIP: To make buttermilk, mix 1 cup (250 ml) milk with 1 tablespoon (15 ml) lemon juice or vinegar and let milk stand for about 10 minutes.

Cajun Chicken

4 boneless skinless chicken breast halves
1 teaspoon hot sauce   5 ml
1 teaspoon Cajun seasoning   5 ml

- Rinse chicken in cool water and dry. Generously brush hot sauce on each side and then sprinkle each side with Cajun seasoning.

- Place chicken in sprayed skillet and brown. Turn and brown other side. Cover and cook slowly for 20 minutes or until fork-tender. Serves 4.

• • • • •

Chicken a la Reuben

4 boneless, skinless chicken breast halves
4 slices Swiss cheese
1 (15 ounce) can sauerkraut, drained   425 g
1 (8 ounce) bottle Catalina salad dressing   250 ml

- Preheat oven to 350° (175° C).

- Arrange chicken breasts in sprayed 9 x 13-inch (23 x 33 cm) baking pan. Place cheese slices over chicken and sauerkraut on top. Cover with Catalina dressing. Bake covered for 30 minutes. Uncover and bake for additional 15 minutes. Serves 4.

• • • • •

Chicken and the Works

6 boneless, skinless chicken breast halves
Paprika
Vegetable oil
2 (10 ounce) cans cream of chicken soup   2 (280 g)
2 cups instant white rice   190 g
1 (10 ounce) package frozen green peas, thawed   280 g

- Sprinkle chicken with a little pepper and paprika and brown in 12-inch (32 cm) skillet with a little oil. Reduce heat, cover and simmer for about 15 minutes. Transfer chicken to plate and keep warm.

- Add soup and 2 cups (500 ml) water to skillet and mix well. Heat to boiling and stir in rice and green peas. Top with chicken breasts, cover and simmer over low heat for about 10 minutes. Serves 6.

• • • • •

Chicken Breast Eden Isle

1 (8 ounce) carton sour cream	225 g
1 (3 ounce) cream cheese, softened	85 g
1 (10 ounce) can cream of chicken soup	280 g
4 boneless, skinless chicken breast halves	
4 strips bacon	
Cooked rice	

• Preheat oven to 350° (175° C).

• Beat sour cream, cream cheese and soup with electric mixer. Wrap each chicken breast with a strip of bacon and place in sprayed 7 x 11-inch (23 x 33 cm) baking dish. Spoon sour cream mixture over chicken. Cover and bake for 1 hour. Uncover last few minutes to brown. Serve over rice. Serves 4.

• • • • •

Chicken Cacciatore

4 boneless, skinless chicken breast halves	
2 cups chunky spaghetti sauce with onions	500 g
1 green pepper, seeded, cut in strips	

• Brown chicken in sprayed skillet and turn frequently to brown on each side; drain. Add spaghetti sauce and green peppers to chicken. Cover skillet and cook on low for 35 minutes or until chicken is tender. Place chicken on platter and pour tomato-pepper mixture over chicken. Serves 4.

TIP: *This dish is very good with shredded parmesan cheese on top, but it's not mandatory for a really great chicken dish.*

• • • • •

Chicken Crunch

4 - 6 boneless, skinless chicken breast halves	
½ cup Italian salad dressing	125 ml
½ cup sour cream	120 g
2½ cups crushed corn flakes	90 g

• Place chicken in resealable plastic bag. Mix dressing and sour cream and toss with chicken; refrigerate for 1 hour.

• When ready to bake, preheat oven to 375° (190° C).

• Remove chicken from bag and discard marinade. Dredge chicken in corn flakes and place in sprayed 9 x 13-inch (23 x 33 cm) baking dish. Bake uncovered for 45 minutes. Serves 4 to 6.

Chicken Dijon

4 boneless, skinless chicken breast halves
¼ cup dijon-style mustard   **60 g**
2 cups seasoned breadcrumbs   **240 g**

- Preheat oven to 350° (175° C).

- Place chicken breasts in sprayed baking dish and bake for 20 minutes.

- Remove from oven and generously spread mustard generously on both sides of chicken. Coat with breadcrumbs, return to baking dish and bake for 1 hour. Serves 4.

TIP: The mustard gives chicken a tangy flavor and keeps it moist. Don't overcook.

● ● ● ● ●

Chicken Mozzarella

4 boneless, skinless chicken breast halves
½ (28 ounce) jar spaghetti sauce   **½ (795 g)**
4 slices mozzarella cheese

- Preheat oven to 325° (165° C).

- Place chicken breasts in sprayed baking dish, cover with sauce and bake covered for 1 hour.

- Top each breast with 1 slice cheese. Bake uncovered for additional 10 minutes. Serve over spaghetti or noodles, if desired. Serves 4.

● ● ● ● ●

Lemon Chicken

4 boneless, skinless chicken breast halves
1 cup lemon juice   **250 ml**
⅓ cup (⅔ stick) butter, melted   **75 g**

- Place chicken in 9 x 13-inch (23 x 33 cm) glass dish and cover with lemon juice. Marinate for 1 hour in refrigerator and turn often.

- When ready to bake, preheat oven to 350° (175° C).

- Drain liquid off chicken and pour melted butter over chicken. Bake for 1 hour or until tender. Serves 4.

● ● ● ● ●

Chicken Jalapeno

4 boneless, skinless chicken breast halves
2 tablespoons butter, melted   30 ml
½ cup jalapeno jelly   160 g

- Place chicken breasts between 2 sheets heavy-duty plastic wrap and flatten to ¼-inch (6 mm) thickness with meat mallet. Cook chicken in butter in large skillet over medium heat for 5 minutes on each side. Remove to serving platter.

- Stir jelly into pan drippings and bring to a boil. Stir until smooth. Spoon mixture over chicken. Serves 4.

Chicken Parmesan

4 boneless, skinless chicken breast halves
⅓ cup (⅔ stick) butter, melted   75 g
1 cup grated parmesan cheese   100 g

- Preheat oven to 325° (165° C).

- Roll chicken breasts in melted butter and then in parmesan cheese until they coat well.

- Place chicken in sprayed baking pan and drizzle a little extra butter over each piece. Bake for 45 to 50 minutes or until tender. Serves 4.

Chicken Souffle

16 slices bread
Butter
½ cup mayonnaise   110 g
4 boneless, skinless chicken breast halves, cooked, sliced
1 cup shredded cheddar cheese, divided   115 g
5 large eggs, beaten
2 cups milk   500 ml
1 (10 ounce) can cream of mushroom soup   280 g

- Remove crust from bread and butter slices on 1 side of each slice. Spray 9 x13-inch (23 x 33 cm) baking dish and place 8 bread slices in dish butter-side down. Spread mayonnaise, chicken slices and ½ cup (120 ml) cheese over bread. Top with remaining 8 slices bread.

- Mix eggs, milk and 1 teaspoon (5 ml) salt and pour over entire dish. Refrigerate overnight or all day. When ready to bake, spread soup over top and press down with back of spoon.

- Bake covered at 350° (175° C) for 45 minutes. Sprinkle with remaining cheese and bake uncovered for 15 additional minutes. Serves 6 to 8.

Chicken Taco Pie

1 pound boneless, skinless chicken breast halves	455 g
Vegetable oil	
1 (1 ounce) packet taco seasoning mix	30 g
2 green bell peppers, seeded, finely chopped	
1½ cups shredded Mexican 3-cheese blend	170 g
1 (8 ounce) package corn muffin mix	225 g
1 egg	
⅓ cup milk	75 ml

- Preheat oven to 400° (205° C).

- Cut chicken into 1-inch (2.5 cm) chunks and cook on medium-high heat in large skillet with a little oil. Cook for about 10 minutes. Drain and stir in taco seasoning, bell peppers and ¾ cup (175 ml) water. Reduce heat, simmer and cook for additional 10 minutes. Stir several times.

- Spoon into sprayed 9-inch (23 cm) deep-dish pie pan and sprinkle with cheese.

- Prepare corn muffin mix with egg and milk and mix well. Spoon over top of pie and bake for 20 minutes or until top is golden brown. Let stand for about 5 minutes before serving. Serves 4 to 6.

• • • • •

Chicken-Wild Rice Special

1 (6 ounce) package long grain-wild rice mix	170 g
4 boneless, skinless chicken breast halves	
Vegetable oil	
2 (10 ounce) cans French onion soup	2 (280 g)
2 green bell peppers, seeded, julienned	

- In saucepan, cook rice according to package directions and keep warm.

- Brown chicken breasts on both sides in large skillet with a little oil over medium-high heat. Add soup, ¾ cup (175 ml) water and bell peppers. Reduce heat to medium-low, cover and cook for 15 minutes.

- To serve, place rice on serving platter with chicken breasts on top. Serve sauce in gravy boat to spoon over chicken and rice. Serves 4.

• • • • •

Chili-Pepper Chicken

¼ cup (½ stick) butter	55 g
6 boneless, skinless chicken breast halves	
1 (6 ounce) box spicy chicken coating mix	170 g
1 (16 ounce) jar mild salsa	455 g

- Preheat oven to 400° (205° C).

- Melt butter in oven in 9 x 13-inch (23 x 33 cm) glass baking dish and remove from oven.

- Place coating mix in shallow bowl and coat each chicken breast on both sides. Place chicken in baking dish and arrange so pieces are not touching. Bake for 20 minutes or until chicken browns lightly. Serve with heaping spoonful of salsa. Serves 4 to 6.

● ● ● ● ●

Classy Chicken

4 boneless, skinless chicken breast halves	
¼ cup lime juice	60 ml
1 (1 ounce) packet dry Italian salad dressing mix	30 g
¼ cup (½ stick) butter, melted	55 g

- Preheat oven to 325° (165° C).

- Season chicken with a little salt and pepper and place in sprayed shallow baking dish.

- Combine lime juice, salad dressing mix and butter and pour over chicken. Cover and bake for 45 minutes. Uncover and bake for 15 additional minutes. Serves 4.

● ● ● ● ●

Cola Barbecued Chicken

4 - 6 boneless, skinless chicken breast halves	
½ cup ketchup	135 g
1 (12 ounce) can cola	355 ml

- Preheat oven to 350° (175° C). Place chicken in large sprayed skillet. Combine ketchup and cola and pour over chicken. Cover and bake for 1 hour or until tender. Serves 4 to 6.

● ● ● ● ●

Cranberries and Chicken

1 (16 ounce) can whole cranberry sauce   455 g
1 (8 ounce) bottle Catalina salad dressing   250 ml
1 (1 ounce) packet dry onion soup mix   30 g
6 boneless, skinless chicken breast halves

- Mix cranberry sauce, salad dressing and soup mix. Pour over chicken breasts in sprayed 9 x 13-inch (23 x 33 cm) glass baking dish. Marinate overnight.

- When ready to bake, preheat oven to 350° (175° C). Bake for 1 hour. Serves 6.

• • • • •

Creamy Chicken and Veggies

6 small boneless, skinless chicken breast halves
Vegetable oil
1 (16 ounce) bottle creamy Italian dressing   500 ml
1 (16 ounce) package frozen broccoli, cauliflower and
       carrots, thawed   455 g

- Sprinkle chicken with a little salt and pepper. Place a little oil in large, heavy non-stick skillet over medium-high heat. Add chicken breasts and cook 2 minutes on each side. Pour about three-fourths dressing over chicken.

- Cover and simmer for about 8 minutes. Add vegetables, cover and cook for additional 10 minutes or until vegetables are tender. Serves 6.

• • • • •

Creamy Mushroom Chicken

4 boneless, skinless chicken breast halves
Vegetable oil
1 (10 ounce) can cream of mushroom soup   280 g
1 (4 ounce) can sliced mushrooms, drained   115 g
½ cup milk   125 ml

- Sprinkle chicken liberally with salt and pepper. In skillet over high heat with a little oil, brown chicken on both sides.

- While chicken browns, combine soup, mushrooms and milk in saucepan and heat just enough to mix well. Pour over chicken breasts, reduce heat to low and simmer covered for 15 minutes. Serves 4.

• • • • •

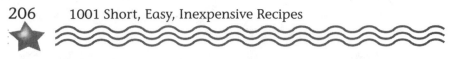

Creamy Tarragon Chicken

1½ cups flour	180 g
6 boneless, skinless chicken breast halves	
2 tablespoons oil	30 ml
1 (14 ounce) can chicken broth	395 g
1 cup milk	250 ml
2 teaspoons dried tarragon	10 ml
1 (4 ounce) can sliced mushrooms, drained	115 g
2 (8 ounce) packages roasted-chicken rice	2 (225 g)

- Mix flour and a little salt and pepper on wax paper and coat chicken. Set aside extra flour. Heat oil in large skillet over medium-high heat, cook chicken breasts and turn once. Cook for about 10 minutes or until light brown. Transfer to plate.

- In same skillet, stir in 2 tablespoons (30 ml) flour-salt mixture. Whisk in broth, milk and tarragon and heat, stirring constantly, until bubbly. Add mushrooms and chicken to skillet. Cover and simmer for 10 to 15 minutes or until sauce thickens.

- Microwave rice according to directions and place on serving platter. Spoon chicken and sauce over rice. Serves 4 to 6.

• • • • •

Crunchy Chip Chicken

1½ cups crushed sour cream potato chips	85 g
1 tablespoon dried parsley	15 ml
1 egg, beaten	
1 tablespoon Worcestershire sauce	15 ml
4 large boneless, skinless chicken breast halves	
¼ cup oil	60 ml

- In shallow bowl, combine potato chips and parsley. In another shallow bowl, combine beaten egg, Worcestershire and 1 tablespoon (15 ml) water. Dip chicken pieces in egg mixture, then dredge chicken in potato chip mixture.

- Heat oil in heavy skillet and fry chicken pieces for about 10 minutes. Turn each piece over and cook for additional 10 minutes until golden brown or until juices are no longer pink. Serves 4.

• • • • •

 Buy in bulk or on sale and freeze breads, butter, coffee, flour, milk (take some out of the container to allow for expansion), nuts and seeds, frozen vegetables.

Crisp Chicken

6 - 8 boneless, skinless chicken breast halves
2 eggs, beaten
Crushed corn flakes

- Preheat oven to 350° (175° C). Dip chicken in eggs and roll in crushed corn flakes until well coated. Place chicken on sprayed baking sheet and bake for 1 hour. Serves 6 to 8.

• • • • •

French Oven Chicken

This recipe will really surprise you. It's delicious!

1 (15 ounce) can whole cranberry sauce   425 g
1 (1 ounce) packet dry onion soup mix   30 g
1 (8 ounce) bottle French salad dressing   250 ml
6 boneless, skinless chicken breast halves

- Combine cranberry sauce, soup mix and salad dressing in bowl and mix until they blend well. Cover and refrigerate until ready to use.

- Place chicken breast halves in sprayed 9 x 13-inch (23 x 33 cm) baking dish and pour cranberry sauce mixture evenly over chicken. Cover and marinate overnight in the refrigerator.

- When ready to bake, preheat oven to 350° (175° C).

- Bake for 1 hour or until tender. Serves 6.

• • • • •

Grilled Lemon Chicken

6 boneless, skinless chicken breast halves
2 teaspoons garlic salt   10 ml
1 tablespoon freshly grated lemon peel   15 ml
2 teaspoons dried thyme   10 ml

- In small bowl, combine garlic salt, lemon peel, thyme and a little pepper. Spray grill with cooking spray and heat coals.

- Sprinkle seasoning mixture over chicken breasts. Grill chicken for 20 to 25 minutes or until chicken is no longer pink and juices run clear. Turn once during cooking. Serves 6.

• • • • •

Grilled Catalina Chicken

4 boneless, skinless chicken breast halves
½ cup Catalina dressing   125 ml

- Trim all visible fat from chicken. Combine dressing and ¼ teaspoon (1 ml) black pepper. Pour into oblong dish, add chicken and turn to coat. Marinate chicken 4 to 6 hours or overnight in refrigerator. Discard marinade.

- When ready to grill, prepare coals and grill chicken for 10 minutes or less on each side. Serves 4.

• • • • •

Fried Chicken Breasts

4 - 6 boneless, skinless chicken breast halves
2 eggs, beaten
30 saltine crackers, finely crushed

- Pound chicken breasts to ¼-inch (6 mm) thickness. (If chicken breasts are very large, cut in half.) In shallow bowl, combine beaten eggs, a little salt and pepper and 3 tablespoons (45 ml) water.

- Dip chicken in egg mixture and then crushed crackers to coat well. Deep fry until golden brown. Drain on paper towels. Serves 4 to 6.

• • • • •

Honey-Mustard Grilled Chicken

¾ cup mayonnaise   170 g
2 tablespoons dijon-style mustard   30 ml
¼ cup honey   85 g
4 boneless, skinless chicken breast halves

- In bowl, combine mayonnaise, mustard and honey and mix well. Brush mayonnaise mixture over each piece of chicken and grill over hot coals until juices run clear. Serves 4.

• • • • •

 Allow ¼ to ½ a whole chicken per serving. Allow ½ pound of chicken per serving if you are grilling or broiling. Allow ¾ pound per serving if frying.

Honey-Orange Glazed Chicken

4 boneless, skinless chicken breast halves
¼ cup honey   85 g
⅓ cup orange marmalade   105 g

- Preheat oven to 350° (175° C).

- Place chicken in 7 x 11-inch (18 x 28 cm) baking dish. Combine honey and marmalade in small bowl. Microwave uncovered for 1 minute or until glaze melts and is hot.

- Stir and spread mixture over chicken. Cover and bake for 30 minutes. Bake uncovered for additional 10 minutes or until chicken is light brown. Serves 4.

• • • • •

Italian Chicken

4 boneless, skinless chicken breast halves
½ cup flour   60 g
1 (8 ounce) bottle Italian salad dressing   250 ml

- Preheat oven to 350° (175° C).

- Remove fat from chicken. Roll halves in flour and place in sprayed 9 x 13-inch (23 x 33 cm) pan.

- Pour dressing over chicken, cover and bake for 1 hour or until tender. Uncover and bake until golden brown. Serves 4.

TIP: This could be prepared in a slow cooker on LOW.

• • • • •

Lemonade Chicken

6 boneless, skinless chicken breast halves
1 (6 ounce) can frozen lemonade concentrate, thawed   175 ml
⅓ cup soy sauce   75 ml
1 teaspoon garlic powder   5 ml

- Preheat oven to 350° (175° C).

- Place chicken in sprayed 9 x 13-inch baking dish. Combine lemonade concentrate, soy sauce and garlic powder and pour over chicken. Cover with foil and bake for 45 minutes. Spoon drippings over chicken and bake uncovered for additional 10 minutes. Serves 6.

• • • • •

Lemon-Lime Chicken Breasts

4 boneless, skinless chicken breast halves
⅓ cup lime juice   75 ml
Lemon pepper

- Pour lime juice over chicken and marinate for 30 minutes in refrigerator. Place chicken in glass pie plate and cover with plastic wrap.

- Prick a few holes in plastic with fork and microwave on HIGH for 8 minutes. Turn and rearrange chicken pieces. Place larger pieces at outside of dish. Microwave for additional 6 minutes or until fork tender and sprinkle with lemon pepper. Serves 4.

• • • • •

Lemon-Pepper Chicken

4 boneless, skinless chicken breast halves
¼ cup soy sauce   60 ml
1 teaspoon lemon pepper   5 ml

- Preheat oven to 350° (175° C). Arrange chicken breasts in sprayed 9 x 13-inch (23 x 33 cm) pan. Sprinkle soy sauce and lemon pepper over chicken. Bake for 1 hour or until tender. Serves 4.

• • • • •

Mandarin Chicken

1 (11 ounce) can mandarin oranges, drained   310 g
1 (6 ounce) can frozen orange juice concentrate   175 ml
1 tablespoon cornstarch   15 ml
4 boneless, skinless chicken breast halves
2 tablespoons garlic-and-herb seasoning   30 ml
2 tablespoons butter   30 ml

- In saucepan, combine oranges, orange juice concentrate, ⅔ cup (150 ml) water and cornstarch. Cook on medium heat, stirring constantly, until mixture thickens. Set aside.

- Sprinkle chicken breasts with seasoning and place in skillet with butter. Cook about 7 minutes on each side until brown. Lower heat and spoon orange-juice mixture over chicken. Cover and simmer for about 20 minutes. (Add a little water if sauce gets too thick.) Serves 4.

• • • • •

Moist and Crunchy
Baked Chicken

½ cup (1 stick) butter, melted	15 g
2 tablespoons mayonnaise	30 ml
1 tablespoon soy sauce	15 ml
1 (6 ounce) can french-fried onions, crushed	170 g
4 boneless, skinless chicken breasts halves	

- Preheat oven to 375° (190° C).

- In shallow bowl, combine melted butter, mayonnaise and soy sauce. Place crushed onions in another shallow bowl. Dry chicken breasts with paper towels and dip into butter mixture. Dredge each chicken breast in crushed onions.

- Place in sprayed 11 x 15-inch (30 x 38 cm) baking pan and arrange so that pieces do not touch. Bake 30 to 35 minutes or until chicken juices run clear. Serves 4.

• • • • •

Easy Mushroom Chicken

4 boneless, skinless chicken breast halves	
1 (10 ounce) can cream of mushroom soup	280 g
1 cup sour cream	240 g

- Preheat oven to 275° (135° C).

- Place chicken in sprayed 9 x 13-inch (23 x 33 cm) baking pan. Combine mushroom soup and sour cream and pour over chicken. Bake for 3 hours or until fork-tender. Serves 4.

• • • • •

Onion Chicken

4 - 6 boneless, skinless chicken breast halves	
1 (1 ounce) packet dry onion soup mix	30 g
2 tablespoons butter, melted	30 ml

- Preheat oven to 350° (175° C).

- Trim all visible fat from chicken. Place chicken breasts in sprayed 9 x 13-inch (23 x 33 cm) baking dish. Sprinkle soup mix and melted butter over chicken. Cover and bake for 1 hour. Serves 4 to 6.

• • • • •

Orange-Onion Chicken

4 boneless, skinless chicken breast halves	
1 cup orange juice	250 ml
1 (1 ounce) packet dry onion soup mix	30 g

- Preheat oven to 350° (175° C). Trim any visible fat from chicken.
  Place chicken pieces in sprayed 9 x 13-inch (23 x 33 cm) pan. Pour
  orange juice over chicken and sprinkle with soup mix. Bake for 30
  minutes. Turn chicken and bake for additional30 minutes or until
  tender. Serves 4.

*SPECIAL NOTE: Chicken breast halves are used throughout the Chicken
                Main Dishes, but any pieces of chicken will work with
                these recipes.*

Orange Soda Chicken

4 boneless, skinless chicken breast halves	
1 (12 ounce) can orange soda	355 ml
2 tablespoons Worcestershire sauce	30 ml

- Arrange chicken breasts in a microwave-safe dish. Pour orange soda
  over chicken and sprinkle with Worcestershire sauce. Cover with
  plastic wrap, folding back one corner to vent and microwave on
  HIGH for 4 minutes.

- Rotate dish half turn and microwave for additional 4 minutes.
  Rotate dish half turn again. Cook chicken until juices run clear and
  meat is not pink in center. Serves 4.

Oven-Fried Ginger Chicken

1 cup flour	120 g
1 teaspoon dried ginger	5 ml
½ cup (¼ stick) butter	115 g
4 boneless, skinless chicken breast halves	
½ cup soy sauce	125 ml
Cooked brown rice	

- Preheat oven to 350° (175° C).

- Mix flour, ginger, ½ teaspoon (2 ml) salt and ½ teaspoon (2 ml)
  pepper. Melt butter in sprayed 9 x 9-inch (23 x 23 cm) baking dish.

- Rinse chicken breasts and pat dry. Coat with flour mixture. Arrange
  meaty side down on butter in baking dish. Bake for 30 minutes.

- Turn chicken over and pour soy sauce over chicken. Bake for
  additional 20 to 25 minutes or until done. Serve over rice. Serves 4.

Party Chicken

4 boneless, skinless chicken breast halves
1 (2 ounce) package dried beef, sliced   55 g
2 (10 ounce) cans cream of mushroom soup   2 (280 g)

- Spread dried beef slices in sprayed baking dish and place chicken over beef. Spoon mushroom soup over chicken and refrigerate for 3 hours.

- When ready to bake, preheat oven to 275° (135° C).

- Bake for 2 hours 30 minutes or until chicken is tender. Serves 4.

Pimento Cheese-Stuffed Fried Chicken

4 skinless, boneless chicken breast halves
½ cup milk   125 ml
1 large egg, beaten
2 cups seasoned breadcrumbs   240 g
Vegetable oil
1 (8 ounce) carton pimento cheese   225 g

- Preheat oven to 350° (175° C). Dry chicken breasts with paper towels and sprinkle well with salt and pepper. Combine milk and beaten egg in shallow bowl and mix well. Place breadcrumbs in second shallow bowl.

- Dip chicken in milk mixture and dredge in breadcrumbs. In large skillet over medium-high heat, pour oil to ⅛-inch (4 mm) depth and cook chicken for about 10 to 12 minutes on each side. Transfer to sprayed baking sheet.

- Hold chicken with tongs and cut slit in thickest part of each chicken breast to form pocket. Spoon about 2 tablespoons (30 g) pimento cheese into each pocket and bake for about 3 minutes or until cheese melts. Serves 4.

Ritzy Baked Chicken

4 boneless, skinless chicken breast halves
1 cup sour cream   240 g
1 cup crushed Cheez It® crackers

- Preheat oven to 325° (165° C). Roll chicken breasts in sour cream, then crushed crackers. Place in sprayed baking dish and bake for 1 hour or until tender. Serves 4.

• • • • •

Pepperoni Chicken

6 boneless, skinless chicken breast halves
24 pepperoni slices
6 mozzarella cheese slices

- Preheat oven to 350° (175° C). Brown chicken on both sides in well sprayed skillet. Place chicken in sprayed 9 x 13-inch (23 x 33 cm) pan and arrange 4 pepperoni slices over each piece of chicken.

- Bake for 30 minutes, remove from oven and top each with cheese. Bake additional 5 minutes or until chicken is tender and juices run clear. Serves 6.

• • • • •

Roasted Chicken and Vegetables

1 (10 ounce) can cream of mushroom soup	280 g
1 teaspoon dried oregano	5 ml
8 - 10 new red potatoes, halved	
1 (16 ounce) package fresh baby carrots	455 g
4 large boneless, skinless chicken breast halves	

- Preheat oven to 375° (190° C). In sprayed 9 x 13-inch (23 x 33 cm) baking pan, combine soup, oregano, potatoes and carrots. Place chicken breast halves over vegetables and season with a little salt and pepper.

- Bake uncovered for 55 minutes or until chicken is no longer pink. Serves 4 to 6.

• • • • •

Russian Chicken

1 (8 ounce) bottle Russian salad dressing	250 ml
1 (1 ounce) packet dry onion soup mix	30 g
1 (8 ounce) jar apricot preserves	225 g
6 boneless, skinless chicken breast halves	

- Preheat oven to 300° (150° C).

- Combine Russian dressing, soup mix and apricot preserves; mix well. Pour mixture over chicken in sprayed 9 x 13-inch (23 x 33 cm) baking dish. Cover and bake for 1½ hours. Uncover and bake additional 30 minutes. Serves 6.

• • • • •

Skillet Chicken and Peas

4 - 5 boneless, skinless chicken breast halves	
2 (10 ounce) cans cream of chicken soup	2 (280 g)
½ teaspoon paprika	2 ml
2 cups instant rice	190 g
1 (10 ounce) package frozen green peas	280 g

- Heat a little oil in very large skillet. Add chicken and cook until brown. Transfer chicken to plate and keep warm.

- To skillet, add soup, 1¾ cups (425 ml) water, paprika and ½ teaspoon (2 ml) pepper. Heat to boiling, stir in rice and peas and reduce heat. Top with chicken and cook on low heat for 15 minutes. Serves 4 to 5.

• • • • •

Chicken-Broccoli Skillet

4 - 5 boneless, skinless chicken breast halves	
2 (10 ounce) cans cream of chicken soup	2 (280 g)
2 cups instant white rice	190 g
1 (16 ounce) package frozen broccoli florets, thawed	455 g
Paprika	

- In very large skillet with a little oil, brown chicken breasts on both sides and simmer for 10 minutes. Remove chicken and keep warm. Add soup and 2 cups (500 ml) water to skillet. Bring to boil and stir in instant rice and broccoli.

- Top with chicken sprinkled with a little pepper and paprika. Cover and cook on low for 15 minutes or until liquid evaporates. Serves 4 to 5.

• • • • •

Basic seasonings to keep on hand include: salt, black peppercorns for grinding fresh, chili powder, ground cinnamon, ground cumin, garlic powder, dried onion flakes and dried oregano.

Spiced Chicken

1 tablespoon paprika	15 ml
1 teaspoon ground cumin	5 ml
½ teaspoon cayenne pepper	2 ml
½ teaspoon coriander	2 ml
½ teaspoon oregano	2 ml

4 - 5 boneless, skinless chicken breasts, halved lengthwise
Extra-virgin olive oil

- In small bowl combine paprika, cumin, cayenne pepper, coriander, oregano and 1 teaspoon (5 ml) salt.

- In large shallow baking dish, place chicken pieces and drizzle with a little olive oil to coat. Rub each piece with spice mix and let stand about 10 minutes.

- Heat large skillet over medium-high heat and brown chicken pieces. Reduce heat, cover and simmer about 10 minutes on each side. Serves 4 to 5.

• • • • •

Sweet 'n Spicy Chicken over Rice

1 pound boneless, skinless chicken breasts, cubed	455 g
1 (1 ounce) packet taco seasoning	30 g
1 (16 ounce) jar chunky salsa	455 g
1 (8 ounce) jar peach preserves	225 g

- Place cubed chicken in resealable plastic bag, add taco seasoning and toss to coat. In large skillet with a little oil, brown chicken and cook on medium-low for 5 minutes.

- In saucepan, combine salsa, preserves and ¼ cup (60 ml) water. Heat and stir until salsa and preserves mix well. Stir into skillet with chicken. Bring mixture to boil. Reduce heat, cover and simmer for 15 minutes. Serve over hot, cooked rice. Serves 4 to 6.

• • • • •

Sunday Chicken

4 boneless, skinless chicken breast halves	
1 (10 ounce) can cream of mushroom soup	280 g
1½ cups shredded cheddar cheese	170 g

- Place chicken in sprayed 9 x 13-inch (23 x 33 cm) pan and bake at 350° (175° C) for 30 minutes. Remove from oven and spread soup over chicken. Bake for 30 minutes. Remove from oven and sprinkle cheese over top. Cook additional 5 minutes. Serves 4.

Swiss Chicken

4 boneless, skinless chicken breast halves
4 slices Swiss cheese
1 (10 ounce) can cream of chicken soup   280 g
¼ cup chicken broth   60 ml
½ cup herb-seasoned stuffing   25 g
¼ cup (½ stick) butter, melted   55 g

- Preheat oven to 350° (175° C).

- Arrange chicken in sprayed 9 x 13-inch (23 x 33 cm) pan. Top with cheese slices. Combine soup and broth in saucepan and heat just enough to mix well.

- Spoon evenly over chicken and sprinkle with stuffing mix. Drizzle butter over stuffing. Bake uncovered for 45 to 55 minutes. Serves 4.

• • • • •

Taco Chicken over Spanish Rice

1¼ cups flour   150 g
2 (1 ounce) packets taco seasoning   2 (30 g)
2 large eggs, beaten
8 boneless, skinless chicken breast halves
2 (15 ounce) cans Spanish rice   2 (425 g)
1 cup shredded Mexican 4-cheese blend   115 g

- Preheat oven to 350° (175° C).

- Mix flour and taco seasoning in large shallow bowl. Mix eggs and 3 tablespoons (45 ml) water in another shallow bowl and beat together. Dip each chicken breast in egg mixture. Dredge in flour-taco seasoning mixture, pressing to apply lots of flour mixture.

- Place in sprayed 11 x 15-inch (28 x 38 cm) baking pan and arrange so that chicken pieces do not touch. Bake for 55 to 60 minutes or until juices run clear.

- About 10 minutes before chicken is done, place Spanish rice in saucepan and stir in cheese. Heat, stirring constantly, just until cheese melts. Spoon onto serving platter and place chicken pieces over hot rice. Serves 6 to 8.

• • • • •

Whole chicken and turkey are the best buys. *A whole bird generally has the best price and it only takes about 15 minutes to remove bones from meat for freezing.*

Tequila-Lime Chicken

½ cup lime juice	125 ml
¼ cup tequila	60 ml
1½ teaspoons chili powder	7 ml
1½ teaspoons minced garlic	7 ml
6 boneless, chicken breast halves with skins	

- In large plastic bag that seals, combine all ingredients except chicken and mix well. Add chicken breasts, seal bag and turn to coat. Refrigerate 10 hours or overnight.

- Remove breasts from marinade and sprinkle chicken with a little salt and pepper. Discard marinade. Grill, skin-side down, for 5 to 7 minutes. Turn and cook 10 minutes or until juices run clear. Remove to platter, cover and let stand for 5 minutes before serving. Serves 6.

• • • • •

Honey-Mustard Chicken Tenders

1 pound boneless, skinless chicken tenders	455 g
3½ tablespoons honey-mustard salad dressing	45 ml
1 (3 ounce) can french-fried onions, crushed	85 g

- Preheat oven to 375° (190° C).

- Coat chicken with dressing and roll in crushed onions. Place chicken in sprayed baking pan and bake for 25 minutes or until chicken is done. Serves 4.

• • • • •

Stir-Fry Chicken and Veggies

1¼ cups instant rice	145 g
¼ cup (½ stick) butter	55 g
1½ pounds chicken tenderloin strips	680 g
1 (16 ounce) package frozen stir-fry vegetables	455 g
½ cup stir-fry sauce	125ml

- Cook rice according to package directions and keep warm. In large non-stick skillet, melt butter and stir-fry chicken strips for about 5 minutes or until light brown.

- Stir in vegetables and cook for additional 8 minutes. Pour in stir-fry sauce and mix well. Cover and cook for 2 minutes or until hot. Serves 4 to 6.

• • • • •

Sweet-and-Sour Chicken

1 cup apricot preserves	320 g
1 (1 ounce) packet onion soup mix	30 g
1 (8 ounce) bottle Russian dressing	225 g
1 (2 pound) package frozen chicken tenderloin strips, thawed	910 g
Cooked rice	

- Preheat oven to 400° (205° C).

- Mix preserves, soup mix and dressing. In sprayed 9 x 13-inch (23 x 33 cm) baking pan, pour mixture over chicken and bake for 40 minutes to 1 hour or until juices from chicken run clear. Serve over rice. Serves 4 to 6.

• • • • •

Ranch Chicken

½ cup grated parmesan cheese	50 g
1½ cups crushed corn flakes	60 g
1 (1 ounce) packet ranch salad dressing mix	30 g
2 pounds chicken drumsticks	910 g
½ cup (1 stick) butter, melted	115 g

- Preheat oven to 350° (175° C).

- Combine cheese, corn flakes and dressing mix. Dip washed, dried chicken in butter and dredge in corn flake mixture. Place in sprayed 9 x 13-inch (23 x 33 cm) baking dish and bake uncovered for 50 minutes. Serves 6.

• • • • •

Baked Buttermilk Chicken

To save money, buy whole chickens and cut them up. It will be fun to guess what some of the "mystery" pieces are.

1 (2 – 3 pound) chicken, cut in serving pieces	910 g - 1.4 kg
½ cup buttermilk*	125 ml
1 cup Italian seasoned breadcrumbs	120 g

- Preheat oven to 350° (175° C).

- Dip chicken in buttermilk and roll in breadcrumbs. Place in sprayed non-stick baking pan and bake for 1 hour or until tender.

TIP: If you don't want to cut up the chicken, buy 2 pounds of pieces you want.

*TIP: To make buttermilk, mix 1 cup (250 ml) milk with 1 tablespoon (15 ml) lemon juice or vinegar and let milk stand for about 10 minutes.

Chipper Chicken

1 (2 - 3 pound) chicken, cut in serving pieces	1.4 kg
½ cup (1 stick) butter, melted	115 g
3 cups potato chips, crushed	170 g

- Preheat oven to 350° (175° C).

- Dip chicken in melted butter and roll in crushed potato chips.

- Bake in sprayed 9 x 13-inch (23 x 33 cm) pan for 1 hour or until tender. Serves 4 to 6.

Honey-Glazed Chicken

¾ cup flour	90 g
1 (2 – 3 pound) chicken, quartered	
¼ cup (½ stick) butter, divided	55 g
⅓ cup packed brown sugar	75 g
⅓ cup honey	115 g
1 tablespoon light soy sauce	15 ml

- Preheat oven to 350° (175° C).

- In shallow bowl, combine flour and 1 teaspoon (5 ml) each of salt and pepper. Cut wing tips off and dredge chicken quarters in flour mixture. Place 2 tablespoons (30 ml) butter in large, heavy skillet and brown chicken on both sides.

- Transfer to sprayed 9 x 13-inch (23 x 33 cm) baking dish. In same skillet, place remaining butter, brown sugar, honey and soy sauce and bring just to boiling; stir constantly. Pour mixture over chicken. Bake uncovered for 35 to 40 minutes and baste several times with pan drippings. Serves 4 to 6.

Honey-Mustard Chicken

⅓ cup dijon-style mustard	85 g
¾ cup honey	255 g
2 tablespoons dried dill weed	30 ml
1 (2½ pound) chicken, quartered	1.1 kg

- Preheat oven to 350° (175° C).

- Combine mustard, honey and dill. Arrange chicken quarters in sprayed 9 x 13-inch (23 x 33 cm) baking dish. Spoon mustard mixture over chicken.

- Turn chicken over and make sure mustard mixture covers all sides of chicken. Bake covered for 35 minutes. Uncover and bake for additional 10 minutes. Serves 4 to 6.

Irish Chicken

1 (2½ pound) chicken, cut into serving pieces	1.1 kg
1 egg, beaten	
1½ cups dry instant potato flakes	90 g
2 tablespoons butter	30 ml

- Preheat oven to 375° (190° C). Dip each chicken piece in egg and roll in potato flakes. Repeat with all chicken pieces.

- Melt butter in shallow baking pan, place chicken in pan and bake for 30 minutes. Turn chicken over and bake for additional 20 minutes. Serves 4 to 6.

• • • • •

Oven-Fried Chicken

1 (2 - 3 pound) chicken, cut in serving pieces	910 g - 1.4 kg
¼ cup (½ stick) butter, melted	55 g
1 cup dry seasoned breadcrumbs	120 g

- Preheat oven to 350° (175° C). Wash and dry chicken. Coat well each piece of chicken with melted butter and roll in breadcrumbs. Bake in sprayed 9 x 13-inch (23 x 33 cm) pan for 50 minutes to 1 hour. Serves 4 to 6.

• • • • •

Easy Roast Chicken

1 (2½ pound) whole chicken	1.1 kg
1 onion, peeled	
5 tablespoons butter, melted	70 g

- Preheat oven to 350° (175° C). Rinse chicken inside and out with cool water and dry with paper towels.

- Place peeled onion inside chicken cavity and brush butter over chicken. Tie legs together and place in foil-lined broiler pan. Roast chicken for 20 minutes per pound. Baste often with additional butter.

- Chicken is done when juices run clear. Serves 6.

TIP: *Other good foods to put in the cavity of chicken include lemon, lime, orange and apple.*

• • • • •

Zesty Orange Chicken

½ cup white cooking wine	125 ml
1 cup orange marmalade	320 g
1 (2 – 3 pound) chicken, quartered	
2 (11 ounce) cans mandarin oranges, drained	2 (310 g)
1½ cups instant brown rice	145 g

- Preheat oven to 325° (165° C). Combine wine and marmalade in sprayed 9 x 13-inch (23 x 33 cm) baking dish. Add chicken quarters and turn to coat chicken.

- Bake for 40 minutes uncovered and baste occasionally. Add oranges during last 5 minutes of cooking. Serve over hot, cooked, buttered rice. Serves 4 to 6.

Cheesy Chicken and Potatoes

1 (20 ounce) package frozen hash browns with bell peppers and onions, thawed	565 g
1 tablespoon minced garlic	15 ml
2 - 2½ cups bite-size chunks rotisserie chicken	280 - 350 g
1 bunch green onions, sliced	
1 cup shredded cheddar cheese	115 g

- Add a little oil to large skillet over medium-high heat and cook potatoes for 7 minutes, turning frequently. Add garlic, chicken, green onions and ⅓ cup (75 ml) water and cook for additional 5 to 6 minutes. Remove from heat and stir in cheese. Serve immediately right from skillet. Serves 4 to 6.

TIP: It's usually cheaper to buy fresh vegetables and cut them up yourself, but sometimes it's just so much easier that it's okay to rationalize buying the packaged vegetables. Hash browns with bell peppers and onions is a prime example.

Spaghetti Toss

1 (10 ounce) package thin spaghetti	280 g
1 (10 ounce) package frozen sugar snap peas	280 g
2 tablespoons butter	30 ml
3 cups cooked chicken	420 g
⅔ cup stir-fry sauce	150 ml

- Cook spaghetti according to package directions. Stir in sugar snap peas and cook for 1 additional minute. Drain and stir in butter until it melts. Spoon into bowl. Cut chicken into strips and add to spaghetti with stir-fry sauce. Serves 6.

• • • • •

Deluxe Dinner Nachos

Nachos:

1 (14 ounce) package tortilla chips, divided	395 g
1 (8 ounce) package shredded Velveeta® cheese, divided	225 g
1 (8 ounce) can chopped jalapenos, divided	225 g

Deluxe Optional Topping:

1 (11 ounce) can Mexicorn® with liquid	310 g
1 (15 ounce) can jalapeno pinto beans, drained	425 g
2 cups skinned, chopped rotisserie chicken	280 g
1 bunch fresh green onions, chopped	
Salsa	

- Preheat oven to 400° (205° C).

- Place about three-quarters tortilla chips in sprayed baking dish. Sprinkle half cheese and lots of jalapenos on top. Bake just until cheese melts.

- Combine corn, beans and chicken in saucepan. Heat over medium heat, stirring constantly, until mixture is hot. Spoon mixture over nachos, place dish in oven and bake for about 10 minutes. Sprinkle remaining cheese and green onions over top and serve immediately. Garnish with remaining jalapenos, remaining tortilla chips and salsa. Serves 4 to 6.

TIP: *As a main course, 2 cups chicken for 4 to 6 people is a pretty inexpensive way to go.*

• • • • •

Lemony Chicken and Noodles

1 (8 ounce) package fettuccine noodles	225 g
1 (10 ounce) package frozen sugar snap peas, thawed	280 g
1 (14 ounce) can chicken broth	395g
1 teaspoon fresh grated lemon peel	5 ml
2 cups cooked, cubed, skinless chicken	280 g
½ cup whipping cream	125 ml

- In large saucepan with boiling water, cook noodles according to package directions. Add snap peas to noodles 1 minute before noodles are done. Drain and return to saucepan.

- Add broth, lemon peel, cubed chicken and ½ teaspoon (2 ml) each of salt and pepper. Heat, stirring constantly, until thoroughly hot. Over low heat, gently stir in cream. Serve hot. Serves 4 to 6.

Savory Chicken and Mushrooms

1 (16 ounce) package frozen chopped bell peppers and onions   455 g
1 (8 ounce) package fresh mushrooms, sliced   225 g
1 (10 ounce) can cream of mushroom soup   280 g
1 cup milk   250 ml
1 cooked chicken, skinned, boned, chopped
3 cups cooked instant rice

- In large skillet with a little oil, cook bell peppers and onions and mushrooms about 5 minutes or until onions are translucent; stir frequently.

- Stir in mushroom soup and milk, mix well and add chicken pieces with a little salt and pepper. Bring to a boil, reduce heat and cook for about 10 minutes. Serve over rice. Serves 6 to 8.

TIP: *Watch for specials at the grocery store on rotisserie chickens. It's a fast way to get cooked chicken.*

• • • • •

Alfredo Chicken Spaghetti

1 (8 ounce) package thin spaghetti, broken in thirds   225 g
2 teaspoons minced garlic   10 ml
1 (16 ounce) jar alfredo sauce   455 g
¼ cup milk   60 ml
1 (10 ounce) package frozen broccoli florets, thawed, drained 280 g
2 cups cooked, diced chicken   280 g

- Cook spaghetti according to package directions and drain. Place back in saucepan and stir in garlic, alfredo sauce and milk and mix well.

- Add drained broccoli florets and cook on medium heat for about 5 minutes or until broccoli is tender; stir several times. Add more milk if mixture gets too dry. Stir in diced chicken. Serves 4 to 6.

• • • • •

Make once, eat twice. Many dishes, particularly casseroles, can be frozen and cooked later. Make two casseroles at the same time and put one in the oven and the other in the freezer for up to 3 months. Double the recipe for other meals such as Sloppy Joes, chili, soups and stews, meat loaf, etc. and freeze what's left for another meal.

Adobe Chicken

2 cups cooked brown rice	390 g
1 (10 ounce) can diced tomatoes and green chilies, drained	280 g
3 cups cooked, chopped chicken	420 g
2 (8 ounce) package shredded Monterey Jack cheese, divided	2 (225 g)

- Preheat oven to 325° (165° C).

- Combine rice, tomatoes and green chilies, chicken, and one package of cheese. Spoon into sprayed 7 x 11-inch (18 x 28 cm) baking dish. Bake covered for 30 minutes. Uncover, sprinkle remaining cheese over casserole and return to oven for 5 minutes. Serves 4 to 6.

• • • • •

Caesar-Salad Pizza

1 (12 inch) Italian pizza crust	32 cm
1 (8 ounce) package shredded mozzarella cheese	225 g
1 (6 ounce) package cooked chicken breast strips	170 g
2 cups shredded lettuce	110 g
¾ cup shredded parmesan cheese	75 g
½ (8 ounce) bottle Caesar dressing	½ (250 ml)

- Preheat oven to 400° (205° C).

- Top pizza crust with mozzarella cheese and bake for 8 minutes or until cheese melts.

- In bowl, combine chicken strips, lettuce and parmesan cheese. Pour about half of Caesar dressing over salad and toss. Top hot pizza with salad and cut into wedges. Serve immediately. Serves 4.

• • • • •

Chicken and Broccoli Casserole

1 (10 ounce) can cream of chicken soup	280 g
½ cup mayonnaise	110 g
1 teaspoon curry powder	5 ml
1 (16 ounce) package frozen broccoli florets	455 g
4 chicken breast halves, cooked, cubed	
1 cup crushed cornbread dressing	60 g

- Preheat oven to 350° (175° C).

- Combine soup, mayonnaise and curry powder. Season with a little salt and pepper. Layer broccoli, chicken and soup mixture in sprayed 1-quart (1 L) baking dish. Top with layer of dressing crumbs. Bake for 30 to 40 minutes. Serves 4 to 6.

Chicken and Noodles

4 boneless, skinless chicken breast halves, cubed	
1 (8 ounce) package egg noodles	225 g
2 (10 ounce) cans cream of mushroom soup	2 (280 g)

- In saucepan, cover chicken with water and boil until tender. Add more water if needed. Add egg noodles and cook until tender. Drain. Stir in soup and heat thoroughly. Serves 4 to 6.

• • • • •

Chicken-Cornbread Casserole

4 cups cornbread, crumbled	355 g
¼ cup chopped green bell pepper	35 g
⅓ cup chopped onion	55 g
2 cups cooked, chopped chicken	280 g
1 (10 ounce) can cream of chicken soup	280 g
1 (14 ounce) can chicken broth	395 g

- Preheat oven to 350° (175° C). Combine cornbread, bell pepper and onion. Mix well. Place half mixture in sprayed 2-quart (2 L) baking dish. Spread chicken over cornbread mixture.

- Combine soup and broth and pour over chicken. Place other half of cornbread mixture over chicken and press down. Bake for 45 minutes. Serves 4 to 6.

TIP: *The small box of Jiffy® cornbread mix is a great timesaver and inexpensive if you don't want to buy a large package of cornmeal.*

• • • • •

Chicken-Parmesan Spaghetti

1 (16 ounce) package frozen chicken cutlets, thawed	455 g
Seasoned breadcrumbs	
1 (28 ounce) jar spaghetti sauce	795 g
2 (5 ounce) packages grated parmesan cheese, divided	2 (145 g)
1 (8 ounce) package thin spaghetti, cooked	225 g

- Preheat oven to 400° (205° C). Boil cutlets in enough water to cover until all pink is gone. Drain and coat with seasoned breadcrumbs. In sprayed 9 x 13-inch (23 x 33 cm) baking dish, place chicken and top each with about ¼ cup (65 g) spaghetti sauce and heaping tablespoon (15 ml) parmesan. Bake for 15 minutes.

- Place cooked spaghetti on serving platter and top with cutlets. Sprinkle remaining cheese over cutlets. Heat remaining spaghetti sauce and serve with chicken and spaghetti. Serves 6 to 8.

Chicken Quesadillas

1 (7 ounce) package frozen, cooked chicken strips, thawed	200 g
1 (10 ounce) can fiesta nacho cheese soup	280 g
1 (16 ounce) jar chunky salsa, divided	455 g
8 - 10 (8 inch) flour tortillas	8 10 (20 cm)

- Preheat oven to 400° (205° C). Coarsely shred chicken strips. In bowl, combine soup and half the salsa and mix well.

- Lay tortillas out on flat surface and spoon about ¼ to ⅓ cup (60 ml to 75 ml) mixture on half of each tortilla to within ½-inch (1.2 cm) of edge. Sprinkle slivers of chicken over soup-salsa mixture.

- Fold tortillas over, moisten edges with a little water and press edges of tortillas to seal. Place on 2 sprayed baking sheets and bake for 5 to 6 minutes or until tortillas brown. Serves 4 to 6.

Chicken Spaghetti

3 boneless, skinless chicken breast halves, cooked	
1 (10 ounce) can diced tomatoes and green chilies	280 g
1 (10 ounce) can cream of mushroom soup	280 g
1 (8 ounce) package shredded cheddar cheese	225 g
1 (8 ounce) package shredded Velveeta® cheese	225 g
1 (12 ounce) package spaghetti	340 g

- Preheat oven to 350° (175° C). Shred cooked chicken into large bowl. Add tomatoes and green chilies, soup, and both cheeses. Boil spaghetti according to package directions. Drain. Add to chicken mixture and mix well. Pour into sprayed 3-quart (3 L) baking dish, cover and bake for 35 minutes.   Serves 4 to 5.

Chicken Tetrazzini

1 (12 ounce) package spaghetti, cooked	340 g
1 (10 ounce) can cream of mushroom soup	280 g
1 (10 ounce) can cream of chicken soup	280 g
1 cup milk	250 ml
4 cups cooked, shredded chicken	560 g
1 (16 ounce) package shredded sharp cheddar cheese	455 g
1 (4 ounce) can diced pimentos, drained well	115 g
1 (5 ounce) package grated parmesan cheese	145 g

- Preheat oven to 350° (175° C). Cook spaghetti according to package directions.   Add remaining ingredients except parmesan and mix well. Transfer to sprayed 9 x 13-inch (23 x 33 cm) baking dish. Top with parmesan cheese. Bake uncovered for 20 to 30 minutes. Serves 6 to 8.

Creamy Chicken Bake

1 (8 ounce) package egg noodles	225 g
1 (16 ounce) package frozen broccoli florets, thawed	455 g
¼ cup (½ stick) butter, melted	55 g
1 (8 ounce) package shredded cheddar cheese	225 g
1 (10 ounce) can cream of chicken soup	280 g
1 cup half-and-half cream	250 ml
3 cups cooked, cubed chicken breasts	420 g

- Preheat oven to 325° (165° C).

- Cook noodles according to package directions and drain. Combine noodles and broccoli in large bowl. Add butter and cheese and stir until cheese melts. Stir in chicken soup, half-and-half cream, chicken and a little salt and pepper.

- Spoon into sprayed 2½-quart (2.5 L) baking dish. Bake covered for about 40 minutes. Serves 6 to 8.

• • • • •

Elegant Chicken and Rice

3 cups cooked, shredded chicken	420 g
1 (6 ounce) package long grain-wild rice mix, cooked	170 g
1 (10 ounce) can cream of celery soup	280 g
1 (4 ounce) jar chopped pimentos, drained	115 g
1 cup mayonnaise	225 g
1 (15 ounce) can French-style green beans, drained	425 g
1 (3 ounce) can french-fried onions	85 g

- Preheat oven to 350° (175° C).

- Combine all ingredients except fried onions. Pour into sprayed 3-quart (3 L) baking dish. Bake for 20 minutes. Top with fried onions and bake additional 5 to 10 minutes. Serves 4 to 6.

• • • • •

Roasted Chicken with Red Peppers

1 (14 ounce) can chicken broth	395 g
1 (8 ounce) can whole kernel corn, drained	225 g
2 cups cooked, cubed chicken	280 g
1 cup roasted chopped red bell peppers	260 g

- In saucepan over medium-high heat, combine broth, corn, chicken and roasted bell peppers. Cover and simmer for about 3 minutes. Serves 4 to 6.

• • • • •

Hurry-Up Enchiladas

2 cups cooked, cubed chicken breasts	280 g
1 (10 ounce) can cream of chicken soup	280 g
1 (16 ounce) jar chunky salsa, divided	455 g
8 (6 inch) flour tortillas	8 (15 cm)
1 (10 ounce) can fiesta nacho cheese soup	280 g

- In saucepan, heat and stir chicken, chicken soup and half salsa. Spoon about ½ cup (125 ml) chicken mixture down center of each tortilla. Use all of chicken mixture.

- Roll tortillas around filling and place seam-side down in sprayed 9 x 13-inch (23 x 33 cm) glass baking dish. In saucepan, combine fiesta nacho cheese soup, remaining salsa and ½ cup (125 ml) water and pour over enchiladas.

- Cover with wax paper and microwave, turning twice, on HIGH for 5 minutes or until filling bubbles. Serves 6 to 8.

• • • • •

Sweet-and-Sour Chicken and Veggies

1 (3 ounce) package chicken-flavored ramen noodles	85 g
1 (16 ounce) package frozen broccoli, cauliflower and carrots	455 g
3 boneless, skinless chicken breast halves, cooked, cut in strips	
⅔ cup sweet-and-sour sauce	150 ml
1 tablespoon soy sauce	15 ml

- In large saucepan, cook noodles and vegetables in 2 cups (500 ml) water (set aside noodle seasoning packet) for 10 minutes or until liquid absorbs. Add seasoning packet, chicken, sweet-and-sour sauce, soy sauce, and a little salt and pepper. Heat on low-medium heat and stir until hot. Serves 4 to 6.

• • • • •

Save money by cutting up 2 or 3 whole chickens at one time. Prepare the parts you want to fry, grill, broil, etc. and stew the other parts for casseroles, soups, stews and other dishes. The stewing liquid becomes a great broth for soups.

Cheddar Cheese
Chicken Casserole

1 (8 ounce) package small egg noodles	225 g
3 tablespoons butter	45 ml
1 (10 ounce) package chopped frozen chopped bell peppers and onions	280 g
1 (10 ounce) can cream of chicken soup	280 g
1 (4 ounce) can sliced mushrooms, drained	115 g
1 (8 ounce) carton sour cream	225 g
4 cups cooked, diced chicken	560 g
1 (12 ounce) package shredded cheddar cheese	340 g

- Preheat oven to 325° (165° C).

- Cook noodles according to package directions and drain. Melt butter in skillet and saute bell peppers and onions.

- In large bowl, combine noodles, sauteed mixture, remaining ingredients and ½ teaspoon (2 ml) pepper. Pour into sprayed 9 x 13-inch (23 x 33 cm) baking dish.

- Cover and bake for 35 to 40 minutes or until bubbly around edges of casserole. Serves 6.

• • • • •

Chicken Pockets

1 (3 ounce) package chive and onion cream cheese, softened	85 g
1½ cups cooked, cubed chicken	210 g
¼ cup (½ stick) butter, softened	115 g
1 (8 ounce) can refrigerated crescent rolls	225 g
Parmesan cheese	

- Preheat oven to 350° (175° C).

- Blend cream cheese, chicken, butter and ¼ teaspoon (1 ml) salt with mixer. Separate crescent roll dough into 4 rectangles and press seams together.

- Spoon mixture into center of each rectangle. Pull 4 corners up and twist together. Seal sides by pinching together. Sprinkle top with parmesan cheese. Bake on unsprayed baking sheet for 20 to 25 minutes. Serves 4.

TIP: Options for cooked chicken are canned chicken, leftover chicken or boil chicken as needed.

• • • • •

Chicken Pot Pie

1 (15 ounce) package frozen double piecrust	425 g
1 (15 ounce) can mixed vegetables, drained	425 g
1 (10 ounce) can cream of celery soup	280 g
1 (10 ounce) can cream of chicken soup	280 g
1½ cups cooked, chopped chicken	210 g

- Preheat oven to 375° (190° C). Place 1 crust in pie pan. Mix remaining ingredients with a little pepper. Pour into crust and top with remaining crust. Prick vent holes in crust to allow steam to escape. Bake for 45 minutes or until golden brown. Serves 4.

TIP: Options for cooked chicken are canned chicken, leftover chicken or boil chicken as needed.

• • • • •

Creamy Chicken-Pasta

1 (10 ounce) package penne pasta	280 g
1 tablespoon olive oil	15 ml
3 cups cooked chopped chicken	2 (340 g)
½ cup prepared pesto	30 ml
¾ cup whipping cream	175 ml

- In large saucepan, cook penne pasta according to package directions. Drain and place back in saucepan. Gently stir in oil, chicken, pesto, whipping cream, and a little salt and pepper.

- Place saucepan over medium-low heat and simmer, but do not let mixture boil; cream must absorb into pasta. Spoon into serving bowl and serve immediately. Serves 6 to 8.

TIP: Options for cooked chicken are canned chicken, leftover chicken or you can boil a piece of chicken as needed.

• • • • •

 Leftover chicken and turkey have many uses. *Freeze leftovers in usable portions for pot pies, slices for sandwiches, chopped for soups and stews, cubed for casseroles and chopped in salads. Make fast microwave meals by freezing meats and vegetables in the same container.*

Southwest Pizza

1 (12 inch) pre-baked pizza crust	32 cm
¾ cup guacamole	175 g
1½ cups cooked chicken, chopped	210 g
½ cup roasted red peppers, drained, sliced	130 g
1 (4 ounce) can sliced ripe olives, drained	115 g
1 (8 ounce) package shredded Mexican 4-cheese blend	225 g

- Preheat oven to 350° (175° C).

- Place pizza crust on sprayed cookie sheet and spread guacamole over crust. Top with chicken, red peppers and olives and spread evenly. Top with cheese. Bake for 15 minutes or just until cheese bubbles and is light brown. Cut pizza into wedges to serve. Serves 4.

TIP: Options for cooked chicken are canned chicken, leftover chicken or boil chicken as needed.

• • • • •

Smoked Turkey Puffs

1 pound smoked turkey, chopped	455 g
1½ cups finely shredded cheddar cheese	170 g
12 eggs	
2 cups milk	500 ml
Dash Worcestershire sauce	
Freshly ground pepper	

- Preheat oven to 350° (175° C).

- Divide turkey equally in 6 sprayed individual bowls or egg cups, 4 inches (10 cm) in diameter. Divide cheese among each bowl. Place eggs, milk, Worcestershire sauce and ½ teaspoon (2 ml) each of salt and pepper in blender. Blend until frothy.

- Pour egg mixture (about 1 cup/250 ml per bowl) over cheese. Bowls will be quite full. Bake for 30 to 35 minutes or until brown and puffed. Serves 4 to 6.

• • • • •

If planning to freeze a casserole, do not season it before freezing. Freezing may cause the seasoning to deteriorate. Wait until the casserole is thawed and ready to bake or reheat before seasoning it.

Turkey Casserole

1 (6 ounce) package herb-seasoned stuffing mix	170 g
1 cup canned whole cranberry sauce	280 g
6 (¼ inch thick) slices turkey	6 (6 mm)
1 (15 ounce) jar turkey gravy	425 g

- Preheat oven to 375° (190°C).

- Prepare stuffing according to package directions. In medium bowl, combine stuffing and cranberry sauce.

- Place turkey slices in sprayed 9 x 13-inch (23 x 33 cm) baking dish and pour gravy on top. Spoon stuffing mixture over casserole. Bake for about 15 minutes or until hot and bubbly. Serves 4 to 6.

• • • • •

Turkey for Supper

4 (¼ inch thick) smoked turkey breast slices	4 (6 mm)
1 (8 ounce) package cream cheese, softened	225 g
¼ cup mayonnaise	55 g
1½ cups hot chunky salsa	395 g

- Place turkey slices on serving platter. In mixing bowl beat cream cheese and mayonnaise with mixer or blender. Fold in salsa. Place one-fourth cream cheese mixture on each slice turkey. Serve cold. Serves 4.

• • • • •

Choose meals that stretch your meat dollar. *Use pasta, rice, potatoes, canned beans or whole grains as a base or try international flavors that use less meat such as stir-fry Asian dishes, Indian vegetarian or other ethnic cuisines.*

Chilly Night's Turkey Bake

1 (6 ounce) package chicken stuffing mix	170 g
1½ pounds turkey, cut into 1 inch (2.5 cm) strips	680 g
1 (10 ounce) can cream of chicken soup	280 g
½ cup sour cream	120 g
1 (16 ounce) bag frozen mixed vegetables, thawed, drained	455 g

- Preheat oven to 375° (190° C).

- Sprinkle ½ cup (25 g) dry stuffing mix evenly in sprayed 9 x 13-inch (23 x 33 cm) baking dish. In bowl, combine remaining stuffing and 1 cup (250 ml) water and stir just until moist.

- Place turkey strips over dry stuffing mix in baking dish. In bowl, mix soup, sour cream and vegetables, spoon over turkey strips and top with prepared stuffing. Bake uncovered for 25 minutes. Serves 6 to 8.

TIP: *Consider cooking turkey more than just once or twice a year. It's a great value for a healthy meat and there are lots of ways to use leftover turkey.*

• • • • •

A turkey of 16 to 20 pounds is a better buy than a small turkey because the ratio of meat to bone is greater. A turkey weighing 12 pounds or less yields about 1 serving per pound; a turkey weighing more than 12 pounds yields approximately 1 serving per ¾ pound. If you do not want to cook a big turkey, ask the butcher to cut it in half; freeze one-half to cook later.

Purse-Strings Beef

Beef adds great flexibility to your menu choices. It is easily "stretched" and less expensive cuts are made tender and delicious with the right cooking methods.

Asian Beef-Noodles

1¼ pounds lean ground beef	565 g
1 (16 ounce) package frozen oriental stir-fry mixture	455 g
2 (3 ounce) packages oriental-flavored ramen noodles	2 (85 g)
½ teaspoon ground ginger	2 ml
3 tablespoons thinly sliced green onions	45 ml

- In large skillet, brown ground beef and drain. Add ½ cup (125 ml) water, and a little salt and pepper, simmer for 10 minutes and transfer to separate bowl. In same skillet, combine 2 cups (500 ml) water, vegetables, broken up noodles, both seasoning packets and ginger. Bring to a boil and reduce heat.

- Cover and simmer for 3 minutes or until noodles are tender; stir occasionally. Return beef to skillet and stir in green onions. Serve right from skillet. Serves 6 to 8.

• • • • •

Baked Hamburger

1½ pounds lean ground beef	680 g
1 (6 ounce) package seasoned croutons	168 g
2 (10 ounce) cans cream of celery soup	2 (280 g)
1 soup can milk	

- Preheat oven to 350° (175° C).

- Pat ground beef into sprayed 9 x 13-inch (23 x 33 cm) baking dish. Mix croutons, soup and milk. Pour over meat and bake for 1 hour. Serves 6 to 8.

• • • • •

 Don't be too shy to ask for price matching at your grocery store. Check the papers and take the ad with you when shopping. Just ask the clerk for price matching and they will already know the price or they'll look it up. This not only saves you money, but will save a trip to another store.

Barbecups

1 pound lean ground beef	455 g
½ cup barbecue sauce	130 g
1 (10 count) can refrigerated biscuits	
½ cup shredded cheddar cheese	55 g

- Preheat oven to 400° (205° C).

- Brown ground beef and drain. Stir in barbecue sauce. Separate dough into 10 biscuits. Place biscuits into 10 sprayed muffin cups. Firmly press in bottom and on sides.

- Spoon ¼ cup (60 ml) meat mixture into each biscuit. Sprinkle with cheese. Bake for 10 to 12 minutes. Cool 1 minute and remove from pan. Serves 6.

• • • • •

Beef Patties in Creamy Onion Sauce

1½ pounds lean ground beef	680 g
½ cup chunky salsa	130 g
1⅓ cups buttery cracker crumbs	80 g
2 (10 ounce) cans cream of onion soup	2 (280 g)
Biscuits	

- In large bowl, combine beef, salsa and cracker crumbs and form into 6 to 8 patties. In sprayed skillet over medium heat, brown patties. Reduce heat and add ¼ cup (60 ml) water. Cover and simmer for 15 minutes.

- In saucepan, combine soup, 1 teaspoon (5 ml) pepper and ½ cup (125 ml) water or milk. Heat and mix well. Pour onion sauce over beef patties and simmer for additional 10 minutes. Serve over hot biscuits. Serves 4 to 6.

• • • • •

The large packages of ground round or ground chuck meat are usually the best buys for hamburgers. The pre-made hamburger patties are a lot more expensive than making your own.

Delicious Meat Loaf

1½ pounds lean ground beef	680 g
⅔ cup dry Italian-seasoned breadcrumbs	80 g
1 (10 ounce) can golden mushroom soup, divided	280 g
2 eggs, beaten	
2 tablespoons butter	30 ml

- Preheat oven to 350° (175° C).

- Combine beef, breadcrumbs, half mushroom soup and eggs in bowl and mix thoroughly. Shape firmly into 8 x 4-inch (20 x 10 cm) loaf pan and bake for 45 minutes.

- Mix butter, remaining soup and ¼ cup (60 ml) water in small saucepan, heat thoroughly and serve sauce over meatloaf. Serves 6 to 8.

• • • • •

Beef-Spinach Bake

2 (10 ounce) packages frozen spinach, thawed, drained	2 (280 g)
1 pound lean ground beef	455 g
1 large onion, chopped	
1 (8 ounce) carton fresh mushrooms, sliced	225 g
1 (8 ounce) carton sour cream	225 g
1½ teaspoons Italian seasoning	7 ml
1 cup shredded cheddar cheese, divided	115 g

- Preheat oven to 350° (175° C).

- Squeeze spinach between paper towels to completely remove excess moisture. Sprinkle 1 teaspoon (5 ml) salt over ground beef and cook in skillet. Add onion and mushrooms. Cook for about 5 minutes.

- Remove from heat and stir in spinach, sour cream, ½ teaspoon (2 ml) salt, Italian seasoning and half cheese. Pour into sprayed shallow 2-quart (2 L) baking dish. Sprinkle remaining cheese over top. Bake uncovered for 20 minutes. Serves 4 to 6.

A shaped meat loaf adds flair to the meal and it is so easy. Just place the meat loaf mixture in a ring mold, invert the mold onto a baking pan and bake. The hollow in the center can be filled with vegetables, mashed potatoes, rice or whatever your family likes. If you don't have a ring mold, put a custard cup or ramekin or other similarly shaped object in the center of the baking pan and just mold the meat loaf around it, remove the custard cup and bake.

Bueno Taco Casserole

2 pounds lean ground beef	910 g
1½ cups taco sauce	375 g
2 (15 ounce) cans Spanish rice	2 (425 g)
1 (8 ounce) package shredded Mexican 4-cheese blend, divided	225 g

- Preheat oven to 350° (175° C).

- In skillet, brown ground beef and drain. Add taco sauce, Spanish rice and half cheese. Spoon into sprayed 3-quart (3 L) baking dish.

- Cover and bake for 35 minutes. Sprinkle remaining cheese on top and bake uncovered for additional 5 minutes. Serves 6 to 8.

• • • • •

Creamy Mushroom Beef over Rice

1 pound ground beef	455 g
1 (10 ounce) can golden cream of mushroom soup	280 g
2 cups cooked rice	315 g

- Brown beef in skillet, crumble and drain. Stir in soup, diluted with ½ can water or milk. Stir and simmer for 20 minutes and serve over hot rice. Serves 4.

• • • • •

Easy Casserole Supper

1 pound lean ground beef	455 g
¼ cup rice	45 g
1 (10 ounce) can French onion soup	280 g
1 (3 ounce) can french-fried onions	85 g

- Preheat oven to 325° (165° C).

- Brown ground beef, drain and place in sprayed 7 x 11-inch (18 x 28 cm) baking dish. Mix rice, onion soup and ½ cup (125 ml) water and pour into baking dish. Cover and bake for 40 minutes. Sprinkle fried onions over top and bake uncovered for additional 10 minutes. Serves 4.

• • • • •

 Large casseroles should be thawed completely in the refrigerator before cooking. Smaller casseroles can be cooked frozen.

Easy Enchiladas

10 corn tortillas	
1 pound lean ground beef	455 g
1 large onion, chopped	
1 (12 ounce) package shredded cheddar cheese, divided	340 g
1 (10 ounce) can cream of onion soup	280 g
1 cup milk	250 ml

- Preheat oven to 300° (150° C).

- Wrap tortillas in paper towels and heat in microwave. Brown beef and onion in skillet. Season with 1 teaspoon (5 ml) pepper.

- Sprinkle each tortilla with 2 tablespoons (30 ml) cheese and top with 1½ tablespoons (22 ml) meat mixture. Roll tightly and place in sprayed 9 x 13-inch (23 x 33 cm) baking dish.

- Heat soup with milk. Pour over enchiladas. Sprinkle with remaining cheese. Bake for 20 to 30 minutes or until hot and bubbly. Serves 6 to 8.

• • • • •

Easy Mexican Casserole

1 pound lean ground beef	455 g
1 (10 ounce) can enchilada sauce	280 g
1 (10 ounce) can cream of chicken soup	280 g
1 (10 ounce) can cream of mushroom soup	280 g
1 (13 ounce) package corn chips. divided	370 g
1½ cups shredded cheddar cheese	170 g

- Preheat oven to 350° (175° C).

- Brown meat and drain. Add enchilada sauce and soups. Place three-fourths bag of chips in sprayed 9 x 13-inch (23 x 33 cm) baking dish. Pour meat mixture over chips. Top with cheese and remaining chips. Bake for 20 minutes. Serves 6.

• • • • •

 Don't have conventional buns for burgers? *Shape ground beef to fit the bread you have. Make square patties for sliced bread, oval for French or Italian loaves, log shapes for hot dog buns or other long rolls.*

Grilled Cheeseburgers on Rye

1 pound lean ground beef	455 g
4 slices cheddar cheese	
1 (4 ounce) can diced green chilies	115 g
8 slices rye bread	
¼ cup (½ stick) butter	55 g

- Make 4 beef patties and cook as desired. Place slice of cheese on each and top with 1 spoonful of green chilies. Place each patty between two slices of bread. Spread both sides of sandwich with butter and grill butter-side down in hot iron skillet and brown both sides. Serves 4.

• • • • •

Hamburger Stroganoff

1 pound ground beef	455 g
2 (10 ounce) cans cream of mushroom soup	2 (280 g)
½ cup milk	125 ml
1 (16 ounce) package noodles	455 g
¼ cup (½ stick) butter	55 g

- Brown beef and drain well. Stir soup and milk into crumbled beef and mix well. Cook for 10 minutes or until mixture heats well. Stir often.

- Cook noodles according to package directions and drain. Stir in butter and serve beef mixture over noodles. Serves 4.

• • • • •

Hamburger-Potato Casserole

2 pounds ground beef	910 g
1 (10 ounce) can cream of mushroom soup	280 g
1 (1 pound) package tater tots	455 g

- Preheat oven to 350° (175° C).

- Press meat into sprayed 9 x 13-inch (23 x 33 cm) pan to make bottom layer. Spread soup over meat. Tater tots form top layer. Bake casserole for 45 to 55 minutes. Serves 6 to 8.

TIP: Potatoes could be second layer and then top with soup.

• • • • •

Hi-Ho Meat, Potatoes and Gravy

1¼ pounds lean ground beef	565 g
⅓ cup seasoned breadcrumbs	40 g
1 egg, beaten	
⅓ cup finely minced onion	55 g
1 (22 ounce) carton refrigerated mashed potatoes, heated	625 g

- In large bowl, combine all ingredients except potatoes and shape into 6 patties. Cook patties over medium heat in sprayed large skillet for 3 to 4 minutes on each side. Transfer patties to glass dish to serve. Keep warm. Serves 6.

Gravy:

3 tablespoons flour	20 g
1½ cups milk	375 ml

- In same skillet with drippings from patties, add flour and ½ teaspoon (2 ml) each of salt and pepper. Stir to mix well. Turn heat to high and slowly pour milk into skillet while stirring constantly until gravy thickens.

- To serve, pour gravy over patties and mashed potatoes. Serves 6.

• • • • •

Hobo Dinner

1 pound ground beef	455 g
4 onion slices	
4 potatoes	
1 teaspoon seasoned salt	5 ml

- Preheat oven to 350° (175° C).

- Shape ground beef into patties and slice potatoes ½-inch (1.2 cm) thick. Place each patty on square of foil and top with 2 or 3 potato slices. Place slice of onion over top and season to taste. Fold each foil package tightly, place in pan and bake for 45 minutes. Serves 4.

• • • • •

 Check out www.grocerysavingtips.com for free coupons and lots of money-saving tips.

Homemade Chorizo Sausage

1 pound ground beef	455 g
1 onion, chopped	
1 (1 ounce) packet chili seasoning mix	30 g

- Combine all ingredients and mix well. Cover and refrigerate overnight to blend flavors. Use in recipes requiring spicy meat, soups, casseroles and Mexican dishes such as burritos and tacos. Serves 4.

• • • • •

Irish-Italian Spaghetti

1 pound lean ground beef	455 g
1 (10 ounce) can cream of mushroom soup	280 g
1 (10 ounce) can tomato soup	280 g
1 (8 ounce) package spaghetti	225 g
1 cup shredded mozzarella cheese	115 g

- Brown meat and season with 1 teaspoon (5 ml) each of salt and pepper. Stir in soups. Cover and simmer for 30 minutes. Cook spaghetti according to package directions. Drain and add to sauce. Mix well. Top with cheese. Serves 4 to 6.

• • • • •

Kids' Favorite Casserole

1 pound ground beef	455 g
2 tablespoons chopped onion	30 ml
1 (15 ounce) can baked beans	425 g

- Brown ground beef and onion together and drain well. Stir in baked beans and cook until mixture heats thoroughly. Serves 4 to 6.

• • • • •

Bagged veggies and salads are a great convenience, but the savings are substantial if you slice and dice them yourself. Individual packets of oatmeal can cost five times as much as a regular canister. Single servings and pre-sliced cheese are also much more expensive.

Meal-in-One

1 pound lean ground beef	455 g
1 (15 ounce) can French-style green beans, drained	425 g
1 (18 ounce) package frozen tater tots, thawed	510 g
1 (10 ounce) can cream of mushroom soup	280 g

- Preheat oven to 350° (175° C).

- Brown ground beef and season with a little salt and pepper. In sprayed 10-inch (25 cm) deep-dish pie pan, layer ground beef, green beans and tater tots. Spread soup over ingredients. Bake for 1 hour. Serves 4 to 6.

• • • • •

Mexican Casserole

1 (13 ounce) bag corn chips, divided	370 g
2 pounds lean ground beef	910 g
1 (15 ounce) can Mexican stewed tomatoes	425 g
1 (8 ounce) package shredded Mexican 4-cheese blend	225 g

- Preheat oven to 350° (175° C).

- Partially crush half bag chips and place in sprayed 9 x 13-inch (23 x 33 cm) baking dish. Brown ground beef and drain. Add stewed tomatoes and cheese and mix well. Pour into baking dish and sprinkle finely crushed remaining chips over top. Bake uncovered for 40 minutes. Serves 6 to 8.

• • • • •

Mexican Meat Loaf

1½ pounds lean ground beef	680 g
1 (10 ounce) can diced tomatoes and green chilies	280 g
1½ cups soft breadcrumbs	90 g
1 egg	
3 tablespoons onion flakes	45 ml
¾ cup shredded cheddar cheese	85 g

- Preheat oven to 375° (190° C).

- Mix together ground beef, tomatoes and green chilies, breadcrumbs, egg, onion flakes, and 1¼ teaspoons (6 ml) salt. Shape into loaf and place in sprayed shallow pan. Bake for 1 hour. Sprinkle cheese on top. Bake until cheese melts. Serves 4 to 6.

• • • • •

Onion Burgers

2 pounds ground beef	**910 g**
1 (1 ounce) packet onion soup mix	**30 g**
Hamburger buns	

- Preheat oven to 350° (175° C).

- Combine beef with soup mix and ½ cup (125 ml) water and mix well. Shape mixture into 8 burgers and place in baking dish. Bake uncovered for 15 minutes or until brown. Serve on hamburger buns. Serves 8.

• • • • •

Onion-Beef Bake

3 pounds lean ground beef	**1.4 kg**
1 (1 ounce) packet dry onion soup mix	**30 g**
2 (10 ounce) cans French onion soup	**2 (280 g)**

- Preheat oven to 350° (175° C).

- Combine beef, soup mix and ½ cup (125 ml) water. Mix well and shape into patties about ½-inch (1.2 cm) thick. Cook in large skillet and brown on both sides.

- Transfer patties to sprayed 9 x 13-inch (23 x 33 cm) baking dish. Pour soup over patties. Cover and bake for about 35 minutes. Serves 6 to 8.

• • • • •

Oriental Burgers

1 ½ pounds ground beef	**680 g**
½ cup chopped water chestnuts	**70 g**
½ cup teriyaki sauce	**125 ml**

- Combine meat and water chestnuts and shape mixture into 6 burgers. Place in glass baking dish and pour teriyaki sauce over burgers. Marinate covered in refrigerator for several hours or overnight. Discard marinade.

- When ready to cook, fry in skillet until brown on both sides. Serve as main dish or sandwich. Serves 6.

• • • • •

Pinto Bean Pie

1 pound lean ground beef	455 g
1 onion, chopped	
2 (15 ounce) cans pinto beans with liquid, divided	2 (425 g)
1 (10 ounce) can diced tomatoes and green chilies	
with liquid, divided	280 g
1 (3 ounce) can french-fried onions	85 g

- Preheat oven to 350° (175° C).

- In skillet, brown beef and onion and drain. In sprayed 2-quart (2 L) baking dish, layer 1 can beans, half beef-onion mixture and half can tomatoes and green chilies. Repeat layers. Top with fried onions and bake uncovered for 30 minutes. Serves 4 to 6.

• • • • •

Porcupine Meatballs

1 cup instant rice	95 g
1 egg, beaten	
1 pound lean ground beef	455 g
2 teaspoons grated onion	10 ml
2½ cups tomato juice	625 ml
½ teaspoon sugar	2 ml

- Mix rice, egg, beef and onion with a little salt and pepper. Shape into meatballs and brown in skillet. Add tomato juice and sugar and bring to a boil. Cover and simmer for 15 to 20 minutes. Serves 4 to 6.

• • • • •

Potato-Beef Bake

1 pound lean ground beef	455 g
1 (10 ounce) can sloppy Joe sauce	280 g
1 (10 ounce) can fiesta nacho cheese soup	280 g
1 (32 ounce) package frozen hash-brown potatoes, thawed	1 kg

- Preheat oven to 400° (205° C).

- In skillet, cook beef over medium heat until no longer pink and drain. Add sloppy Joe sauce and soup. Place hash browns in sprayed 9 x 13-inch (23 x 33 cm) baking dish. Top with beef mixture. Cover and bake for 25 minutes. Uncover and bake for additional 10 minutes. Serves 4 to 6.

• • • • •

Potato-Beef Casserole

4 medium potatoes, peeled, sliced	
1¼ pounds lean ground beef, browned, drained	565 g
1 (10 ounce) can cream of mushroom soup	280 g
1 (10 ounce) can vegetable-beef soup	280 g

- Preheat oven to 350° (175° C).

- In large bowl, combine all ingredients plus ½ teaspoon (2 ml) each of salt and pepper. Transfer to sprayed 3-quart (3 L) baking dish. Bake covered for 1 hour 30 minutes or until potatoes are tender. Serves 4 to 6.

• • • • •

Shepherd's Pie

1 pound lean ground beef	455 g
1 (1 ounce) packet taco seasoning mix	30 g
1 cup shredded cheddar cheese	115 g
1 (11 ounce) can Mexicorn®, drained	310 g
2 cups prepared instant mashed potatoes	420 g

- Preheat oven to 350° (175° C).

- In skillet, brown beef and cook for 10 minutes. Drain. Add taco seasoning and ¾ cup (175 ml) water and cook additional 5 minutes.

- Spoon beef mixture into sprayed 8-inch (20 cm) square baking pan. Sprinkle cheese on top. Spread corn over beef and cheese. Spread mashed potatoes over top. Bake for 25 minutes or until top is golden brown. Serves 4 to 6.

• • • • •

Check your receipts. *The prices are programmed by humans and humans make mistakes. Bring it to the store's attention so you pay the right price. Your receipt is also a great way to start a spreadsheet or notebook on price comparisons for the products you purchase often.*

Salisbury Steak and Gravy

1½ pounds extra-lean ground beef	680 g
1 egg, beaten	
½ cup chili sauce	135 g
¾ cup seasoned breadcrumbs	90 g
Vegetable oil	

- In medium bowl, combine all ingredients except oil and mix well. Shape into 6 to 8 patties ¾-inch (1.8 cm) thick. In large skillet with a little oil, brown patties for about 5 minutes on each side. Set aside in warm oven.

Brown Gravy:

2 (14 ounce) cans beef broth	2 (395 g)
2 tablespoons cornstarch	30 ml
1 (8 ounce) can sliced mushrooms	225 g

- Add beef broth and cornstarch mixed with ¼ cup (60 ml) water to skillet and stir until cornstarch mixture dissolves. Cook and stir over high heat until mixture thickens. Add mushrooms and cook until hot and gravy bubbles. Spoon gravy over patties to serve. Serves 4 to 6.

• • • • •

Simple Family Filet Mignon

1½ pounds very lean ground beef	680 g
1 (1 ounce) packet dry onion soup mix	30 g
1 teaspoon minced garlic	2 ml
6 slices bacon	

- Preheat broiler.

- In bowl, combine beef, onion soup mix and garlic and mix well. Form into 6 thick patties that are flat on top. Wrap slice of bacon around outside of each patty and secure with toothpick. Place in shallow baking pan and broil for about 10 minutes on each side. Serves 4 to 6.

• • • • •

Pasta, whether macaroni, noodles, spaghetti or any of the fun shapes, is a great way to make leftovers into a fresh and economic meal. Bits of meat or tuna also can stretch a meal.

Skillet Beef and Pasta

1 (8 ounce) package spiral pasta (rotini)	225 g
1 (14 ounce) can beef broth	395 g
1 pound lean ground beef	455 g
2 (11 ounce) cans Mexicorn®, drained	2 (310 g)
1 (16 ounce) package cubed Mexican Velveeta® cheese	455 g

- Cook pasta according to directions, but use 4½ cups (1.1 L) water and beef broth instead of 6 cups (1.4 L) water. While pasta cooks, brown beef in large skillet and drain. Stir in corn and cheese and cook on low heat until cheese melts.

- Drain pasta thoroughly. Gently stir cooked pasta into beef mixture until pasta coats well. Spoon mixture into serving bowl. Serves 4 to 6.

• • • • •

Sour Cream Tacos

1 pound lean ground beef	455 g
1 large onion, diced	
2 teaspoons minced garlic	10 ml
1 (10 ounce) can tomato soup	280 g
1 (8 ounce) package shredded Velveeta® cheese	225 g
1 (1 pint) carton sour cream	480 g
Corn or tortilla chips	

- Preheat oven to 350° (175° C).

- Brown beef, onion and garlic in skillet. Add soup, cheese and sour cream, heat and stir constantly until cheese melts.

- Line sprayed 7 x 11-inch (18 x 28 cm) baking dish with chips and pour mixture on top. Bake for 20 minutes. Serves 4 to 6.

• • • • •

Buy ground beef on sale. Season, shape into individual servings, repackage and freeze. Make hamburger patties, small or large meat loaves, meat balls, etc. Separate servings with wax paper or plastic wrap and place in a sealed plastic bag.

Southwest Grilled Burgers

1½ pounds lean ground beef	680 g
¾ cup hot chipotle salsa, divided	200 g
¼ cup seasoned breadcrumbs	30 g
6 hamburger buns	
6 slices pepper-Jack cheese	

- Heat grill.

- In large bowl, combine ground beef, ¼ cup (60 ml) salsa and seasoned breadcrumbs and mix well. Shape mixture into 6 (½-inch/1.2 cm thick) patties and grill patties for about 14 minutes or broil in oven for about 12 minutes. Turn once during cooking.

- Place buns cut-side down on grill and cook about 2 minutes or until buns toast lightly. Place 1 slice cheese on each cooked patty and cook just long enough for cheese to begin to melt. Move patties and cheese to bottom halves of buns, add 1 tablespoon (15 ml) salsa to each and top with top halves of buns. Serves 4 to 6.

• • • • •

 # Southwest Spaghetti

1½ pounds lean ground beef	680 g
1 tablespoon chili powder	15 ml
1 (15 ounce) can tomato sauce	425 g
1 (10 ounce) package spaghetti, broken up, cooked	280 g
1 tablespoon beef bouillon granules	15 ml
Shredded cheddar-Jack cheese	

- Brown beef until no longer pink. Drain and place in slow cooker. Add chili powder, tomato sauce, spaghetti, 2⅓ cups (560 ml) water and beef bouillon granules. Mix well. Cover and cook on LOW for 6 to 7 hours. When ready to serve, cover generously with cheese. Serves 4 to 6.

• • • • •

 Many recipes add cracker crumbs, oats or breadcrumbs to meat loaf mixtures. This adds volume to the meat loaf, stretching the servings. Some of these recipes date to the Great Depression when it was necessary to make every penny count when putting a meal together.

Spanish Hamburgers

1 pound lean ground beef	455 g
1 large onion, chopped	
1 (10 ounce) can tomato soup	280 g
1 teaspoon chili powder	5 ml
4 hamburger buns	

- Brown ground beef and onion. Drain. Add soup and chili powder to hamburger mixture. Stir and simmer until hot. Serve over hamburger buns. Serves 4.

• • • • •

Spanish Meat Loaf

1 pound ground beef	455 g
1 (15 ounce) can Spanish rice, drained	425 g
1 egg, beaten	

- Preheat oven to 350° (175° C).

- Combine all ingredients and mix well. Pour into sprayed loaf pan and bake for 1 hour. Drain off excess liquid. Serves 4.

• • • • •

Spaghetti Pizza

½ cup milk	125 ml
1 egg	
1 (16 ounce) package thin or angel hair pasta, cooked	455 g
1 (26 ounce) spaghetti sauce	735 g
1 pound ground beef, cooked, drained	455 g
1 (12 ounce) package shredded mozzarella cheese	340 g

- Preheat oven to 350° (175° C).

- Mix milk and egg and toss with spaghetti. Spread pasta in sprayed 9 x 13-inch (23 x 33 cm) baking pan. Top with spaghetti sauce. Crumble beef on top. Sprinkle with cheese. Bake for 30 minutes. Serves 4 to 6.

• • • • •

Make a double batch of meat loaf to have plenty for sandwiches and a delicious second meal.

Speedy Gonzales Special

1½ pounds lean ground beef	680 g
1 (1.5 ounce) packet taco seasoning mix	45 g
1 (12 count) package tostada shells	

- Preheat oven to 300° (150° C).

- In skillet, brown and crumble ground beef. Add 1 cup (250 ml) water and taco seasoning and heat to boiling. Reduce heat and simmer for about 12 minutes. While beef cooks, heat 6 to 8 tostada shells on baking sheet in oven.

Topping:

1 (10 ounce) package shredded lettuce	280 g
2 - 3 vine-ripened tomatoes, chopped, drained	
1 (8 ounce) package shredded cheddar cheese	225 g
1 (16 ounce) container chunky salsa	455 g

- In serving bowl, combine about 2 cups (155 g) shredded lettuce, chopped tomatoes and cheese and toss. When ready to serve, place about 2 heaping tablespoons (30 ml) beef on each shell and spread out. Top with heaping spoonfuls of lettuce-cheese mixture. Let each person add salsa. Serve immediately. Serves 4 to 6.

• • • • •

Speedy Spaghetti

1 (16 ounce) package spaghetti	455 g
1 pound ground beef	455 g
1 (26 ounce) jar chunky garden-style spaghetti sauce with tomatoes, garlic and onions	735 g
1 cup shredded cheese 115 g	

- Preheat oven to 350° (175° C).

- Cook spaghetti according to package directions and drain well. Brown meat, crumble and drain. Stir spaghetti sauce into meat and heat thoroughly.

- Pour drained spaghetti onto large platter and spread meat sauce over spaghetti or combine spaghetti and meat sauce and mix thoroughly. Top with shredded cheddar cheese and heat until cheese melts. Serves 4 to 6.

• • • • •

Spinach-Stuffed Shells

1 (12 ounce) package jumbo macaroni shells	340 g
2 (9 ounce) packages frozen creamed spinach	2 (255 g)
1 (15 ounce) carton ricotta cheese	425 g
1 (8 ounce) package shredded mozzarella cheese	225 g
½ pound ground beef	225 g
1 (26 ounce) jar spaghetti sauce	735 g

- Preheat oven to 350° (175° C).

- Prepare pasta according to package directions, and drain well. Prepare spinach and cool slightly. Add ricotta, mozzarella and 1 teaspoon (5 ml) salt to spinach. Stuff each shell with 1 tablespoon (15 ml) mixture

- In skillet, cook meat and add spaghetti sauce. Place shells in sprayed 9 x13-inch (23 x 33 cm) baking dish and pour sauce over all. Bake for 30 minutes. Serves 6 to 8.

• • • • •

Stuffed Green Peppers

4 green bell peppers	
1 pound ground beef or ground round, browned, drained	455 g
1 (15 ounce) can Spanish rice	425 g

- Preheat oven to 350° (175° C).

- Blanch or place bell peppers in boiling water and cook for several minutes. Remove and dip in cold water to stop cooking process. This brings out the flavor and color of the peppers. Cool.

- Cut off tops of peppers and remove seeds and membranes. Stuff peppers with cooked meat mixed with Spanish rice, placed in sprayed casserole dish and bake for 20 minutes. Serves 4.

TIP: *You may stuff peppers that have not been boiled or blanched. Place them in sprayed casserole dish with a little water and bake for 25 minutes.*

• • • • •

 Save energy when you use your oven by planning to bake several dishes at the same time. Many dishes can be reheated quickly in either the oven or a microwave.

Beef Tips and Noodles

1½ pounds stew meat, fat trimmed	680 g
2 (10 ounce) cans cream of onion soup	2 (280 g)
1 (8 ounce) package noodles	225 g

- Brown stew meat in sprayed skillet. When brown, add soup diluted with 1 cup (250 ml) water. Simmer for 3 hours and stir occasionally. Cook noodles according to package directions. Serve beef tips over noodles. Serves 6.

• • • • •

Taco Pie

1 pound lean ground beef	455 g
1 (11 ounce) can Mexicorn®, drained	310 g
1 (8 ounce) can tomato sauce	225 g
1 (1 ounce) packet taco seasoning	30 g
1 (9 inch) frozen piecrust	23 cm
1 cup shredded cheddar cheese	115 g

- Preheat oven to 350° (175° C).

- In large skillet, brown and cook ground beef until no longer pink. Stir in corn, tomato sauce and taco seasoning. Keep warm. Place piecrust in pie pan and bake for 5 minutes.

- Spoon ground beef mixture into piecrust and spread evenly. Sprinkle cheese over top and bake for additional 20 minutes or until filling is bubbly. Let stand for 5 minutes before slicing to serve. Serves 6.

• • • • •

Brisket and Sauce

1 (4 - 6 pound) brisket	1.8 - 2.7 kg
1 (8 ounce) bottle chili sauce	225 g
1 (12 ounce) can cola soda, not diet	355 ml
1 (1 ounce) packet dry onion soup mix	30 g

- Preheat oven to 325° (165° C).

- Place brisket in roasting pan with lid. Combine chili sauce, soda and onion soup mix and mix well. Pour over brisket, cover and bake for 3 to 5 hours or for 30 minutes per pound until tender. Pour sauce into gravy boat and serve with brisket. Serves 6 to 8.

• • • • •

Good Night Beef Brisket

1 (3 - 4 pound) brisket, trimmed	1.4 - 1.8 kg
1 tablespoon Worcestershire sauce	15 ml
1 teaspoon seasoned salt	5 ml

- Place brisket, lean-side up, in baking pan about same size as brisket. Sprinkle Worcestershire sauce generously over meat. Smooth on meat with back of spoon.

- Sprinkle seasoned salt over brisket. Turn brisket over, fat-side up, and repeat seasoning process. Cover tightly and refrigerate overnight.

- Remove from refrigerator 30 minutes before cooking.

- Preheat oven to 300° (150° C).

- Bake uncovered for 4 hours or until fork tender. Baste only with liquid that forms in bottom of pan. Do not add water. Slice across grain. Serves 6 to 8.

• • • • •

Oven Brisket

1 (5 - 6 pound) trimmed brisket	2.3 - 2.7 kg
1 (1 ounce) packet onion soup mix	30 g
1 (12 ounce) can cola	355 ml
1 (10 ounce) bottle steak sauce	280 g

- Preheat oven to 325° (165° C).

- Place brisket, fat-side up, in roasting pan. Combine onion soup mix, cola and steak sauce and pour over brisket. Cover and bake for 4 to 5 hours or until tender.

- Remove brisket from pan, pour off drippings and refrigerate drippings and brisket separately overnight.

- The next day, trim all fat from meat, slice and reheat. Skim off top layer of fat from drippings; reheat and serve sauce over brisket. Serves 6 to 8.

• • • • •

 To tenderize meats cooked in liquid, add about 1 teaspoon vinegar to the water to tenderize without affecting the flavor of the cooking liquid or the meat.

Overnight Brisket

2 tablespoons liquid smoke	30 ml
1 (3 - 4 pound) brisket	1.4 - 1.8 kg
Garlic powder	

- Rub liquid smoke on sides of brisket and sprinkle with garlic powder. Wrap tightly in foil and refrigerate overnight.

- When ready to bake, preheat oven to 275° (135° C).

- Sprinkle with more garlic powder and rewrap in foil. Bake in large baking dish for 6 hours or bake at 325° (165° C) for 5 hours. Serve immediately or refrigerate overnight again and slice the next day. Serves 6 to 8.

TIP: When you serve this as leftovers, pour barbecue sauce over the slices and reheat.

• • • • •

Party Brisket

1 (5 pound) beef brisket	2.3 kg
1 (6 ounce) can frozen lemon juice concentrate, thawed	175 ml
1 (1 ounce) packet dry onion soup mix	30 g

- Preheat oven to 250° (120° C).

- Trim all visible fat from meat. Stir enough thawed lemon juice concentrate into soup mix to make smooth paste.

- Place brisket in 9 x 13-inch (23 x 33 cm) pan or in roasting pan. Spread lemon-onion paste over meat and cover tightly with foil or lid. Bake for 5 to 6 hours or until fork-tender. Serves 6 to 8.

• • • • •

Western Brisket

1 (6 pound) boneless beef brisket	2.7 kg
2 tablespoons Worcestershire sauce	30 ml
¼ cup liquid smoke	60 ml

- Preheat oven to 275° (135° C).

- Place brisket in pan and pour Worcestershire sauce and liquid smoke over brisket. Cover and bake for 5 to 7 hours or until tender. Serves 6 to 8.

• • • • •

Barbecued Beef Brisket

1 (4 pound) brisket	1.8 kg
1 (3.5 ounce) bottle liquid smoke	100 g
1 (6 - 8 ounce) bottle barbecue sauce	170 - 225 g

- Place brisket in baking pan. Pour liquid smoke over meat and rub into brisket. Cover and refrigerate overnight.

- When ready to bake, preheat oven to 275° (135° C).

- Bake covered for 5 hours. Remove from oven, slice and pour barbecue sauce over brisket. Serves 6 to 8.

TIP: Bottom round roast is one of the least expensive cuts of beef. The best way to cook it is slowly in liquid. It's great for chicken-fried steak, shredded beef, Swiss steak, pot roast and beef sandwiches.

• • • • •

Corned Beef Brisket

1 (3 - 4 pound) corned beef brisket	1.4 - 1.8 kg
2 tablespoons mustard	30 ml
¼ cup packed brown sugar	55 g

- Cook corned beef over low heat in pot with enough water to almost cover for 2 hours 30 minutes.

- Preheat oven to 350° (175° C).

- Remove beef from pot, place in 9 x 13-inch (23 x 33 cm) roasting pan and poke holes in meat with fork.

- Mix mustard and brown sugar until creamy and paste forms. Spread mixture over entire brisket and bake for 1 hour 30 minutes or until tender. Serves 4 to 6.

• • • • •

One of the best ways to save money on meats is to serve smaller portions. Smaller portions are healthier and will cost less. Load up on vegetables and fruits.

Corned Beef Supper

1 (4 - 5 pound) trimmed corned beef brisket   1.8 - 2.3 kg
4 large potatoes, peeled, quartered
6 carrots, peeled, halved
1 head cabbage

- Place corned beef in roasting pan, cover with water and bring
  to boil. Reduce heat, cook on low for 3 hours and add water if
  necessary.

- Add potatoes and carrots. Cut cabbage into eighths and lay over
  potatoes, carrots and brisket. Bring to boil, reduce heat and cook
  for additional 30 to 40 minutes or until vegetables are done. Slice
  corned beef across grain. Serves 6 to 8.

• • • • •

New England Corned Beef

1 (4 pound) corned beef brisket   1.8 kg
20 whole cloves
½ cup maple syrup   125 ml

- Place beef in large roasting pan, cover with water and bring to a boil.
  Reduce heat, cover and cook on low heat for 3 hours 30 minutes
  to 4 hours until done. Remove from water and place on rack in
  roasting pan.

- Preheat oven to 375° (190° C).

- Score top and stud with cloves. Pour maple syrup over meat and bake
  for 20 minutes or until brown. Baste during cooking. Serves 4 to 6.

• • • • •

Know the less expensive cuts of meat. *Cuts of meat, like
tri-tip roast, chuck roast, flat-iron steak, fajita or skirt steak,
round steak, and brisket can be just as delicious as pricier
ones. The secret is to cook them long and slow with plenty
of liquid so they don't dry out.*

Lemon-Herb Pot Roast

1 teaspoon minced garlic	5 ml
2 teaspoons lemon pepper	10 ml
1 teaspoon dried basil	5 ml
1 (3 - 3½ pound) boneless beef chuck roast	1.4 - 1.6 kg
1 tablespoon oil	15 ml
3 potatoes	

- Preheat oven to 325° (165° C).

- Combine garlic, lemon pepper and basil and press evenly into surface of beef. In large, heavy pan, heat oil over medium-high heat until hot and brown roast.

- Add 1 cup (250 ml) water. Cover and bake for 3 hours. Quarter potatoes and add to roast. Cover and cook for additional 45 minutes. Serves 6 to 8.

• • • • •

 # Slow Cooker Roast Beef

4 potatoes, peeled and quartered	
2 onions, sliced	
1 (3 - 4 pound) chuck roast	1.4 - 1.8 kg
½ teaspoon garlic powder	2 ml
½ teaspoon seasoned salt	2 ml

- Place half potatoes and onions in slow cooker. Place roast on top of vegetables and add remaining potatoes and onions over top.

- Pour ½ cup (125 ml) water over meat and vegetables and cover. Cook on LOW for 10 to 12 hours or on HIGH for 5 to 6 hours. Serves 4 to 6.

• • • • •

 The slow cooker is exceptionally useful for creating really tender and tasty meat dishes. You can also cook budget cuts of meat slowly on top of the stove or in the oven, but these methods require constant attention.

Coffee Beef Roast

1 (3 - 5 pound) chuck roast	1.4 -2.3 kg
1 cup vinegar	250 ml
2 cups brewed strong black coffee	500 ml

- Place roast in glass dish or pan. Pour vinegar over meat. Cover and refrigerate for 24 hours or longer and drain.

- Place roast in a large skillet and brown on all sides. Pour coffee over meat. Add 2 cups (500 ml) water and cover. Simmer for 4 to 6 hours (depending on the size of roast). Add more water if needed. Serves 4 to 6.

• • • • •

Caraway Seed Roast

1 (3 pound) chuck roast	1.4 kg
1 tablespoon caraway seed	15 ml
1 teaspoon garlic powder	5 ml
1 tablespoon seasoned pepper	15 ml

- Preheat oven to 325 (165° C).

- Trim all visible fat from roast. Sprinkle caraway seeds, garlic powder and seasoned pepper over roast. Place on rack in roasting pan and cover or wrap in foil. Bake for 3 hours or until tender. Serves 6.

TIP: *Beef is muscle. Muscles that get the most use are the toughest: round steak, flank steak, skirt steak, flat-iron steak and brisket. Beef that gets the least use and has marbling is the most tender: tenderloin, porterhouse, T-bone, strip, filet mignon and rib eye.*

• • • • •

Pay attention to loss leaders in grocery stores. They are the products with big ads and special sales that get you into the stores. The grocery stores make very little on these products, but are counting on you shopping for other products while you're there.

Baked Pot Roast and Peppers

1 (3 - 4 pound) beef pot roast	1.4 - 1.8 kg
1 (10 ounce) can beef broth	280 g
1 green bell pepper, seeded, julienned	
1 red bell pepper, seeded, julienned	

- Preheat oven to 325° (165° C).

- Brown roast on all sides in sprayed skillet. Place in roasting pan and pour broth and 1 cup (250 ml) water evenly over beef. Cover tightly and bake for 1 hour.

- Reduce heat to 275° (135° C) and bake for additional 4 hours or until done. Add bell peppers 20 minutes before roast is done. Serves 6.

• • • • •

Pot Roast

3 pound chuck roast or london broil	1.4 kg
2 (10 ounce) cans cream of mushroom soup	2 (280 g)
2 (10 ounce) cans French onion soup	2 (280 g)
Lemon pepper	

- Preheat oven to 325° (165° C).

- Place roast in roasting pan. Pour soups over roast and sprinkle roast with lemon pepper. Cover and bake for 4 to 5 hours. Serves 6 to 8.

TIP: The soups make a great gravy.

• • • • •

Yankee Pot Roast

1 (4 - 5 pound) beef chuck roast	1.8 - 2.3 kg
2 (10 ounce) cans French onion soup	2 (280 g)
6 potatoes, peeled, quartered	

- Preheat oven to 325° (165° C). Brown meat on all sides in iron skillet or large heavy pan. Add soup, cover and bake for 3 to 4 hours or until roast is fork-tender.

- Add potatoes after meat cooks for 2 hours and continue cooking until done. Serves 4 to 6.

• • • • •

London Broil Supreme

⅓ cup chopped onion	55 g
⅓ cup chopped celery	35 g
½ teaspoon garlic powder	2 ml
1 (3 pound) chuck roast	1.4 kg
1 (14 ounce) can beef broth	395 g

- Preheat oven to 350° (175° C).

- Combine onion and celery and place in sprayed roasting pan.
  Combine garlic powder with 1 teaspoon (5 ml) pepper and rub over
  roast. Place fat-side up over vegetables.

- Bake uncovered for 2 hours 30 minutes to 3 hours. Let stand for
  15 minutes before carving. Add beef broth, stir to remove brown bits
  in pan and heat. Strain and discard vegetables. Serve liquid with
  roast. Serves 6 to 8.

• • • • •

Mushroom-Onion Round Steak

3 - 4 pounds round steak	1.4 - 1.8 kg
1 (10 ounce) can cream of mushroom soup	280 g
½ (1 ounce) packet dry onion soup mix	½ (30 g)

- Preheat oven to 325° (165° C).

- Brown or sear meat on all sides. Place steak on 2 to 3 sheets foil,
  spread soup over meat and sprinkle with soup mix. Wrap steak
  tightly, place in pan and bake for 3 to 4 hours or until done.
  Serves 6 to 8.

• • • • •

Electric Skillet Roast Beef

3 tablespoons oil	45 ml
2 pounds round steak	910 g
1 large onion, chopped	

- Heat oil in electric skillet to 350° (175° C). Place roast in skillet and
  brown each side. Sprinkle with black pepper and top with onion.

- Reduce heat to 250° (120° C) and add enough water to fill skillet
  halfway up. Cover and cook for 3 hours or until fork tender.
  Serves 2 to 4.

• • • • •

Husband's Favorite Flank Steak

2 pounds flank steak	910 g
¼ cup soy sauce	60 ml
¼ cup Worcestershire sauce	60 ml

- Score flank steak with sharp knife and place in glass baking dish. Combine soy sauce and Worcestershire sauce and pour over steak. Marinate steak in refrigerator for 2 to 4 hours. Turn steak several times.

- Remove steak from marinade (discard marinade) and broil or grill to desired doneness. Turn with tongs and broil other side. Set aside for 10 minutes before slicing. Serves 2 to 4.

• • • • •

Marinated Grilled Steak

1 lemon	
½ cup soy sauce	125 ml
3 tablespoons oil	45 ml
2 tablespoons Worcestershire sauce	30 ml
1 clove garlic, minced	
Chopped green onion	
2 pounds flank steak	910 g

- Squeeze juice from lemon. Mix all ingredients except steak to make marinade. Pour over steak. Refrigerate for 4 to 12 hours and turn occasionally. Discard marinade.

- Grill meat over hot coals as desired or broil. Serves 6 to 8.

• • • • •

South Seas Flank Steak

1 flank steak	
¼ cup soy sauce	60 ml
¼ cup pineapple juice	60 ml

- Pour soy sauce and pineapple juice in shallow 9 x 13-inch (23 x 33 cm) dish. Lay flank steak in mixture and turn to coat both sides. Marinate for 1 hour and turn every 15 minutes. Remove steak from marinade and broil or grill. Discard marinade. Serves 2 to 4.

• • • • •

Beef and Broccoli

1 pound round steak	455 g
1 onion, chopped	
1 (10 ounce) can cream of broccoli soup	280 g
1 (10 ounce) package frozen chopped broccoli, thawed	280 g
1 (12 ounce) package medium noodles, cooked	340 g

- Slice beef across grain into very thin strips. In large skillet brown steak strips and onion in a little oil and stir several times. Reduce heat and simmer for 10 minutes. Stir in soup and broccoli and heat. When ready to serve, spoon beef mixture over noodles. Serves 6.

• • • • •

Simple Beef Stroganoff

1 pound round steak, cut into thin strips	455 g
½ cup sliced onion	55 g
2 tablespoons butter	30 ml
1 (10 ounce) can cream of mushroom soup	280 g
½ cup sour cream	120 g
Cooked noodles	

- Brown meat in skillet and drain. Cook onion in butter until tender. Add soup, sour cream and ½ cup (125 ml) water. Bring to boil; reduce heat and simmer for 45 minutes or until tender. Serve over noodles. Serves 4 to 6.

• • • • •

 # Slow Cooker Steak Delight

1½ pounds tenderized round steak, trimmed	680 g
1 (1 ounce) package brown gravy mix	30 g
1 (10 ounce) can diced tomatoes and green chilies	280 g
1 (1 ounce) packet onion soup mix	30 g
1½ tablespoons Cajun seasoning	22 ml

- Cut steak into serving pieces. Cook gravy mix with 1 cup (250 ml) water according to package directions. Combine tomatoes and green chilies, soup mix and Cajun seasoning in blender. Put all ingredients in slow cooker and cook on HIGH for 4 hours. Serves 4 to 6.

TIP: The butcher will tenderize any cut of beef you want.

• • • • •

Smothered Steak

1½ pounds (¾-inch thick) beef round steak	680 g/1.8 cm
⅓ cup flour	40 g
3 tablespoons oil	45 ml
3 medium onions, sliced	
1 (10 ounce) can beef broth	280 g
1 tablespoon lemon juice	15 ml
1 teaspoon garlic powder	5 ml

- Cut meat into serving-size pieces. Sprinkle flour on both sides of steak and hit several times with meat tenderizer (mallet). In large skillet, brown steak in oil and top with onion slices.

- In medium bowl, combine remaining ingredients. Pour over steak, bring to boil and reduce heat to simmer. Cover and cook slowly for 1 hour. Check steak while cooking and add a little water if needed. Serves 4 to 6.

• • • • •

Southwestern Steak

1 pound tenderized round steak	455 g
Flour	
Vegetable oil	
2 teaspoons beef bouillon granules	10 ml
1 (15 ounce) can Mexican stewed tomatoes	425 g
¾ cup salsa	200 g

- Preheat oven to 325° (165° C).

- Cut beef into serving-size pieces and dredge in flour. In skillet, brown steak in a little oil. Stir bouillon granules into ½ cup (125 ml) boiling water and add tomatoes and salsa. Pour over steak, cover and bake for 1 hour. Serves 4.

• • • • •

 Use a meat tenderizer device (meat hammer) on thinner cuts of meat to tenderizer them. Thin cuts of round steak can be tenderized at home or by the butcher.

Pepper Steak

1¼ pounds round steak, cut into strips	565 g
Vegetable oil	
1 (14 ounce) can beef broth	395 g
1 (16 ounce) package frozen chopped bell peppers	
and onions, thawed	455 g
2 tablespoons cornstarch	30 ml

- Sprinkle pepper over steak. In large skillet with a little oil, brown steak strips. Pour beef broth over steak and add bell peppers and onions, ¾ cup water (175 ml), and 1 teaspoon (5 ml) salt. Bring to a boil, reduce heat and simmer for 15 minutes.

- In small bowl, combine cornstarch and ¼ cup water (60 ml) and pour into skillet. Stir and cook over medium heat until mixture thickens. Serves 4.

• • • • •

Round Steak in
Rich Mushroom Sauce

1 pound boneless beef round steak, cut in strips	455 g
2 tablespoons vegetable oil	30 ml
1 (14 ounce) can beef broth	395 g
2 teaspoons minced garlic	10 ml
1 (10 ounce) can cream of mushroom soup	280 g
1 (8 ounce) can sliced mushrooms	225 g
1 (8 ounce) package angel hair pasta, cooked, drained	225 g

- Brown steak strips in large non-stick skillet with oil over medium-high heat. Add beef broth, garlic, generous amount of pepper and ½ soup can of water. Heat to boiling, reduce heat and simmer for 15 minutes.

- Combine mushroom soup, mushrooms and 1 cup (250 ml) water in saucepan and heat just enough to mix well. Pour over steak and simmer for additional 15 minutes. Serve over angel hair pasta. Serves 4 to 6.

TIP: *You could use sirloin steak instead of round.*

TIP: *Less expensive cuts of beef are less tender than expensive cuts, but many times have more flavor. The key is to cook tougher beef slowly and make sure it doesn't dry out.*

• • • • •

Creamed Dried Beef

2 (2.25 ounces) packages thinly sliced dried beef, chopped   2 (65 g)
3 tablespoons flour   45 ml
2½ cups hot milk   625 ml
Toasted bread

- Fry thin dried beef slices in sprayed skillet until crisp. Stir in flour with beef, slowly add milk and cook until mixture is thick. Stir constantly. (The beef is so salty that no salt is needed.) Serve hot over toasted bread. Serves 4.

• • • • •

Pantry Chili Pie

2 (20 ounce) cans chili without beans   2 (565 g)
1 (13 ounce) package original corn chips, divided   370 g
1 onion, diced, divided
1 (12 ounce) package shredded cheddar cheese, divided   340 g

- Preheat oven to 350° (175° C).

- In saucepan, heat and stir chili over low heat. In sprayed 9 x13-inch (23 x 33 cm) glass baking dish, layer half corn chips, half chili, half onions and half cheese. Repeat layers except cheese.

- Cover and bake for 20 minutes, top with remaining cheese and bake just until cheese melts. Serve from baking dish. Serves 6.

• • • • •

Hot Tamale Pie

1 (24 ounce) package corn chips   680 g
2 (15 ounce) cans chili without beans   2 (425 g)
1 (16 ounce) can tamales   455 g
12 - 15 slices Velveeta® cheese

- Preheat oven to 350° (175° C).

- Arrange corn chips in lightly sprayed 9 x 13-inch (23 x 33 cm) baking dish. Heat chili and spread over chips. Slice tamales and arrange over chili. Top with cheese slices. Bake for 20 to 30 minutes. Serves 4 to 6.

• • • • •

Chili and Tamales

1 (15 ounce) can tamales	425 g
1 (15 ounce) can chili without beans	425 g
1 cup shredded cheddar cheese	115 g

- Remove wrappers from tamales and heat in microwave for 2 minutes. Heat chili in saucepan, stirring often. Pour hot chili over tamales and top with cheese. Serves 4.

TIP: Serve with tortilla chips.

• • • • •

Liver and Onions

Bacon drippings or vegetable oil	
1 pound calves liver	455 g
Flour	
1 (10 ounce) can French onion soup	280 g
½ soup can water	

- Heat bacon drippings or oil in large skillet over medium-high heat. Season liver with a little salt and pepper and dredge in flour. Brown both sides in skillet.

- Pour soup and water over liver and stir to loosen crumbs in bottom and sides of skillet. Cover and reduce heat. Cook for about 15 to 20 minutes or until gravy thickens. Serves 4.

• • • • •

If frozen meat or poultry becomes "freezer burned", soak for 1 or 2 hours in a water-baking soda solution. Use 2 tablespoons soda to 1 quart water.

Penny-Pinching Pork

Pork chops, hams, pork roast and the fantastic variety of sausage are all delicious and easy to coordinate with veggies, salads and more.

Creamy Mushroom Pork Chops

4 - 6 pork chops
1 (10 ounce) can cream of mushroom soup   280 g
1 soup can milk

- Fry pork chops in large skillet until almost done. Drain. Put back
  into pan and add soup and milk. Cover and simmer for about
  30 minutes or until done. Serves 4 to 6.

• • • • •

Crunchy Pork Chops

1 cup crushed saltine crackers   60 g
¼ cup biscuit mix   30 g
1 egg, beaten
4 boneless pork chops
Oil

- In shallow bowl, combine crushed crackers, biscuit mix and
  ¾ teaspoon (4 ml) salt. In second shallow bowl, combine beaten egg
  and 2 tablespoons (30 ml) water. Dip pork chops into egg mixture
  and dredge in cracker mixture. Heat a little oil in heavy skillet; cook
  pork chops for about 15 minutes and turn once. Serves 4.

• • • • •

Delicious Pork Chops

¾ cup biscuit mix   90 g
1 teaspoon paprika   5 ml
¾ cup Italian salad dressing   175 ml
1 cup Italian breadcrumbs   120 g
3 tablespoons vegetable oil   45 ml
4 pork chops

- Mix biscuit mix and paprika in shallow bowl. Pour dressing in
  second bowl and breadcrumbs in third bowl. Dip pork chops in
  biscuit mixture, in salad dressing and then breadcrumbs.

- In skillet, heat oil and cook pork chops for 5 to 8 minutes or until
  both sides brown lightly. Reduce heat to low, cover and cook for
  about 15 minutes longer. Drain on paper towels. Serves 4.

• • • • •

Dijon Pork Chops

4 - 6 pork chops
½ cup packed brown sugar   110 g
2 teaspoons dijon-style mustard   10 ml

- Preheat oven to 350° (175° C).

- Arrange pork chops in sprayed 7 x 11-inch (18 x 28 cm) baking dish.
  Combine sugar and mustard in small dish and mix well. Spread
  mixture on top of chops and bake covered for 45 minutes. Uncover
  and bake for additional 10 minutes or until brown. Serves 4 to 6.

• • • • •

Lemon-Pepper Pork Chops

4 butterfly pork chops
¾ teaspoon garlic salt   4 ml
¾ teaspoon lemon pepper   4 ml
Vegetable oil
½ cup chopped pecans   55 g
3 tablespoons lemon juice   45 ml
1 (9 ounce) package microwave-ready rice, cooked   255 g

- Sprinkle both sides of pork chops with garlic salt and lemon pepper.
  In large skillet, heat a little oil over medium-high heat. Add chops
  and cook for about 5 minutes on each side until chops brown lightly.
  Reduce heat, add several tablespoons (15 ml) water, cover and
  simmer for 10 minutes.

- Transfer pork chops to serving plate and keep warm. Top with
  pecans. Stir lemon juice into pan drippings, heat and stir constantly
  until they blend. Spoon drippings on pork chops and serve over rice.
  Serves 4.

• • • • •

*Get serious about coupons; coupons can even double
your savings when an item is on sale. Buy a Sunday paper;
it is the largest single source of grocery coupons. Go online
and check the store's Web site and manufacturer's Web sites
for any special offers.*

Mexicali Pork Chops

1 (1 ounce) packet taco seasoning	30 g
4 pork chops	
1 tablespoon oil	15 ml
½ cup salsa	130 g

- Rub taco seasoning over pork chops. In skillet, brown pork chops in oil over medium heat. Add 2 tablespoons (30 ml) water, turn heat to low, cover and simmer for about 40 minutes. Spoon desired amount of salsa over pork chops. Serves 4.

• • • • •

Onion Pork Chops

6 pork chops	
1 (10 ounce) can French onion soup	280 g
1 tablespoon mustard	15 ml
Cooked rice	

- Preheat oven to 350° (175° C).

- Arrange pork chops in sprayed baking dish. In bowl, combine onion soup and mustard and mix well. Pour over pork chops, cover and bake for 30 minutes.

- Uncover and bake for additional 15 to 20 minutes or until pork chops are brown. Serve over rice. Serves 6.

• • • • •

Orange-Dijon Chops

1 cup orange marmalade	320 g
3 tablespoons dijon-style mustard	45 ml
3 tablespoons soy sauce	45 ml
4 – 6 pork chops	

- In small saucepan over low heat, stir marmalade, dijon-style mustard and soy sauce until preserves melt. When ready to grill, sprinkle both sides of pork chops with salt and pepper.

- Place chops on grill about 5 inches (13 cm) from heat. Cook until pork is no longer pink in center. Turn once during cooking and brush with preserves mixture last 2 minutes of cooking time.

- When ready to serve, heat remaining preserves mixture to boiling and serve hot with pork chops. Serves 4 to 6.

• • • • •

Onion-Smothered Pork Chops

6 (½-inch thick) pork chops	6 (1.2 cm)
1 tablespoon oil	15 ml
½ cup (1 stick) butter, divided	115 g
1 onion, chopped	
1 (10 ounce) can cream of onion soup	280 g
3 cups instant brown rice	564 g

- Preheat oven to 325° (165° C).

- In skillet, brown pork chops in oil and simmer for about 10 minutes. Remove pork chops and set aside.

- In same skillet, add half butter and saute chopped onion. (Pan juices are brown from pork chops so onions will be brown from juices already in skillet.) Add soup and ½ cup (125 ml) water and stir well. Sauce will have a pretty, light brown color.

- Cook rice according to package directions and add remaining butter to rice. Place in sprayed 9 x 13-inch (23 x 33 cm) baking pan and place pork chops over rice. Pour onion-soup mixture over pork chops. Cover and bake for 40 minutes. Serves 6.

• • • • •

Orange-Honey Pork Chops

2 tablespoons vegetable oil	30 ml
6 pork chops	
1½ cups orange juice	375 ml
½ cup honey	115 g
2 teaspoons mustard	10 ml
2 cups instant brown rice	375 g

- In large skillet over medium-high heat, heat oil and brown pork chops on both sides.

- In bowl, combine orange juice, honey and mustard and pour over pork chops.

- Heat liquid and pork chops to boiling, reduce heat and simmer about 20 minutes. Cook rice according to package directions. (Rice should be ready when pork chops are done.) Serves 6.

• • • • •

 Ask for a rain check if the store runs out of an advertised special. *Stores want to keep your business and that means giving you appropriate service.*

Pork Chop Casserole

4 - 6 pork chops	
3 potatoes, peeled, sliced	
1 onion, sliced	
1 (10 ounce) can cream of mushroom soup	280 g
½ cup milk	125 ml

- Preheat oven to 350° (175° C).

- Brown pork chops in skillet. Place potatoes in sprayed 9 x 13-inch (23 x 33 cm) pan. Layer onions on top.

- Combine soup and milk and cover onions with three-fourths soup-milk mixture. Place browned pork chops on top. Spread remaining soup mixture. Bake covered for 1 hour. Serves 4 to 6.

• • • • •

Pork Chop Cheddar Bake

8 boneless pork chops	
1 (10 ounce) can cream of mushroom soup	280 g
1 cup rice	185 g
1½ cups shredded cheddar cheese	170 g
⅓ cup chopped bell pepper	50 g
1 (4 ounce) can sliced mushrooms, drained	115 g
1 (3 ounce) can french-fried onions	85 g

- Preheat oven to 325° (165° C).

- Brown pork chops lightly. Drain and place in sprayed 9 x 13-inch (23 x 33 cm) baking dish. In same skillet, combine soup, 1¼ cups (310 ml) water, rice, cheese, bell pepper and mushrooms and mix well. Pour over pork chops.

- Cover and bake for 1 hour. Top with french-fried onions. Bake uncovered for additional 15 minutes. Serves 8.

• • • • •

Casseroles are cost-effective dishes, whether main courses, side dishes or even desserts. They give new life to leftovers, respond well to herbs and seasonings and can be frozen or refrigerated until ready to use.

Pork Chops and Apples

6 thick-cut pork chops
Flour
Oil
3 baking apples

- Preheat oven to 325° (165° C).

- Sprinkle pork chops with salt and pepper. Dip pork chops in flour, coat well and brown in skillet with a little oil. Place in sprayed 9 x 13-inch (23 x 33 cm) baking dish.

- Add ⅓ cup (75 ml) water and bake covered for 45 minutes. Peel, halve and seed apples. Place halves over each pork chop. Bake for additional 10 to 15 minutes. (DO NOT overcook apples.) Serves 4 to 6.

• • • • •

Pork Chop Scallop

4 pork chops	
2 tablespoons butter	**30 ml**
1 (5 ounce) box scalloped potatoes	**140 g**
⅔ cup milk	**150 ml**

- In skillet brown pork chops in butter. Remove chops and set aside. Empty potatoes and packet of seasoning sauce mix into skillet. Stir in water and milk according to package directions. Heat to boiling.

- Reduce heat and place chops on top. Cover and simmer for 35 minutes or until potatoes and pork chops are tender. Serves 4.

• • • • •

Pork Chop Special

4 - 6 pork chops	
½ cup rice, cooked	**95 g**
2 (10 ounce) cans cream of mushroom soup	**2 (280 g)**

- Preheat oven to 375° (190° C).

- Brown pork chops on both sides and drain. Place cooked rice in sprayed baking dish and lay browned chops over rice. Pour soup over pork chops, cover and bake for 40 minutes. Serves 4 to 6.

• • • • •

Stuffed Pork Chops

4 boneless center-cut pork chops
Vegetable oil

Stuffing:

2 slices rye bread, diced	
⅓ cup chopped onion	55 g
⅓ cup chopped celery	35 g
⅓ cup diced apples	40 g
½ cup chicken broth	125 ml

- Preheat oven to 400° (205° C).

- Make 1-inch (2.5 cm) wide slit on side of pork chop and insert knife blade toward other side, but not through pork chop. Sweep knife back and forth and carefully cut pocket opening larger.

- In bowl, combine rye bread pieces, onion, celery, apples and broth and mix well. Stuff chops with stuffing mixture and press to use all stuffing mixture. Place chops in heavy skillet with a little oil and saute each chop about 3 minutes on each side. Transfer to sprayed or nonstick baking dish and bake uncovered for 10 minutes. Serves 4.

• • • • •

Tangy Pork Chops

4 - 6 pork chops	
¼ cup Worcestershire sauce	60 ml
¼ cup ketchup	70 g
½ cup honey	170 g

- Preheat oven to 325° (165° C).

- In skillet, brown pork chops. Place in shallow baking dish. Combine Worcestershire, ketchup and honey. Pour over pork chops. Cover and bake for 45 minutes. Serves 4 to 6.

• • • • •

 Colorful foods add flair to meals when you entertain – without busting the budget. If you have a main dish of meat, plan a variety of color in vegetables.

Sweet-and-Sour Pork Cutlets

¾ cup flour	90 g
4 pork cutlets	
2 tablespoons butter, divided	30 ml
¾ cup orange juice	175 ml
⅓ cup dried sweetened cranberries (Craisins®)	40 g
1 tablespoon dijon-style mustard	15 ml
1 tablespoon brown sugar	15 ml

- Place flour in shallow bowl and dredge cutlets in flour. Brown pork cutlets in heavy skillet with 1 tablespoon (15 ml) butter and turn once. Add orange juice, cranberries, mustard, brown sugar and remaining butter. Cook on high until mixture bubbles. Reduce heat and simmer for about 5 minutes. Serves 4.

• • • • •

Cranberry-Glazed Pork Roast

1 (3 pound) pork shoulder roast	1.4 kg
1 teaspoon seasoned salt	5 ml
1 (16 ounce) can whole cranberry sauce	455 g
¼ cup packed brown sugar	55 g

- Preheat oven to 325° (165° C).

- Sprinkle seasoned salt and ½ teaspoon (2 ml) pepper over roast, place in roasting pan and bake for 3 hours or until fork-tender. (If using meat thermometer, it should register 185°/85° C.)

- Remove roast, pour off drippings and trim fat. Return meat to pan. Mash cranberry sauce with fork, stir in brown sugar and mix well.

- Increase oven to 350° (175° C).

- Cut deep gashes in meat, brush generously with cranberry sauce and bake for 30 minutes. Brush often with glaze. Serves 6.

• • • • •

Grocery stores are not your only resource. You may find great deals at pharmacies, warehouse club stores, discount grocery stores, big-box superstores such as Walmart, Target and Kmart (which frequently accept competitor's coupons), surplus stores, etc.

Delectable Apricot Ribs

4 pounds baby back pork ribs	1.8 kg
1 (16 ounce) jar apricot preserves	455 g
⅓ cup soy sauce	75 ml
¼ cup packed light brown sugar	55 g
2 teaspoons garlic powder	10 ml

- Place ribs in sprayed large slow cooker. In bowl, combine preserves, soy sauce, brown sugar and garlic powder and spoon over ribs. Cover and cook on LOW for 6 to 7 hours. Serves 4 to 6.

• • • • •

Apricot-Glazed Ham

1 (29 ounce) can apricots with syrup	805 g
¾ cup apricot preserves	180 ml
1 small baked, boneless ham	

- Preheat oven 325° (165° C). Drain syrup from apricots and save fruit. Bring syrup to a boil, reduce heat and simmer for 10 minutes or until liquid reduces to half. Remove from heat, stir in preserves and apricots and set aside.

- Bake ham for 2 hours and baste often with glaze during last hour of baking. Serve remainder with ham. Serves 8.

• • • • •

Honey Ham

1 (5 pound) fully cooked boneless ham	2.3 kg
¼ cup honey	85 g
½ cup packed brown sugar	110 g

- Preheat oven to 325° (165° C).

- Score ham, wrap in foil and bake for 30 minutes in broiling pan. Combine honey and brown sugar and mix well.

- Remove ham from oven, pull foil open and spread honey glaze over ham. Rewrap in foil and bake for additional 1 hour. Cool for 15 minutes before serving. Serves 6 to 8.

• • • • •

Peach-Pineapple Baked Ham

1 (4 - 5 pound) shank or butt ham	1.8 - 2.3 kg
¼ cup dijon-style mustard, divided	60 g
1 cup peach preserves	320 g
1 cup pineapple preserves	320 g

- Preheat oven to 350° (175° C).

- Spread half mustard on ham. Place ham in sprayed shallow baking pan and bake for 2 hours.

- Combine remaining mustard and both preserves. Heat in microwave oven for 20 seconds (or in small saucepan on low heat for 2 to 3 minutes). Pour over ham and bake for additional 15 minutes. Serves 6 to 8.

• • • • •

Ham Slices with Cranberry Relish

1 (3 pound) boneless cooked ham	1.4 kg

Cranberry Relish:

1 (16 ounce) can whole cranberry sauce	455 g
1 cup orange marmalade	320 g
1 (8 ounce) can crushed pineapple, drained	225 g
¾ cup coarsely chopped pecans	80 g

- Preheat oven to 250° (120° C).

- Slice enough ham for each person. Serve room temperature or warmed. To warm ham, place slices in foil and bake for 15 minutes.

- In small bowl, combine relish ingredients and place in freezer to chill just until ready to serve. This relish can be served cold or warm over ham. Serves 6 to 8.

• • • • •

 The best time to buy ham is around the holidays. They are usually on sale and you can package the leftovers for individual dinners.

Honey-Orange Ham

1 (1 pound) fully cooked slice ham	455 g
3 tablespoons frozen orange juice concentrate, thawed	45 ml
3 tablespoons honey	65 g
¼ teaspoon ginger	1 ml

- Place ham slice in large skillet. In small bowl, combine orange juice concentrate, honey and ginger. Spread mixture over ham and cook on low-medium heat for about 4 minutes, turn and brush again with juice-honey mixture. Cook for additional 4 to 5 minutes. Serves 4.

• • • • •

Hawaiian Ham Steak

1 (8 ounce) can sliced pineapple with liquid	225 g
2 tablespoons brown sugar	30 ml
1 pound center-cut ham slice	455 g

- Pour liquid from sliced pineapple into skillet and stir in brown sugar. Make slashes in fat around ham slice to keep it from curling. Place ham in skillet with juice mixture.

- Cook on medium-low heat for 10 minutes per side. Top with pineapple slices.

- Cook on medium to low heat until sauce becomes thick and serve with pineapple slice on each serving. Serves 4.

• • • • •

Grilled Ham and Apples

½ cup orange marmalade	160 g
1 tablespoon butter	15 ml
¼ teaspoon ground ginger	1 ml
1 pound (½-inch thick) ham slice	455 g (1.2 cm)
2 apples, seeded, sliced	

- Combine marmalade, butter and ginger in 1 cup (250 ml) glass measuring cup or other microwave-safe container. Microwave for 1 minute and stir once. Place ham slice on grill and cover grill with grill lid.

- Grill for about 5 to 10 minutes, turn occasionally and baste with marmalade mixture. Place apple slices on ham and grill for additional 5 to 10 minutes. Serves 4 to 6.

• • • • •

Ham with Red-Eye Gravy

6 (¼-inch thick) slices country ham	6 (6 mm)
¼ cup (½ stick) butter	55 g
¼ cup packed brown sugar	55 g
½ cup strong brewed black coffee	125 ml

- Saute ham in butter over low heat until light brown and turn several times. Remove ham from skillet and keep warm.

- Stir brown sugar into pan drippings and heat until sugar dissolves; stir constantly. Add coffee and simmer for 5 minutes. Season gravy with a little pepper. Serve over ham slices. Serves 4 to 6.

• • • • •

Pasta, Ham and Veggies

1 (8 ounce) package bow-tie (farfalle) pasta	225 g
1 (10 ounce) package frozen broccoli florets, thawed	280 g
1 (10 ounce) package green peas, thawed	280 g
1 (16 ounce) jar alfredo sauce	455 g
1 pound cooked ham, cubed	455 g

- In large saucepan, cook pasta according to package directions. Add broccoli and peas during last 3 minutes of cooking time. Drain well.

- Add alfredo sauce and ham. Cook and stir gently over very low heat to keep ingredients from sticking to pan. Serves 8.

• • • • •

Remember that grocery stores (like every other store) are designed to help you spend more money. End of aisle displays, island displays and goods at chest-level height on the shelves will be more expensive and more attractive to impulse buying. These items will always be positioned where they're easier to reach. Check out the lower shelves and the higher shelves and compare price and value.

Stovetop Ham Supper

1 (12 ounce) package spiral pasta	340 g
3 tablespoons butter, sliced	45 g
2 - 3 cups cooked, cubed ham	280 - 420 g
1 teaspoon minced garlic	5 ml
1 (16 ounce) package frozen broccoli, cauliflower and carrots	455 g
½ cup sour cream	120 g
1 (8 ounce) package shredded cheddar cheese, divided	225 g

- Preheat oven to 375° (190° C).

- Cook pasta in large saucepan, according to package directions, drain and stir in butter while still hot. Add ham, garlic and 1 teaspoon (5 ml) salt.

- Cook vegetables in microwave according to package directions and stir, with liquid, into pasta-ham mixture. Stir in sour cream and half cheese. Mix until they blend well.

- Spoon into sprayed 3-quart (3 L) baking dish. Bake for 15 minutes or just until bubbly around edges. Sprinkle remaining cheese on top and let stand just until cheese melts. Serves 6 to 8.

• • • • •

Ham and Potatoes Olé

1 (24 ounce) package frozen hash browns with onions and peppers, thawed	680 g
3 cups leftover cooked, cubed ham	420 g
1 (10 ounce) can cream of chicken soup	280 g
1 (10 ounce) can fiesta nacho cheese soup	280 g
1 cup hot salsa	265 g
1 (8 ounce) package shredded cheddar-Jack cheese	225 g

- Preheat oven to 350° (175° C).

- Combine potatoes, ham, soups and salsa in saucepan and heat just enough to mix well. Spoon into sprayed 9 x 13-inch (23 x 33 cm) baking dish.

- Cover and bake for 40 minutes. Sprinkle cheese over casserole and bake uncovered for additional 5 minutes. Serves 8.

• • • • •

Super Supper Frittata

2 cups cooked rice	315 g
1 (10 ounce) box frozen green peas, thawed	280 g
1 cup cooked, cubed ham	140 g
Vegetable oil	
8 large eggs, beaten	
1 cup shredded pepper-Jack cheese, divided	115 g
1 teaspoon dried thyme	5 ml
1 teaspoon sage	5 ml

- Preheat broiler.

- In large cast-iron skillet with oven-proof handle, heat rice, peas and ham for 3 to 4 minutes with a little oil or until mixture is thoroughly hot. In separate bowl, whisk eggs, three-fourths cheese, thyme, sage and 1 teaspoon (5 ml) salt.

- Add to mixture in skillet and shake pan gently to distribute evenly. On medium heat, cover and cook, without stirring, until set on bottom and sides.

- Eggs will still be runny in center. Sprinkle remaining cheese over top. Place in oven and broil for about 5 minutes or until frittata is firm in center. Serves 4 to 6.

• • • • •

Guacamole Ham Wrap

¾ cup prepared guacamole	180 g
4 (8 inch) spinach tortillas	4 (20 cm)
¾ cup salsa	200 g
½ (8 ounce) package shredded 4-cheese blend	½ (225 g)
¾ pound leftover cooked ham, cut in thin strips	340 g
Shredded lettuce	

- Spread guacamole over half of each tortilla and layer salsa, cheese, ham strips and lettuce to within 2 inches (5 cm) of edges. Roll tightly. Serves 4.

• • • • •

Watch the timing of sales. Some items are on sale every other week, others every three weeks and some are on sale once a month. If you watch and take notes, you can time your menu and shopping list for the sales.

Ham-Broccoli Stromboli

1 (10 ounce) package refrigerated pizza dough	280 g
1 (10 ounce) package frozen chopped broccoli	280 g
1 (10 ounce) can cream of celery soup	280 g
3 cups cooked, diced ham	420 g
1 cup shredded cheddar cheese	115 g

- Preheat oven to 400° (205° C).

- Unroll dough onto sprayed baking sheet. Cook broccoli according to package directions. Mix broccoli, soup and ham. Spread ham mixture down center of dough. Top with cheese.

- Fold long sides of dough over filling. Pinch short side to seal. Bake uncovered for 20 minutes or until golden brown. Slice and serve. Serves 4.

• • • • •

Ham Quesadillas

2 cups shredded ham	280 g
½ cup chunky salsa	130 g
2 teaspoons chili powder	10 ml
¾ cup whole kernel corn, drained	125 g
8 large whole-wheat tortillas	
1 (8 ounce) package shredded Mexican 4-cheese blend	225 g

- In large bowl, combine shredded ham, salsa, chili powder and corn. Spread mixture over 4 tortillas to within ½-inch (1.2 cm) of edge and sprinkle cheese on top.

- Top with remaining tortillas and cook 1 quesadilla at a time on medium-high heat in large nonstick skillet for about 5 minutes. Turn after 2 minutes or when light golden brown. Cut in wedges to serve. Serves 6 to 8.

TIP: Serve with pinto beans and guacamole.

• • • • •

If you can, shop for groceries without the kids. *All too often, they will beg for products you really don't need or want them to have. You will wind up spending more with kids in tow.*

Mac 'n Cheese Casserole

4 eggs	
1½ cups milk	375 ml
1 (12 ounce) package macaroni, cooked	340 g
1 (8 ounce) package shredded cheddar cheese	225 g
2 cups cooked cubed ham	280 g
¾ cup seasoned breadcrumbs	90 g

- Preheat oven to 350° (175° C).

- In large bowl, lightly beat eggs and milk with a little salt and pepper. Stir in macaroni, cheese and cubed ham. Spoon into sprayed 7 x 11-inch (18 x 28 cm) baking dish, sprinkle breadcrumbs on top and bake uncovered for 30 minutes. Serves 4 to 6.

• • • • • •

Ham-It-Up with Wild Rice

1 (6 ounce) package instant long grain-wild rice mix	170 g
1 (10 ounce) package frozen broccoli spears, thawed	280 g
1 (8 ounce) can whole kernel corn, drained	225 g
3 cups cooked, cubed ham	420 g
1 (10 ounce) can cream of mushroom soup	280 g
1 cup mayonnaise	225 g
1 teaspoon mustard	5 ml
1 cup shredded cheddar cheese	115 g
1 (3 ounce) can french-fried onions	85 g

- Preheat oven to 350° (175° C).

- Prepare rice according to package directions. Spoon into sprayed 3-quart (3 L) baking dish. Top with broccoli, corn and ham.

- In saucepan, combine soup, mayonnaise, mustard and shredded cheese and heat just enough to mix well. Spread over top of rice-ham mixture. Cover and bake for about 20 minutes. Sprinkle fried onions over top. Return to oven and bake uncovered for additional 15 minutes. Serves 6 to 8.

• • • • • •

Plan menus for a week or longer. *Take advantage of specials, sales and coupons. Manufacturer coupons are often available on their Web sites.*

Hopping John

2 (15 ounce) cans jalapeno black-eyed peas with liquid	2 (425 g)
¾ pound ham, chopped	340 g
1 cup chopped onion	160 g
2 cups hot cooked rice	315 g
½ cup chopped green onions	50 g

- Combine peas, ham and onion in saucepan. Bring to boil, reduce heat and simmer 15 minutes. Stir in hot rice and green onions. Serves 4.

• • • • •

Noodles-Ham-Veggie Mix

1 (8 ounce) package medium egg noodles	225 g
2 (10 ounce) cans cream of celery soup	2 (280 g)
1½ cups half-and-half cream	375 ml
1 (8 ounce) can whole kernel corn, drained	225 g
1 (16 ounce) package frozen broccoli, cauliflower and carrots, thawed	455 g
3 cups cooked cubed ham	420 g
1 (8 ounce) package shredded cheddar-Jack cheese, divided	225 g

- Preheat oven to 350° (175° C).

- Cook noodles according to package directions and drain. In large bowl, combine soup, half-and-half cream, corn, broccoli-cauliflower-carrot mixture, ham ½ teaspoon (2 ml) pepper and mix well. Fold in egg noodles and half the cheese.

- Spoon into sprayed 9 x 13-inch (23 x 33 cm) baking dish. Cover and bake for 45 minutes. Sprinkle remaining cheese over top of casserole. Bake uncovered for additional 10 minutes or until cheese bubbles. Serves 6 to 8.

• • • • •

There are certain foods that will change texture if frozen. Potatoes will become mushy, mayonnaise may separate, sauces containing eggs and milk may curdle. Cheese does not freeze well and should be used as a topping when the casserole is thawed and baked or reheated.

Planet Pizza

1 (8 ounce) can crescent dinner rolls	225 g
1 (8 ounce) can tomato sauce	225 g
½ pound sliced bacon, fried	225 g
½ cup sliced fresh mushrooms	35 g
1 teaspoon ground oregano	5 ml
1 cup shredded mozzarella cheese	115

- Preheat oven to 375° (190° C).

- Place dough on cookie sheet. Flatten to form 1 large rectangle. Spread tomato sauce over dough evenly and crumble bacon over tomato sauce. Sprinkle with mushrooms, oregano and cheese. Bake for 15 minutes or until cheese bubbles. Serves 4.

• • • • •

Spaghetti and Meatballs

1 (18 ounce) package frozen cooked meatballs, thawed	510 g
1 (28 ounce) jar spaghetti sauce	795 g
1 (8 ounce) package spaghetti	225 g
1 (5 ounce) package grated parmesan cheese	140 g

- In large microwave baking dish, heat meatballs on HIGH for 3 to 5 minutes, stirring occasionally. Add spaghetti sauce and microwave for additional 2 minutes or until hot.

- Cook spaghetti according to package directions and drain well. Pour onto serving plate and spoon meatball-sauce mixture over spaghetti. Top with cheese. Serves 4.

• • • • •

Mini Pizzas

1 (14 ounce) package English muffins	395 g
1 pound bulk sausage, cooked, drained	455 g
1½ cups pizza sauce	380 g
1 (4 ounce) can sliced mushrooms, drained	115 g
1 (8 ounce) package shredded mozzarella cheese	225 g

- Preheat broiler.

- Split muffins and layer ingredients on each muffin half in order listed, ending with cheese. Broil until cheese melts. Serves 4 to 6.

• • • • •

Quesadilla Pie

1 (4 ounce) can diced green chilies	115 g
½ pound sausage, cooked	225 g
1 (8 ounce) package shredded cheddar cheese	225 g
3 eggs, well beaten	
1½ cups milk	375 ml
¾ cup biscuit mix	90 g
Hot salsa	

- Preheat oven to 350° (175° C).

- Sprinkle green chilies, cooked sausage and cheddar cheese in sprayed 9-inch (23 cm) pie pan.

- In separate bowl, combine eggs, milk and biscuit mix. Pour mixture over chilies, sausage and cheese and bake for 30 to 40 minutes. Serve with salsa on top of each slice. Serves 4 to 6.

• • • • •

Sausage-Potato Casserole

2 (10 ounce) cans cream of mushroom soup	2 (280 g)
1 cup milk	250 ml
1 pound ground sausage, divided	455 g
2 (15 ounce) cans whole potatoes, drained, sliced	2 (425 g)
1 (8 ounce) package shredded cheddar cheese, divided	225 g

- Preheat oven to 375° (190° C).

- Combine soup and milk. Brown sausage until thoroughly cooked. Place half potatoes in sprayed 9 x 13-inch (23 x 33 cm) baking dish.

- Pour half soup mixture over potatoes and add half of sausage. Spread with half cheese. Repeat layers. Bake for 25 minutes. Serves 6 to 8.

• • • • •

Use cooking energy wisely. For example, a slow cooker operates on less energy than an oven; an oven operates on less energy than stovetop cooking. And the slow cooker doesn't heat up your kitchen. Because of the speed of the cooking, a microwave oven will use less energy than a regular oven.

Sausage Souffle

8 slices white bread, cubed	
1 (8 ounce) package shredded sharp cheddar cheese	225 g
1 pound link sausage, cut in thirds	455 g
5 eggs	
2¾ cups milk, divided	675 ml
¾ teaspoon dry mustard	4 ml
1 (10 ounce) can cream of mushroom soup	280 g

- Place bread cubes in sprayed 9 x 13-inch (23 x 33 cm) pan and top with cheese. Brown and drain sausage and place on top of cheese. Beat eggs with 2¼ cups (560 ml) milk and mustard and pour over sausage. Cover and refrigerate overnight.

- Heat soup and remaining milk in saucepan just enough to mix well and pour over bread and sausage. Bake at 300° (150° C) for 1 hour 30 minutes until set. Serves 6 to 8.

• • • • •

Sausage Rice Casserole

1 pound pork sausage	455 g
3 cups cooked rice	315 g
1 (10 ounce) can golden cream of mushroom soup	280 g

- Preheat oven to 350° (175° C). Fry sausage, crumble and drain. Combine sausage, rice and mushroom soup and mix well. Pour into sprayed 9-inch (23 cm) square baking dish and bake for 30 minutes. Serves 6.

• • • • •

Sausage and Wild Rice

2 tablespoons butter	30 ml
1 medium onion, chopped	
1 (4 ounce) can mushroom pieces, drained	115 g
1 pound smoked sausage, thinly sliced	455 g
Dash poultry seasoning	
1 (6 ounce) box long grain-wild rice mix	170 g

- Melt butter in large skillet. Add onions and mushrooms and saute until onion is translucent and tender. Add sausage and cook for 10 to 15 minutes. Add a little poultry seasoning. Cook rice according to package directions. When done, stir into sausage mixture and toss. Serves 4 to 6.

• • • • •

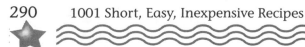

Italian Sausage and Ravioli

1 (16 ounce) package sweet Italian pork sausage, casing removed	455 g
1 (28 ounce) jar chunky mushroom and green pepper spaghetti sauce	795 g
1 (24 ounce) package frozen cheese-filled ravioli, cooked, drained	680 g
½ cup grated parmesan cheese	50 g

- In large skillet over medium heat, brown sausage and stir until meat is no longer pink. Stir in spaghetti sauce and heat to boiling. Add ravioli and stir gently until it is hot. Pour into serving dish and sprinkle with parmesan cheese. Serves 6 to 8.

• • • • •

Bratwurst and Sauerkraut

1 (1 pound) fully-cooked bratwurst	455 g
2 (15 ounce) cans sauerkraut, drained	2 (425 g)
¼ cup packed brown sugar	55 g

- Cook bratwurst in well greased skillet and turn often for 5 minutes until brown. Add sauerkraut to skillet and sprinkle with brown sugar. Cover and cook over low heat for 10 minutes. Serves 6.

• • • • •

Colorful Sausage Supper

¼ cup olive oil, divided	60 ml
1 pound cooked Polish sausage, cut into (¼-inch/6 mm) slices	455 g
1 red bell pepper, seeded, julienned	
3 small zucchini, sliced	
3 small yellow squash, sliced	
1 (12 ounce) package penne pasta	340 g
1 (26 ounce) jar spaghetti sauce, heated	735 g

- In large skillet with 2 tablespoons (30 ml) oil, saute sausage, bell pepper, zucchini and squash until vegetables are tender-crisp. Keep warm. Cook pasta according to package directions, drain and stir in remaining oil. Add a little salt and pepper.

- Spoon into large serving bowl and spread heated spaghetti sauce over pasta. Use slotted spoon to top with sausage-vegetable mixture. Serve immediately. Serves 8.

• • • • •

New Orleans Franks

1 medium onion, chopped
1 clove garlic, minced
3 tablespoons butter, melted   45 ml
2 (15 ounce) cans diced tomatoes   2 (425 q)
6 - 10 frankfurters, divided
5 cups cooked rice   790 g

- Saute onion and garlic in butter in saucepan until tender. Add
  ½ teaspoon (2 ml) salt, dash of pepper and tomatoes. Mix well.
  Dice 2 frankfurters and add to tomato mixture. Cook over low
  heat for 15 to 20 minutes.

- Add remaining whole frankfurters. Cook until frankfurters are
  plump and sauce is thick. Arrange frankfurters on rice and pour
  sauce over all. Serves 6 to 8.

• • • • •

Cheese-n-Weiner Crescents

8 large wieners
4 slices American cheese, each cut into 6 strips
1 (8 count) can refrigerated crescent dinner rolls

- Preheat oven to 375° (190° C).

- Slit wieners within ½-inch (1.2 cm) of edge and insert 3 strips
  cheese in each slit. Separate crescent dough into 8 triangles and
  roll wieners inside dough. Place rolls cheese-side down on sprayed
  baking sheet and bake for 12 to 15 minutes or until golden brown.
  Serves 6 to 8.

• • • • •

Use coupons. *Go online before you shop and check out
the sites of your favorite brands – and check the grocery
store's Web site as well. Newspapers and store circulars
also have coupons.*

Crescent Pizza

1 (8 ounce) can crescent dinner rolls	225 g
1 (6 ounce) jar spaghetti sauce	170 g
1 (3.5 ounce) package pepperoni slices	100 g
1 (8 ounce) package shredded mozzarella cheese	225 g

- Preheat oven to 375° (190° C).

- Separate crescent rolls into 4 rectangles and seal perforations.
  Place on sprayed baking sheet. Spread spaghetti sauce over dough.
  Arrange 8 pepperoni slices on each 5 x 7-inch (13 x 18 cm) rectangle.
  Top with cheese.

- Bake for 14 to 16 minutes or until crust is golden brown. Serves 2 to 4.

● ● ● ● ●

Choose convenience foods carefully. *Convenience foods can be great timesavers, but may not be the cheapest way to go. Rotisserie chicken plus a bag salad can be a terrific timesaver for a busy day, but cost about twice as much as buying a whole chicken and cutting up a salad. You have to decide what your time is worth.*

Seafood Savers
&
Veggie Dinners

*Fish is one of the quickest meats
to prepare and is easily flavored
to suit your taste. And sometimes
a meatless meal just fills the bill.*

Golden Catfish Fillets

2 eggs	
¾ cup flour	90 g
¾ cup cornmeal	120 g
1 teaspoon garlic powder	5 ml
6 - 8 (4 - 8 ounce) catfish fillets	6 - 8 (115 - 230 g)
Vegetable oil	

- In shallow bowl, beat eggs and 2 tablespoons (30 ml) water until foamy. In another shallow bowl, combine flour, cornmeal, garlic powder and a little salt. Dip fillets in eggs, then coat with flour-cornmeal mixture.

- Heat ¼-inch (6 mm) oil in large skillet. Fry fish over medium-high heat for about 4 to 5 minutes on each side. Serves 6 to 8.

• • • • •

Oven-Fried Catfish

4 - 6 catfish fillets	
1½ cups buttermilk*	375 ml
1 cup seasoned breadcrumbs	120 g
2 cups crushed corn flakes	75 g

- Preheat oven to 400° (205° C).

- Dry catfish fillets with paper towels. Place buttermilk in plastic freezer bag, add catfish fillets and turn to coat fish well. Seal and marinate about 20 to 30 minutes. Remove fillets from buttermilk and discard buttermilk.

- Sprinkle fillets with a little salt and pepper. Place breadcrumbs and crushed corn flakes in shallow bowl, dredge fillets in mixture and press mixture gently onto each fillet. Place in sprayed baking pan and bake for 20 to 25 minutes (depending on size of fillets) or until fish flakes easily. Serve immediately. Serves 4 to 6.

TIP: To make buttermilk, mix 1 cup (250 ml) milk with 1 tablespoon (15 ml) lemon juice or vinegar and let milk stand about 10 minutes.

• • • • •

The "fresh" fish you see in the meat department display may well have been frozen on the fishing vessel and then thawed for display. Frozen fillets may be the better buy and fresher, too.

Grilled Catfish

4 catfish fillets
Olive oil
½ teaspoon garlic powder   2 ml
½ teaspoon lemon pepper   2 ml

- Sprinkle catfish fillets with olive oil and rub in. Sprinkle fillets with seasonings plus ½ teaspoon (2 ml) salt.

- Cover grill rack with foil and place fish on foil directly over medium hot coals. Grill for about 3 to 5 minutes per side or until fish flakes easily. Serves 4.

• • • • •

Spicy Fish Amandine

6 - 8 fish fillets
¼ cup (½ stick) butter, melted   55 g
1½ teaspoons Creole seasoning   7 ml
½ cup sliced almonds, toasted   95 g

- Preheat oven to 350° (175° C).

- Dip each fillet in butter and arrange fillets in sprayed 9 x 13-inch (23 x 33 cm) baking dish. Sprinkle with Creole seasoning and almonds.

- Bake for 20 to 25 minutes or until fish flakes easily when tested with fork. Serves 6.

• • • • •

Flounder Italiano

4 - 6 frozen flounder fillets
1½ cups spaghetti sauce   380 g
½ cup shredded mozzarella cheese   55 g

- Preheat oven to 350° (175° C).

- Place fillets in sprayed 9 x 13-inch (23 x 33 cm) pan and pour spaghetti sauce over fillets.

- Bake uncovered for 30 minutes, sprinkle with cheese and bake for additional 5 minutes or until cheese melts. Serves 4.

• • • • •

Flounder au Gratin

½ cup fine dry breadcrumbs	60 g
¼ cup grated parmesan cheese	25 g
1 pound flounder fillets	455 g
⅓ cup mayonnaise	75 g

- Preheat oven to 350° (175° C).

- In shallow dish, combine crumbs and cheese. Brush both sides of fish with mayonnaise and coat with crumb mixture. Arrange fish in single layer in sprayed shallow pan and bake for 20 to 25 minutes or until fish flakes easily with fork. Serves 3 to 4.

• • • • •

Buttered Flounder

2 pounds flounder fillets	910 g
⅔ cup (1⅓ stick) butter	150 g
3 tablespoons fresh cilantro leaves	45 ml
1 tablespoon lime juice	15 ml

- Preheat broiler.

- Place fillets in sprayed large broiler pan. Broil for about 3 to 4 minutes and carefully turn fillets over with tongs and not with fork. Broil for additional 3 minutes or until fish flakes easily when tested with fork.

- In saucepan, heat and stir butter, cilantro leaves and lime juice. Just before serving, spoon mixture over flounder. Serves 6 to 8.

• • • • •

Beer-Battered Fish

1 pound flounder fillets	910 g
Oil	
1 cup biscuit mix	120 g
1 (12 ounce) can beer	355 g

- In large saucepan or fish cooker, heat fillets in 1 to 2 inches (2.5 to 5 cm) oil; remove and keep warm. In mixing bowl, combine biscuit mix and just enough beer to make a batter (not too thin).

- Use tongs to dip 1 fillet at a time in batter. Place battered fillets in hot oil and cook. Drain on paper towels and fry remaining fillets. Serves 3 to 4.

• • • • •

Lemon-Pepper Fish Fillets

1½ pounds cod fillets	680 g
1 tablespoon plus 1 teaspoon olive oil	20 ml
¼ teaspoon lemon pepper	1 ml

- Preheat oven to 375° (190° C).

- Arrange fillets in sprayed baking dish. Drizzle with oil and season with salt and lemon pepper. Bake for 10 to 12 minutes or until fish is opaque. Serves 4.

• • • • •

South-of-the-Border Baked Cod

4 cod filets
Thick-and-chunky salsa
4 slices cheddar or Monterey Jack cheese

- Preheat oven to 350° (175° C).

- Place fish in sprayed baking pan. Spread salsa over fish and top with cheese slices. Bake until fish flakes when tested with fork. Serves 3 to 4.

• • • • •

Chipper Fish

½ cup Caesar salad dressing	125 ml
1½ cups seasoned breadcrumbs	180 g
1½ - 2 pounds sole or orange roughy fillets	680 - 910 g
1 cup crushed potato chips	55 g

- Preheat oven to 375° (190° C).

- Pour dressing in shallow bowl and breadcrumbs in second shallow bowl. Dip fish in dressing, then in breadcrumbs and coat lightly.

- Place coated fish in sprayed large baking dish. Sprinkle fish lightly with crushed potato chips and bake for 20 to 25 minutes or until fish flakes easily with fork. Serves 6 to 8.

• • • • •

Do not be swayed by a fantastic rock-bottom price on something if your family won't eat it. It's not a good buy if you end up throwing it away.

Bless My Sole

1½ pounds frozen sole or cod, thawed	680 g
1 egg, beaten	
2 tablespoons milk	30 ml
2 cups crushed corn flakes	80 g
Oil	

- Cut fish into serving-size pieces and sprinkle with a little salt and pepper. In shallow bowl, combine egg and milk or water; place corn flake crumbs in second bowl.

- Dip fish in egg mixture and coat well on both sides with crushed flakes. Fry in thin layer of oil in skillet until brown on both sides, about 5 to 8 minutes on each side. Serves 4.

• • • • •

Walnut Roughy

1½ pounds fresh or frozen orange roughy	680 g
½ cup mayonnaise	110 g
3 tablespoons grated parmesan cheese	20 g
1 teaspoon dried basil	5 ml
⅓ cup chopped walnuts	45 g

- Preheat oven to 425° (220° C).

- Cut orange roughy into serving-size pieces and place in sprayed baking pan. Do not let pieces touch.

- In bowl, combine mayonnaise, parmesan cheese and dried basil and spread over fish. Sprinkle with chopped walnuts. Bake uncovered for 14 to 15 minutes or until fish flakes easily. Serves 4 to 6.

• • • • •

Where you live will determine the cost and freshness of fish and shellfish. It can be either a bargain or a luxury. Select fish and shellfish with care as it deteriorates more rapidly than poultry, pork or beef. Canned salmon or tuna can furnish a low-cost meal in just a few minutes. Canned shellfish also has many uses in salads and casseroles.

Orange Roughy with Peppers

1 pound orange roughy filets	455 g
Vegetable oil	
1 onion, sliced	
2 red bell peppers, seeded, julienned	
1 teaspoon dried thyme	5 ml

- Cut fish into 4 serving-size pieces.

- Heat a little oil in skillet, layer onion and bell peppers in oil and sprinkle with thyme and ¼ teaspoon (1 ml) pepper.

- Place fish over bell peppers. Cover and cook fish on medium heat for 15 to 20 minutes or until fish flakes easily. Serves 3 to 4.

• • • • •

Parmesan Orange Roughy

1 egg, beaten	
¼ cup milk	60 ml
1½ cups cracker crumbs	90 g
⅓ cup grated parmesan cheese	35 g
4 large orange roughy fillets	

- Preheat oven to 425° (220° C).

- In shallow bowl, beat egg and milk. In another shallow bowl, combine cracker crumbs and parmesan cheese. Dip fillets in egg mixture, then dredge both sides of fillets in crumb mixture and press to use all crumb mixture.

- Place in sprayed 9 x 13-inch (23 x 33 cm) baking pan. Bake uncovered for 15 to 20 minutes or until fish flakes easily with fork. Serves 4.

• • • • •

Determine staples, the regularly-used items you want to keep on hand in your pantry and refrigerator. Keep them in the same, convenient place all the time. It will make it easier to check your supply before shopping.

Crispy Oven Fish

¾ cup biscuit mix	90 g
⅓ cup yellow cornmeal	35 g
1½ teaspoons chili powder	7 ml
1 egg, beaten	
1½ pounds orange roughy fillets	680 g

- Preheat oven at 425° (220° C).

- Pour several tablespoons (30 ml) oil into 9 x 13-inch (23 x 33 cm) baking pan and place in oven to heat oil.

- In shallow bowl, combine biscuit mix, cornmeal and chili powder. In separate shallow bowl, add 1 tablespoon (15 ml) water to egg and mix well. Dip each piece of fish in egg and then in biscuit-cornmeal mixture to coat well. Place in heated pan. Bake for 20 to 25 minutes or until fish flakes easily with fork. Serves 4.

• • • • •

Crunchy Baked Fish

1 cup mayonnaise	225 g
2 tablespoons fresh lime juice	30 ml
1 - 1½ pounds haddock fillets	455 - 680 g
2 cups finely crushed corn chips	175 g

- Preheat oven to 425° (220° C).

- In small bowl, mix mayonnaise and lime juice. Spread on both sides of fish fillets. Place crushed corn chips on wax paper and dredge both sides of fish in chips.

- Place fillets on foil-covered baking sheet and bake for 15 minutes or until fish flakes easily. Serves 4 to 6.

• • • • •

Never shop when you're hungry. *Hunger will make you pick up all kinds of expensive (and unhealthy) junk and convenience foods. Fatigue will also make you shop unwisely as will emotions because they affect your ability to stay focused and within your budget.*

Haddock Parmigiana

4 (4 ounce) haddock fillets, fresh or frozen	4 (115 g)
1 cup spaghetti sauce	250 g
4 mozzarella cheese slices	

- Preheat oven to 375° (190° C).

- Place haddock in sprayed baking dish. Pour spaghetti sauce over fish, cover both sides and top each with cheese slice.

- Bake for 15 minutes or until cheese bubbles and fish flakes easily when tested with fork. Watch carefully. Serves 4.

• • • • •

Broiled Fish Fillets

4 fish fillets	
⅓ cup mayonnaise	75 g
3 tablespoons parmesan cheese	20 g

- Preheat broiler.

- Spread mayonnaise over each fillet. Sprinkle cheese on top of each and place in sprayed broiler pan.

- Broil 4 to 6 inches (10 - 15 cm) from heat for 5 to 8 minutes or until fish flakes easily when tested with fork. Serves 4.

• • • • •

Crisp Oven-Fried Fish

¼ cup milk	60 ml
1 egg, beaten	
1 cup crushed corn flakes	80 g
¼ cup parmesan cheese	25 g
2 pounds fish fillets	910 g
⅓ cup (⅔ stick) butter, melted	75 g

- Preheat oven to 500° (260° C).

- Mix egg and milk in shallow pan. Mix crumbs and cheese in separate pan. Dip fillet in egg-milk mixture. Roll in crumb mixture.

- Lay fillets side-by-side in sprayed baking dish. Drizzle with melted butter and sprinkle remaining crumbs on top. Bake for 14 minutes. Serves 6 to 8.

• • • • •

Grilled and Dilled Fish Fillets

1 pint plain yogurt	455 g
1 tablespoon lemon juice	15 ml
2 cloves garlic, minced	
1 tablespoon chopped fresh dill	15 ml
Dash hot sauce	
½ cucumber, peeled, thinly sliced	
6 (8 ounce) fish fillets	6 (225 g)

- Preheat broiler.

- Combine yogurt with lemon juice, garlic, dill, ⅛ teaspoon (.5 ml) each of salt and pepper, and hot sauce in medium bowl. Gently stir in cucumber. Place oven rack about 3 inches (8 cm) from heat.

- Broil or grill fish for 8 to 10 minutes or until fish flakes easily. Turn once. Spread yogurt dill sauce over fish before serving. Serves 6.

• • • • •

Salmon Casserole

1 (14 ounce) can salmon, drained	395 g
1 egg, beaten	
1 (10 ounce) can cream of mushroom soup, divided	280 g
2 cups crushed potato chips, divided	160 g

- Preheat oven to 350° (175° C).

- Remove bone and skin from salmon. Combine salmon and beaten egg.

- Arrange half salmon-egg mixture, half soup and half chips in layers in sprayed 8-inch (20 cm) baking dish.

- Repeat layers and end with chips on top. Bake for 20 to 25 minutes. Serves 4 to 6.

• • • • •

 If the family fisherman has brought home more fish than can be used right away, put fillets in sealable plastic bags. fill the bags with water and freeze.

Noodled Tuna Bake

2 (6 ounce) cans tuna, well drained	2 (170 g)
1 (10 ounce) can cream of celery soup	280 g
1 egg, beaten	
1 (3 ounce) can Chinese fried noodles, divided	85 g

- Preheat oven to 350° (175° C).

- In bowl, combine tuna, soup, half can fried noodles and egg. Mix well and pour into sprayed 9-inch (23 cm) square baking dish.

- Bake for 25 minutes, top with remaining noodles and bake for additional 10 minutes. Serves 6.

• • • • •

Swiss Tuna Grill

1 (6 ounce) can white tuna, drained, flaked	170 g
½ cup shredded Swiss cheese	55 g
1 rib celery, finely chopped	
½ cup mayonnaise	110 g
Rye bread	
Butter, softened	

- Combine tuna, cheese, celery, mayonnaise, ½ teaspoon (2 ml) salt and ¼ teaspoon (1 ml) pepper and mix well. Spread on rye bread and top with another slice rye bread.

- Spread top of sandwiches with butter and place butter-side down on hot griddle. Butter other side. Over medium heat, brown sandwich on both sides and serve hot. Serves 4.

• • • • •

 Don't be fooled into buying more of an item than you really want. *When the sale price is 5 for $5, they will sell you 1 for $1. You only have to buy 5 if the offer specifically says "__must__ buy 5".*

Tuna Biscuit Melts

1 (10 ounce) can refrigerated buttermilk biscuits	280 g
1 (12 ounce) can chunk light tuna packed in water, drained	340 g
¾ cup chopped celery	75 g
½ cup sweet pickle relish	125 g
½ cup mayonnaise	110 g
4 slices Swiss cheese	

- Preheat oven to 350° (175° C).

- Bake biscuits according to package directions and cool slightly. Split biscuits and arrange cut-side up on same baking pan.

- In large bowl, combine tuna, celery, pickle relish and mayonnaise. Divide tuna mixture among split biscuits and place half slice cheese over top of tuna.

- Bake for 6 to 7 minutes or until filling is hot and cheese melts. Serves 4 to 6.

• • • • •

 # Tuna Twisters

1 (6 ounce) can tuna, drained	170 g
⅓ cup sweet pickle relish, drained	80 g
½ cup chipotle mayonnaise	110 g
6 - 8 flour tortillas	
1 (8 ounce) package shredded mozzarella cheese	225 g

- Place tuna in bowl and break up chunks with fork to shred. Add pickle relish and mayonnaise and mix well. Lay all tortillas out flat and spread tuna mixture over tortillas. Top with about ⅓ cup (35 g) shredded cheese.

- Mash down ingredients to make rolling tortillas easier. Roll tortilla. Place tortillas seam-side down on microwave-safe tray and microwave on HIGH for about 15 to 20 seconds or until cheese melts. Serves 4 to 6.

• • • • •

 Check the weight when buying a bag of potatoes or other produce. *You may find a bag that is actually heavier than the average weight and it's priced just the same.*

Tuna Toast

1 (10 ounce) can cream of chicken soup	280 g
1 (6 ounce) can white tuna in water, drained	170 g
¼ cup milk	60 ml
3 slices thick Texas toast, toasted both sides	
3 fresh green onions, chopped	

- In saucepan over low heat, combine soup, tuna, dash of pepper and milk or water. Stir until hot.

- Place each slice Texas toast on individual plates and spoon one-third tuna mixture on top of toast. Sprinkle chopped green onion over tuna mixture. Serves 3 to 4.

• • • • •

Tuna Souffle

6 slices white bread, torn	
1 (12 ounce) can evaporated milk	355 ml
2 eggs, beaten	
2 (6 ounce) cans tuna with liquid	2 (170 g)
2 (10 ounce) cans chicken noodle soup	2 (280 g)
1 (10 ounce) can cream of mushroom soup	280 g

- Preheat oven to 350° (175° C).

- Soak torn bread in evaporated milk. Stir in eggs. Add tuna and chicken noodle soup and blend. Pour into 9 x 13-inch (23 x 33 cm) sprayed baking pan. Bake for 30 minutes. Heat cream of mushroom soup, spoon over top of soufflé and bake for additional 10 minutes. Serves 6.

• • • • •

Tuna Potatoes

4 medium potatoes, baked	
1 (6 ounce) can tuna, drained	170 g
1 (8 ounce) package shredded cheddar cheese, divided	225 g
½ cup mayonnaise	110 g
¼ cup chopped onion	40 g

- Preheat oven to 400° (205° C).

- Halve baked potatoes, scoop flesh out of skin carefully and save shell. Mix potato with tuna, half cheese, mayonnaise and onion. Spoon into potato shell. Put remaining cheese on top of potatoes and bake until hot and cheese melts. Serves 4.

• • • • •

Tuna Noodles

1 (8 ounce) package wide noodles, cooked, drained	225 g
2 (6 ounce) cans white tuna, drained	2 (170 g)
1 (10 ounce) can cream of chicken soup	280 g
¾ cup milk	175 ml

- Preheat oven to 300° (150° C).

- Place half noodles in sprayed 2-quart (2 L) baking dish. In saucepan, combine tuna, soup and milk and heat just enough to mix well. Pour half soup mixture over noodles and repeat layers. Cover and bake for 20 minutes. Serves 4 to 6.

• • • • •

No-Panic Crab Casserole

1 (16 ounce) package imitation crabmeat, flaked	455 g
1 cup half-and-half cream	250 ml
1½ cups mayonnaise	335 g
6 eggs, hard-boiled, finely chopped	
1 cup seasoned breadcrumbs, divided	120 g
1 tablespoon dried parsley flakes	15 ml
2 tablespoons butter, melted	30 ml

- Preheat oven to 350° (175° C).

- Combine crabmeat, half-and-half cream, mayonnaise, hard-boiled eggs, ½ cup (60 g) breadcrumbs, parsley and a little salt and mix well.

- Pour into sprayed 2-quart (2 L) baking dish. Combine remaining breadcrumbs and butter and sprinkle over top of casserole. Bake uncovered for 40 minutes. Serves 6.

• • • • •

Stay on task and budget when shopping. Stick to your list. Take a pocket calculator and add up products as you select them, especially the impulsive buys. They are usually the most expensive.

Tomatoes and Crabmeat

1 (8 ounce) package imitation crabmeat, flaked	225 g
2 - 3 large red tomatoes, sliced thick	
½ cup oil	125 ml
¼ cup wine vinegar	60 ml
6 tablespoons sugar	75 g
3 tablespoons ketchup	50 g

- Mound crabmeat on each tomato slice. Combine remaining ingredients with 1 teaspoon (5 ml) salt. Drizzle dressing over each tomato-crabmeat assembly. Serves 4 to 6.

TIP: Serve on bed of shredded lettuce.

• • • • •

Cheese Ravioli and Zucchini

1 (25 ounce) package fresh cheese-filled ravioli	710 g
4 small zucchini, sliced	
2 ribs celery, sliced diagonally	
1 (16 ounce) jar marinara sauce	455 g
¼ cup grated parmesan cheese	25 g

- Cook ravioli according to package directions and drain. Return to saucepan and keep warm. (You can also use frozen chicken ravioli.)

- Place zucchini and celery in another saucepan and pour marinara sauce over vegetables. Cook and stir over medium-high heat for about 8 minutes or until vegetables are tender-crisp. Spoon marinara-vegetable mixture over ravioli and toss gently. Pour into serving bowl and garnish with parmesan. Serves 6.

• • • • •

Use coupons along with special sales at the store. If there is a "buy one, get one free" offer, use a coupon for the item you buy and save more.

Cheese, Spaghetti and Spinach

1 (7 ounce) box ready-cut spaghetti	200 g
2 tablespoons butter	30 ml
1 (8 ounce) carton sour cream	225 g
1 cup shredded cheddar cheese	115 g
1 (8 ounce) package shredded Monterey Jack cheese, divided	225 g
1 (10 ounce) package frozen chopped spinach, thawed, drained	280 g

- Cook spaghetti according to package directions, drain and stir in butter until it melts. In large bowl, combine sour cream, cheddar cheese, half Monterey Jack cheese and spinach. Fold into spaghetti and spoon into sprayed slow cooker.

- Cover and cook on LOW for 2 to 4 hours. When ready to serve, sprinkle with remaining Jack cheese. Serves 6 to 8.

• • • • •

Cheese Enchiladas

12 corn tortillas	
1 (12 ounce) package shredded Mexican 4-cheese blend, divided	340 g
1 small onion, chopped	
2 (10 ounce) cans enchilada sauce	2 (280 g)

- Wrap 6 tortillas in slightly damp paper towel. Place between 2 plates and microwave on HIGH 45 seconds. On each tortilla, place about ⅓ cup (35 g) cheese and 1 tablespoon (15 ml) onion and roll.

- On sprayed 9 x 13-inch (23 x 33 cm) baking dish, place tortillas seam-side down and repeat with remaining tortillas. Pour enchilada sauce on top and sprinkle with remaining cheese and onions. Cover and microwave on MEDIUM for 5 to 6 minutes. Serves 4 to 6.

• • • • •

An occasional meatless meal is less costly and can be just as nutritious. Combine rice and beans for a complete protein or consider quinoa, the only grain that is a complete protein. Legumes and whole grains are another combination with good protein.

Dollar Days Sweets

Cakes

Desserts add that special finishing touch to celebrations. They also "dress up" the simplest meal and make it into a feast.

Chocolate Applesauce Cake

1 (18 ounce) box chocolate cake mix	510 g
1 (16 ounce) can applesauce	455 g
½ - ¾ cup egg substitute (or 3 eggs, beaten)	120 - 185 g

- Combine all ingredients in mixing bowl and blend well. Pour mixture into sprayed 9 x 13-inch (23 x 33 cm) baking pan. Bake according to cake box directions. Serves 12 to 14.

TIP: Use 1 can prepared milk chocolate frosting, if desired.

Old-Fashioned Applesauce Spice Cake

1 (18 ounce) box spice cake mix	510 g
3 eggs	
1¼ cups applesauce	320 g
⅓ cup canola oil	75 ml
1 cup chopped pecans	110 g
1 can prepared vanilla frosting	
½ teaspoon ground cinnamon	2 ml

- Preheat oven to 350° (175° C).

- Combine cake mix, eggs, applesauce and oil in bowl. Beat at medium speed for 2 minutes. Stir in pecans.

- Pour into sprayed, floured 9 x 13-inch (23 x 33 cm) baking pan. Bake for 40 minutes. Cake is done when toothpick inserted in center comes out clean. Cool.

- For frosting, mix prepared vanilla frosting mixed with ground cinnamon. Serves 18.

Apricot Cake

1 (18 ounce) box lemon cake mix	510 g
3 eggs, beaten slightly	
1 (15 ounce) can apricots with liquid, chopped	425 g
1 cup apricot preserves	320 g

- Preheat oven to 350° (175° C).

- In bowl, combine cake mix, eggs and apricots with liquid and mix well. Pour into sprayed, floured 9 x 13-inch (23 x 33 cm) pan and bake for 30 to 35 minutes or until toothpick inserted in center comes out clean. While cake is warm, frost with apricot preserves. Cool and cut into squares. Serves 12 to 14.

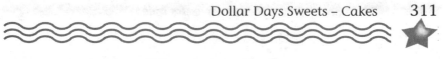

Carrot Cake

1 (18 ounce) box spice cake mix	510 g
2 cups shredded carrots	220 g
1 cup chopped walnuts or pecans	130 g/110 g

- Prepare cake mix according to package directions. Stir in carrots and nuts.

- Bake according to package directions in sprayed, floured 9 x 13-inch (23 x 33 cm) pan. Cool before frosting.

Frosting:

½ cup (1 stick) butter, softened	115 g
1 (8 ounce) package cream cheese, softened	225 g
1 (16 ounce) box powdered sugar	455 g

- Combine butter and cream cheese and beat until creamy. Stir in powdered sugar and beat. Spread on carrot cake. Serves 12 to 14.

• • • • •

Cherry Cake

1 (18 ounce) box French vanilla cake mix	510 g
½ cup (1 stick) butter, melted	115 g
2 eggs	
1 (20 ounce) can cherry pie filling	565 g
1 cup chopped pecans	110 g
Powdered sugar	

- Preheat oven to 350° (175° C).

- Mix all ingredients in large bowl with spoon. Pour into sprayed, floured bundt or tube pan. Bake for 1 hour. Sprinkle sifted powdered sugar on top of cake, if you like. Serves 8.

• • • • •

Cherries-on-a-Cloud

1 prepared angel food cake	
1 (20 ounce) can cherry pie filling	565 g
1 (8 ounce) carton frozen whipped topping, thawed	227 g

- Slice cake. Place 1 slice on each dessert plate and spoon cherry pie filling over cake. Top with whipped topping. Serves 8.

• • • • •

Chocolate-Orange Cake

1 (16 ounce) loaf frozen pound cake, thawed	455 g
1 (12 ounce) jar orange marmalade	340 g
1 (16 ounce) can ready-to-spread chocolate-fudge frosting	455 g

- Cut cake horizontally in 3 layers. Place 1 layer on cake platter. Spread with half of marmalade. Place second layer over first and spread remaining marmalade. Top with third cake layer and spread frosting on top and sides of cake. Refrigerate. Serves 8.

• • • • •

Hawaiian Dream Cake

1 (18 ounce) yellow cake mix	510 g
4 eggs	
¾ cup canola oil	175 ml
½ (20 ounce) can crushed pineapple with liquid	½ (570 g)

- Preheat oven to 350° (175° C).

- Drain pineapple and set aside one-half for glaze. Beat all ingredients and half pineapple liquid in bowl for 4 minutes. Pour into sprayed, floured 9 x 13-inch (23 x 33 cm) baking pan.

- Bake for 30 to 35 minutes or until toothpick inserted in center comes out clean. Cool and spread coconut-pineapple frosting over cake.

Coconut-Pineapple Glaze:

½ (20 ounce) can crushed pineapple with liquid	½ (570 g)
½ cup (1 stick) butter	115 g
1 (16 ounce) box powdered sugar	455 g
1 (6 ounce) can flaked coconut	170 g

- Heat pineapple and butter in saucepan and boil for 2 minutes. Add powdered sugar and coconut. Punch holes in cake with knife and pour hot glaze over cake. Serves 18.

• • • • •

Learn how the grocery store handles special savings programs. Find out on what day they have double or even triple coupons. Sign up for any special discount card.

Pineapple-Cherry Cake

1 (20 ounce) can crushed pineapple, drained	565 g
1 (20 ounce) can cherry pie filling	565 g
1 (18 ounce) box yellow cake mix	510 g
1 cup (2 sticks) butter, softened	230 g
1¼ cups chopped pecans	140 g

- Preheat oven to 350° (175° C).

- Place all ingredients in bowl and mix with spoon. Pour into sprayed, floured 9 x 13-inch (23 x 33 cm) baking dish. Bake for 1 hour 10 minutes. Serves 20.

• • • • •

Fruit Cocktail Cake

1 (18 ounce) box yellow cake mix	510 g
3 eggs	
1 (15 ounce) can fruit cocktail with liquid	425 g

- Preheat oven to 350° (175° C).

- Combine all ingredients in large bowl and mix well. Pour into sprayed, floured 9 x 13-inch (23 x 33 cm) pan and bake for 45 to 50 minutes. Serves 12 to 14.

• • • • •

Quick Fruitcake

1 (15.6 ounce) package cranberry or blueberry quick-bread mix	440 g
½ cup chopped pecans	55 g
½ cup chopped dates	75 g
¼ cup chopped maraschino cherries	40 g
¼ cup crushed pineapple, drained	60 g

- Preheat oven to 350° (175° C).

- Prepare quick-bread batter according to package directions. Stir in remaining ingredients. Pour into sprayed 9 x 5-inch (23 x 13 cm) loaf pan.

- Bake for 60 minutes or until toothpick inserted in center comes out clean. Cool 10 minutes before removing from pan. Serves 18.

• • • • •

Angel-Cream Cake

1 large angel food cake	
1 (18 ounce) jar chocolate ice cream topping	510 g
½ gallon vanilla ice cream, softened	1.9 L
1 (12 ounce) carton whipping topping	340 g
½ cup slivered almonds, toasted	85 g

- Tear cake into large pieces. Stir in chocolate topping to coat pieces of cake and mix in softened ice cream. Work fast! Stir into tube pan and freeze overnight.

- Turn out onto large cake plate and frost with whipped topping. Decorate with almonds and freeze. Serves 18.

• • • • •

Pineapple-Angel Cake

1 (1-step) angel food cake mix	
1 (20 ounce) can crushed pineapple with juice	565 g

- Preheat oven to 350° (175° C).

- Place angel food cake mix in bowl and add in pineapple. Beat according to directions on cake mix box.

- Pour into unsprayed 9 x 13-inch (23 x 33 cm) baking pan; do not spray pan. Bake for 30 minutes. (This is a good low-calorie cake, but if you want it frosted, use a prepared vanilla frosting.) Serves 15.

• • • • •

Strawberry-Angel Delight Cake

1 cup sweetened condensed milk	310 g
¼ cup lemon juice	60 ml
1 pint fresh strawberries, halved	305 g
1 angel food cake	
1 (1 pint) carton whipping cream, whipped	500 ml
Extra strawberries for topping	

- Combine sweetened condensed milk and lemon juice in bowl. Fold in strawberries. Slice cake in half horizontally. Spread strawberry filling on bottom layer and place top layer over filling. Cover with whipped cream and top with extra strawberries. Serves 18.

• • • • •

Chess Cake

1 (18 ounce) box yellow cake mix	510 g
2 eggs	
½ cup (1 stick) butter, softened	115 g

- Preheat oven to 350° (175° C). Beat cake mix, 2 eggs and butter in mixing bowl. Press into sprayed 9 x 13-inch (23 x 33 cm) baking pan.

Topping:

2 eggs	
1 (8 ounce) package cream cheese, softened	230 g
1 (1 pound) box powdered sugar	455 g

- Beat 2 eggs, cream cheese and powdered sugar in bowl and pour over cake batter. Bake for 35 minutes. Serves 18.

Favorite Cake

1 (18 ounce) box butter pecan cake mix	510 g
1 cup almond-toffee bits	240 g
1 cup chopped pecans	110 g
Powdered sugar	

- Preheat oven to 350° (175° C).

- Prepare cake mix according to package directions. Fold in almond-toffee bits and pecans. Pour into sprayed, floured bundt pan.

- Bake for 45 minutes or until toothpick inserted in center comes out clean. Allow cake to cool several minutes and remove cake from pan. Dust with sifted powdered sugar. Serves 18.

Golden Rum Cake

1 (18 ounce) box yellow cake mix with pudding	510 g
3 eggs	
⅓ cup canola oil	75 ml
½ cup rum	125 ml
1 cup chopped pecans	110 g

- Preheat oven to 325° (165° C).

- Blend cake mix, eggs, 1 cup (250 ml) water, oil and rum in bowl. Stir in pecans. Pour into sprayed, floured 10-inch (25 cm) tube or bundt pan. Bake for 1 hour. (If you like, sprinkle sifted powdered sugar over cooled cake.) Serves 18.

• • • • •

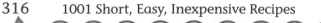

Gooey Butter Cake

4 eggs, divided	
1 (18 ounce) box butter cake mix	510 g
½ cup (1 stick) butter, melted	115 g
1 (16 ounce) box powdered sugar	455 g
1 (8 ounce) package cream cheese, softened	225 g

- Preheat oven to 350° (175° C).

- Beat 2 eggs with cake mix and butter in bowl. Spread mixture into sprayed, floured 9 x-13 inch (23 x 33 cm) baking pan.

- Set aside ¾ cup (90 g) powdered sugar for topping. Mix remaining powdered sugar, remaining 2 eggs and cream cheese in bowl and beat until smooth.

- Spread mixture on top of dough. Sprinkle remaining sugar on top. Bake for 40 minutes. Cake will puff up and then go down when it cools. Serves 18.

• • • • •

Two-Surprise Cake

The first surprise is how easy this recipe is and the second surprise is how good it is! You'll make this more than once.

1 bakery orange-chiffon cake	
1 (15 ounce) can crushed pineapple with juice	425 g
1 (3.4 ounce) package vanilla instant pudding	100 g
1 (8 ounce) carton frozen whipped topping, thawed	225 g
½ cup slivered almonds, toasted	85 g

- Slice cake horizontally to make 3 layers. Mix pineapple, pudding and whipped topping in bowl and blend well. Spread on each layer and cover top of cake. Sprinkle almonds on top and refrigerate. Serves 18.

• • • • •

 Make low-cost whipped topping *by whipping equal parts instant dry milk with cold water. Add some lemon juice when it reaches the soft peak stage; it will add stability and extra flavor.*

Pound Cake

1 cup (2 sticks) butter, softened	230 g
2 cups sugar	400 g
5 eggs	
2 cups flour	240 g
1 tablespoon almond flavoring	15 ml

- Preheat oven to 325° (165° C).

- Combine all ingredients in bowl and beat for 10 minutes at medium speed. Pour into sprayed, floured tube pan. (Batter will be very thick.) Bake for 1 hour. Cake is done when toothpick inserted in center comes out clean. Serves 18.

• • • • •

Aloha Pound Cake

1 (10 inch) bakery pound cake	25 cm
1 (20 ounce) can crushed pineapple with juice	565 g
1 (3.5 ounce) package instant coconut pudding mix	100 g
1 (8 ounce) carton frozen whipped topping, thawed	225 g
½ cup flaked coconut	45 g

- Slice cake horizontally to make 3 layers. Mix pineapple, pudding and whipped topping in bowl and blend well. Spread on each layer and over top. (Stack layers to form cake.) Sprinkle top of cake with coconut and refrigerate. Serves 18.

• • • • •

Blueberry Pound Cake

1 (18 ounce) box yellow cake mix	510 g
1 (8 ounce) package cream cheese, softened	230 g
½ cup canola oil	125 ml
4 eggs	
1 (15 ounce) can whole blueberries, drained	425 g
Powdered sugar	

- Preheat oven to 350° (175° C).

- Combine all ingredients in bowl except blueberries and powdered sugar and beat for 3 minutes. Gently fold in blueberries. Pour into sprayed, floured bundt or tube pan.

- Bake for 50 minutes. Cake is done when toothpick inserted in center comes out clean. Sprinkle sifted powdered sugar over top of cake. Serves 18.

• • • • •

Strawberry Pound Cake

1 (18 ounce) box strawberry cake mix	510 g
1 (3.4 ounce) package instant vanilla pudding mix	100 g
⅓ cup canola oil	75 ml
4 eggs	
1 (3 ounce) package strawberry gelatin	85 g

- Preheat oven to 350° (175° C).

- Mix all ingredients plus 1 cup (250 ml) water in bowl and beat for 2 minutes at medium speed. Pour into sprayed, floured bundt pan.

- Bake for 55 to 60 minutes. Cake is done when toothpick inserted in center comes out clean. Cool for 20 minutes before removing cake from pan. If you would like frosting, use prepared vanilla frosting. Serves 18.

• • • • •

Poppy Seed Bundt Cake

1 (18 ounce) box yellow cake mix	510 g
1 (3.4 ounce) package instant coconut cream pudding mix	100 g
½ cup canola oil	125 ml
3 eggs	
2 tablespoons poppy seeds	20 g
Powdered sugar	

- Preheat oven to 350° (175° C).

- Combine cake mix and pudding mix, 1 cup (250 ml) water, oil and eggs in bowl. Beat on low speed until moist. Beat on medium speed for 2 minutes.

- Stir in poppy seeds. Pour into sprayed, floured bundt pan. Bake for 50 minutes or until toothpick inserted in center comes out clean. Cool for 10 minutes and remove from pan. Dust with sifted powdered sugar. Serves 18.

• • • • •

 According to the Economic Research Service, Americans waste more than 25% of the food they buy. If we cut our food waste, we cut our cost and we cut the amount that goes into landfills.

Cranberry Coffee Cake

2 eggs
1 cup mayonnaise   225 g
1 (18 ounce) box spice cake mix   510 g
1 (16 ounce) can whole cranberry sauce   455 g
Powdered sugar

- Preheat oven to 325° (165° C).

- Beat eggs, mayonnaise and cake mix in bowl. Fold in cranberry
  sauce. Pour into sprayed, floured 9 x 13-inch (23 x 33 cm)
  baking pan.

- Bake for 45 minutes. Cake is done when toothpick inserted in center
  comes out clean. When cake is cool, dust with sifted powdered
  sugar. (If you would rather have frosting than powdered sugar, use
  prepared frosting.) Serves 18.

• • • • •

Tasty Coffee Cake

1 cup sugar   200 g
1 cup oil   250 ml
4 eggs
2 cups flour   240 g
1 teaspoon baking powder   5 ml
1 (20 ounce) can your choice of pie filling   565 g
Powdered sugar

- Preheat oven to 350° (175° C).

- Cream sugar and oil. Add eggs and mix well. Combine flour and
  baking powder and add to mixture. Spread half batter in sprayed
  9 x 13-inch (23 x 33 cm) baking pan.

- Top with pie filling. Spread remaining batter over pie filling. Bake
  for 30 minutes. Dust with powdered sugar. Serves 6 to 8.

• • • • •

*Rather than buy a new set of dishes, mix and match
your existing patterns.* It not only saves money, it happens
to be the latest trend in table settings.

Pumpkin Cupcakes

1 (18 ounce) box spice cake mix	510 g
1 (15 ounce) can pumpkin	425 g
3 eggs	
⅓ cup canola oil	75 ml

- Preheat oven to 350° (175° C).

- Blend cake mix, pumpkin, eggs, oil and ⅓ cup (75 ml) water in bowl. Beat for 2 minutes. Pour batter into 24 paper-lined muffin cups and fill three-fourths full. Bake for 18 to 20 minutes or until toothpick inserted in center comes out clean. (You may want to spread with prepared frosting.) Yields 24 cupcakes.

• • • • •

Easy Cheesecake

2 (8 ounce) packages cream cheese, softened	2 (225 g)
½ cup sugar	100 g
½ teaspoon vanilla	2 ml
2 eggs	
1 (9 ounce) ready graham cracker piecrust	255 g
1 (20 ounce) can pie filling (your choice of flavor)	565 g

- Preheat oven to 350° (175° C).

- Beat cream cheese, sugar, vanilla and eggs in bowl. Pour into piecrust. Bake for 40 minutes. Cool and serve with any pie filling. Serves 6 to 8.

• • • • •

Rise to the challenge. *You can literally save hundreds of dollars if not a thousand dollars or more every year by rising to the challenge of organizing your task and getting the best food values for your family and your budget.*

Dollar Days Sweets

Pies & Cobblers

Desserts add that special finishing touch to celebrations. They also "dress up" the simplest meal and make it into a feast.

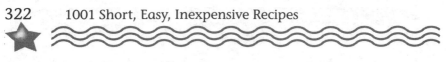

Speedy Banana Pie

1 (3.4 ounce) box banana pudding mix   100 g
2 - 3 bananas, sliced
1 (9 inch) piecrust, baked   23 cm

- Prepare pudding mix as pie according to package directions. Place banana slices in cooled crust and pour pudding over bananas. Garnish with banana slices and let stand for 5 to 10 minutes.

Speedy Meringue:

2 cups miniature marshmallows   90 g

- Preheat broiler.

- Sprinkle miniature marshmallows over top of pie and broil for 2 to 3 minutes until they turn light brown and partially melt. Serves 6 to 8.

• • • • •

Merry-Berry Pie

1 (6 ounce) package strawberry gelatin   170 g
1 cup whole cranberry sauce   280 g
½ cup cranberry juice cocktail   125 ml
1 (8 ounce) carton frozen whipped topping, thawed   230 g
1 (9 inch) baked piecrust   23 cm

- Dissolve gelatin in 1 cup (250 ml) boiling water in bowl. Add cranberry sauce and juice. Refrigerate until it begins to thicken.

- Fold in whipped topping and refrigerate again until mixture mounds. Pour into piecrust. Refrigerate for several hours before serving. Serves 6 to 8.

• • • • •

Cherry-Pecan Pie

1 (14 ounce) can sweetened condensed milk   395 g
¼ cup lemon juice   60 ml
1 (8 ounce) carton frozen whipped topping, thawed   225 g
1 cup chopped pecans   110 g
1 (20 ounce) can cherry pie filling   565 g
2 (6 ounce) ready graham cracker piecrusts   2 (170 g)

- Combine sweetened condensed milk and lemon juice in bowl and stir well. Fold in whipped topping. Fold pecans and pie filling into mixture. Spoon into 2 piecrusts. Refrigerate overnight. Serves 12.

• • • • •

Black Forest Pie

This is a great party dessert.

4 (1 ounce) bars unsweetened baking chocolate	4 (30 g)
1 (14 ounce) can sweetened condensed milk	395 g
1 teaspoon almond extract	5 ml
1½ cups whipping cream, whipped	325 ml
1 (9 inch) baked piecrust	23 cm
1 (20 ounce) can cherry pie filling, chilled	565 g

- Melt chocolate with sweetened condensed milk in saucepan over medium-low heat and stir well to mix. Remove from heat and stir in almond extract. (This mixture needs to cool.)

- When mixture is about room temperature, pour chocolate into whipped cream and fold gently until both are combined.

- Pour into piecrust. To serve, spoon heaping spoonful of cherry filling over each piece of pie. Serves 8 to 10.

• • • • •

Creamy Lemon Pie

1 (8 ounce) package cream cheese, softened	225 g
1 (14 ounce) can sweetened condensed milk	395 g
¼ cup lemon juice	60 ml
1 (20 ounce) can lemon pie filling	565 g
1 (6 ounce) ready graham cracker piecrust	170 g

- Beat cream cheese in bowl until creamy. Add sweetened condensed milk and lemon juice. Beat until mixture is very creamy.

- Fold in lemon pie filling and stir until mixture is creamy and smooth. Pour into piecrust. Refrigerate for several hours before slicing and serving. Serves 8.

• • • • •

 Lemons, oranges and grapefruit should be at room temperature and rolled firmly on a countertop to get the most juice when squeezing. A medium lemon yields about 2 tablespoons juice and about 1 tablespoon zest. If a recipes calls for both zest and juice, zest first and then squeeze the lemon for juice.

Sunny Lemon-Pineapple Pie

1 (14 ounce) can sweetened condensed milk	395 g
1 (20 ounce) can lemon pie filling	565 g
1 (20 ounce) can crushed pineapple, well drained	565 g
1 (8 ounce) carton frozen whipped topping, thawed	225 g
2 (9 inch) cookie-flavored piecrusts	2 (23 cm)

- With mixer, combine condensed milk and lemon pie filling and beat until smooth. Add pineapple and whipped topping and gently fold into pie filling mixture. Pour into 2 piecrusts. Refrigerate. Serves 6 to 8.

• • • • •

Shaker Lemon Pie

2 lemons, sliced thin (peel and all)	
1½ cups sugar	300 g
4 eggs	
2 (9-inch) frozen piecrusts, thawed	2 (23cm)

- Place lemon slices in bowl and pour sugar over them. Mix well and set aside for 2 to 3 hours.

- When ready to bake, preheat oven to 450° (230° C).

- Beat eggs and pour over lemons. Fill an unbaked piecrust. Add top crust and make vents in top. Bake for 15 minutes. Reduce heat to 350° (175° C) and bake until done. Serves 8.

• • • • •

Pink Lemonade Pie

1 (6 ounce) can frozen pink lemonade concentrate. thawed	175 ml
1 (8 ounce) carton frozen whipped topping, thawed	225 g
1 (14 ounce) can sweetened condensed milk	395 g
1 (9 ounce) graham cracker crumb piecrust	255 g

- Combine lemonade concentrate, whipped topping and milk. Mix well and refrigerate. Pour into graham cracker piecrust and freeze. Serves 6 to 8.

• • • • •

 When a staple or item you use regularly is on sale, stock up. Buy a two, three or four-week supply, enough to get to the next time that item will probably be on sale.

Sunny Lime Pie

2 (6 ounce) cartons key lime pie yogurt	2 (170 g)
1 (3 ounce) package lime gelatin	85 g
1 (8 ounce) carton frozen whipped topping, thawed	225 g
1 (6 ounce) graham cracker piecrust	170 g

- In bowl, combine yogurt and dry lime gelatin and mix well. Fold in whipped topping, spread in piecrust and freeze. Take out of freezer 20 minutes before slicing. Serves 6.

• • • • •

Key Lime Pie

1 (6 ounce) can frozen limeade concentrate	175 ml
1 (8 ounce) carton frozen whipped topping, thawed	225 g
1 (14 ounce) can sweetened condensed milk	395 g
1 (9 ounce) graham cracker piecrust	255 g

- Combine all ingredients except piecrust and mix well. Pour into graham cracker or chocolate crumb piecrust. Refrigerate for at least 2 hours before serving. Serves 6 to 8.

• • • • •

Peach Mousse Pie

1 (16 ounce) package frozen peach slices, thawed	455 g
1 cup sugar	200 g
1 (1 ounce) packet unflavored gelatin	30 g
¾ (8 ounce) carton frozen whipped topping, thawed	¾ (225 g)
1 (6 ounce) ready graham cracker piecrust	170 g

- Place peaches in blender and process until smooth. Place in saucepan, bring to a boil and stir constantly. Combine sugar and gelatin in bowl. Stir into hot puree until sugar and gelatin dissolve.

- Pour gelatin-peach mixture into large bowl. Freeze until mixture mounds (about 20 minutes) and stir occasionally.

- Beat mixture at high speed for about 5 minutes until mixture becomes light and frothy. Fold in whipped topping and spoon into graham cracker piecrust. Refrigerate. Serves 8.

• • • • •

Pineapple-Cheese Pie

1 (14 ounce) can sweetened condensed milk	395 g
¼ cup lemon juice	60 ml
1 (8 ounce) package cream cheese, softened	225 g
1 (15 ounce) can crushed pineapple, well drained	425 g
1 (6 ounce) ready graham cracker piecrust	170 g

- Combine sweetened condensed milk, lemon juice and cream cheese in bowl. Whip slowly at first, then beat until smooth. Fold in pineapple and mix well. Pour into piecrust and refrigerate for 8 hours before slicing. Serves 6.

• • • • •

Pineapple Fluff Pie

This pie is light, airy and full of fluff.

1 (20 ounce) can crushed pineapple with juice	565 g
1 (3.4 ounce) package instant lemon pudding mix	100 g
1 (8 ounce) carton frozen whipped topping, thawed	225 g
1 (6 ounce) ready graham cracker crust	170 g

- Combine pineapple and pudding mix in bowl and beat until thick. Fold in whipped topping. Spoon into piecrust. Refrigerate for several hours before serving. Serves 8.

• • • • •

Easy Pumpkin Pie

2 eggs	
1 (20 ounce) pumpkin pie filling	565 g
⅔ cup evaporated milk	150 ml
1 (9 inch) refrigerated deep-dish piecrust	23 cm

- Preheat oven to 400° (205° C).

- Beat eggs lightly in large bowl. Stir in pumpkin pie filling and evaporated milk. Pour into piecrust. Cut 2-inch (5 cm) wide strips of foil and cover crust edges to prevent excessive browning.

- Bake for 15 minutes. Reduce temperature to 350° (175° C) and bake for additional 50 minutes or until knife inserted in center comes out clean. Cool. Serves 6 to 8.

• • • • •

Yum-Yum Strawberry Pie

2 pints fresh strawberries, divided	715 g
1¼ cups sugar	250 g
3 tablespoons cornstarch	45 ml
1 (6 ounce) ready graham cracker piecrust	170 g
1 (8 ounce) carton whipping cream, whipped	250 ml

- Crush half strawberries in saucepan, add sugar, cornstarch and a dash of salt and cook on low heat until thick and clear. Cool.

- Place remaining strawberries in piecrust and cover with cooked mixture. Top with whipped cream and refrigerate. Serves 6 to 8.

• • • • •

Strawberry-Cream Cheese Pie

2 (10 ounce) packages frozen sweetened strawberries, thawed	2 (280 g)
2 (8 ounce) packages cream cheese, softened	2 (225 g)
⅔ cup powdered sugar	80 g
1 (8 ounce) carton frozen whipped topping, thawed	225 g
1 (6 ounce) ready chocolate crumb piecrust	170 g
Fresh strawberries	

- Drain strawberries and set aside ¼ cup (60 ml) liquid. Combine cream cheese, set aside strawberry liquid, strawberries and powdered sugar in bowl and beat well.

- Fold in whipped topping and spoon into piecrust. Refrigerate overnight and garnish with fresh strawberries. Serves 8.

• • • • •

Strawberry Ice Cream Pie

1 (3 ounce) package strawberry gelatin	85 g
1 pint vanilla ice cream, softened	475 ml
1 pint fresh or frozen strawberries	330 g
1 (6 ounce) graham cracker piecrust	170 g

- Prepare gelatin with 1 cup (250 ml) boiling water and mix well until gelatin dissolves.

- Stir in ice cream and then berries. Pour into piecrust. Refrigerate until ready to serve. Serves 6.

• • • • •

Sweet Potato Pie

1 (14 ounce) can sweet potatoes, drained, mashed	395 g
¾ cup milk	175 ml
1 cup packed brown sugar	220 g
2 eggs	
½ teaspoon ground cinnamon	2 ml
1 (9 inch) refrigerated piecrust	23 cm

- Preheat oven to 350° (175° C).

- Combine all ingredients except piecrust plus ½ teaspoon (2 ml) salt in bowl and blend until smooth. Pour into piecrust.

- Bake for 40 minutes or until knife inserted in center comes out clean. (Shield edges of pastry with strips of foil to prevent excessive browning.) Serves 6.

• • • • •

Grasshopper Pie

22 large marshmallows	
⅓ cup creme de menthe liqueur	75 ml
2 (8 ounce) cartons whipping cream, whipped	2 (250 ml)
1 (6 ounce) ready chocolate piecrust	170 g

- Melt marshmallows with creme de menthe in large saucepan over low heat, stirring constantly. Cool and fold whipped cream into marshmallow mixture. Pour filling into piecrust and freeze until ready to serve. Serves 8.

• • • • •

Tumbleweed Pie

½ gallon vanilla ice cream, softened	1.9 L
⅓ cup plus 1 tablespoon Kahlua® liqueur	90 ml
⅓ cup plus 1 tablespoon amaretto liqueur	90 ml
1 (6 ounce) ready chocolate-cookie crust	170 g
¼ cup slivered almonds, toasted	40 g

- Place ice cream, Kahlua® and amaretto in bowl and blend as quickly as possible. Pour into piecrust. Sprinkle almonds over top and freeze. Serves 8.

• • • • •

Cheesecake Pie

2 (8 ounce) packages cream cheese	2 (225 g)
3 eggs	
1 cup sugar, divided	200 g
1½ teaspoons vanilla, divided	7 ml
1 (8 ounce) carton sour cream	230 g

- Preheat oven to 350° (175° C).

- Combine cream cheese, eggs, ¾ cup (150 g) sugar and ½ teaspoon (2 ml) vanilla in bowl. Beat for 5 minutes.

- Pour into sprayed 9-inch (23 cm) pie pan and bake for 25 minutes. Cool for 20 minutes. (Leave oven on.)

- Combine sour cream, ¼ cup (50 g) sugar and 1 teaspoon (5 ml) vanilla. Pour over cooled pie and bake for additional 10 minutes.

- Refrigerate for at least 4 hours. Serve with your favorite fruit topping or pie filling of your choice. Serves 8.

• • • • •

Chocolate Almond Pie

¼ cup milk	60 ml
20 marshmallows	
7 (1.5 ounce) chocolate almond bars	7 (40 g)
1 (8 ounce) carton frozen whipped topping, thawed	225 g
1 (6 ounce) graham cracker piecrust	170 g

- Pour milk into saucepan, add marshmallows and melt over medium heat. Add chocolate bars and melt.

- Remove from heat, cool a little and stir in whipped topping. Pour mixture into piecrust and refrigerate for 2 hours before serving. Serves 6.

■ ■ ■ ■ ■

Basic seasonings are important. *You don't have to buy every seasoning. Learn which seasonings can be substituted for ones you'll use only once. Don't buy in bulk; seasonings lose their flavor with time.*

Chocolate-Cream Cheese Pie

1 (8 ounce) package cream cheese, softened	225 g
¾ cup powdered sugar	90 g
¼ cup cocoa	20 g
1 (8 ounce) container frozen whipped topping, thawed	230 g
1 (6 ounce) ready graham cracker piecrust	170 g
½ cup chopped pecans	55 g

- Combine cream cheese, powdered sugar and cocoa in bowl and beat at medium speed until creamy. Add whipped topping and fold until smooth. Spread into piecrust, sprinkle pecans over top and refrigerate. Serves 6.

• • • • •

Easy Frozen Peanut Butter Pie

¾ cup chunky peanut butter	215 g
1 quart vanilla ice cream, softened	945 ml
1 (9 ounce) graham cracker or chocolate piecrust	255 g

- Combine peanut butter and softened ice cream and mix well. Pour into piecrust and freeze. Serves 6 to 8.

• • • • •

Creamy Peanut Butter Pie

⅔ cup crunchy peanut butter	190 g
1 (8 ounce) package cream cheese, softened	225 g
½ cup milk	125 ml
1 cup powdered sugar	120 g
1 (8 ounce) carton frozen whipped topping, thawed	225 g
1 (6 ounce) ready graham cracker piecrust	170 g

- Blend peanut butter, cream cheese, milk and powdered sugar in bowl and fold in whipped topping. Pour into piecrust. Refrigerate for several hours before serving. Serves 6.

• • • • •

Be aware of when the store marks down items for quick sale because of upcoming expiration dates. You can stock up on meat and bread and freeze for later use.

Chess Pie

½ cup (1 stick) butter, softened	115 g
2 cups sugar	400 g
1 tablespoon cornstarch	15 ml
4 eggs	
1 (9 inch) refrigerated piecrust	23 cm

- Preheat oven to 325° (165° C).

- Cream butter, sugar and cornstarch in bowl. Add eggs one at a time and beat well after each addition.

- Pour mixture in piecrust. Cover piecrust edges with strips of foil to prevent excessive browning. Bake for 45 minutes or until center sets. Serves 6 to 8.

• • • • •

Creamy Pecan Pie

1½ cups light corn syrup	375 ml
1 (3 ounce) package vanilla instant pudding mix	85 g
3 eggs	
2½ tablespoons butter, melted	35 g
2 cups pecan halves	225 g
1 (10 inch) deep-dish piecrust	25 cm

- Preheat oven to 325° (165° C).

- Combine corn syrup, pudding mix, eggs and butter in bowl, mix well and stir in pecans.

- Pour into piecrust. Cover piecrust edges with strips of foil to prevent excessive browning. Bake for 35 to 40 minutes or until center of pie sets. Serves 8.

• • • • •

Dixie Pie

24 large marshmallows	
1 cup evaporated milk	250 ml
1 (8 ounce) carton whipping cream, whipped	250 ml
3 tablespoons bourbon	45 ml
1 (6 ounce) ready chocolate piecrust	170 g

- Melt marshmallows in milk in saucepan over low heat and stir constantly. Do not boil. Cool in refrigerator. Fold into whipped cream while adding bourbon. Pour into chocolate piecrust. Refrigerate for at least 5 hours before serving. Serves 8.

• • • • •

Coffee-Mallow Pie

1 tablespoon instant coffee granules	15 ml
4 cups miniature marshmallows	180 g
1 tablespoon butter	15 ml
1 (8 ounce) carton whipping cream, whipped	250 ml
1 (6 ounce) ready graham cracker piecrust	170 g
½ cup chopped walnuts, toasted	65 g

- Bring 1 cup (250 ml) water in heavy saucepan to a boil and stir in coffee granules until it dissolves. Reduce heat and add marshmallows and butter. Cook and stir over low heat until marshmallows melt and mixture is smooth.

- Set saucepan in ice and whisk mixture constantly until it cools. Fold in whipped cream and spoon into piecrust. Sprinkle with walnuts. Refrigerate for at least 4 hours before serving. Serves 8.

• • • • •

Cheap Million Dollar Pie

24 buttery round crackers, crumbled	
1 cup chopped pecans	240 ml
4 egg whites (absolutely no yolks at all)	
1 cup sugar	240 ml

- Preheat oven to 350° (175° C).

- Mix cracker crumbs with pecans. In separate mixing bowl, beat egg whites until stiff and slowly add sugar while mixing. Gently fold in crumbs and pecan mixture. Pour in pie plate and bake 20 minutes. Cool before serving. Serves 4 to 6.

• • • • •

Mini Crusts for Individual Pies

1 (3 ounce) package cream cheese, softened	85 g
½ cup (1 stick) butter, softened	115 g
1 cup flour	120 g

- Combine all ingredients and mix well. Refrigerate dough.

- When ready to bake, preheat oven to 350° (175° C).

- Shape dough into 24 balls, place in unsprayed mini-muffin pan and press against bottom and sides. Bake until golden brown. Fill with pie filling of your choice. Yields 24 mini piecrusts.

• • • • •

Pat-in-the-Pan Pastry

1⅓ cups flour	160 g
⅓ cup vegetable oil	75 ml
2 tablespoons cold water	30 ml

- Preheat oven to 475° (245° C).

- Combine flour and oil until flour is moistened. Sprinkle 1 tablespoon (15 ml) cold water at a time over flour mixture and toss with fork until water absorbs into dough.

- Gather pastry into ball and press it in bottom and up sides of pie pan. Flute edges of crust and prick bottom and sides with fork. Bake unfilled for 10 to 12 minutes. Yields 1 piecrust.

• • • • •

Apricot Cobbler

So easy and so good!

1 (20 ounce) can apricot pie filling	565 g
1 (20 ounce) can crushed pineapple with liquid	565 g
1 cup chopped pecans	110 g
1 (18 ounce) box yellow cake mix	510 g
1 cup (2 sticks) butter, melted	230 g

- Preheat oven to 375° (190° C).

- Pour and spread pie filling in sprayed, floured 9 x 13-inch (23 x 33 cm) baking dish. Spoon pineapple and liquid over pie filling and sprinkle pecans over pineapple. Sprinkle cake mix over pecans.

- Drizzle melted butter over cake mix and bake for 40 minutes or until light brown and crunchy. Serve hot or at room temperature. (It's great topped with whipped topping.) Serves 15.

• • • • •

Shop once a week or every other week. *This will save you time and money. You will also focus on just what you need and are less likely to buy impulsively.*

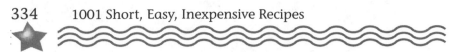

Short-Cut Blueberry Cobbler

2 (20 ounce) cans blueberry pie filling	2 (565 g)
1 (18 ounce) box white cake mix	510 g
1 egg	
½ cup (1 stick) butter, softened	115 g

- Preheat oven to 350° (175° C).

- Spread pie filling in sprayed 9 x 13-inch (23 x 33 cm) baking dish.

- With mixer, combine cake mix, egg and butter and blend well. Mixture will be stiff. Spoon over filling.

- Bake for 45 minutes or until brown. Serves 10 to 12.

• • • • •

Granny's Peach Cobbler

1 (29 ounce) can sliced peaches with syrup	805 g
1 (18 ounce) package butter-pecan or yellow cake mix	510 g
½ cup (1 stick) butter, melted	115 g

- Preheat oven to 325° (165° C).

- Spread peaches in sprayed 9 x 13-inch (23 x 33 cm) pan.

- Sprinkle dry cake mix over peaches and drizzle melted butter over cake mix. Bake for 45 to 55 minutes. Serves 10 to 12.

• • • • •

Check the "per unit" pricing label on the shelf to determine which size of an item is the better buy. Sometimes a smaller size is on sale and has a lower price per unit than the large "economy" size.

Dollar Days Sweets

Cookies, Bars & Brownies

Desserts add that special finishing touch to celebrations. They also "dress up" the simplest meal and make it into a feast.

Lemon Drops

½ (8 ounce) carton frozen whipped topping, thawed   ½ (225 g)
1 (18 ounce) box lemon cake mix   510 g
1 egg
Powdered sugar

- Preheat oven to 350° (175° C).

- Stir whipped topping into lemon cake mix in bowl with spoon.
  Add egg and mix thoroughly. Shape into balls and roll in sifted
  powdered sugar. Bake for 8 to 10 minutes. Do not overcook. Yields
  3 dozen cookies.

• • • • •

Orange Balls

1 (12 ounce) box vanilla wafers, crushed   340 g
½ cup (1 stick) butter, melted   115 g
1 (16 ounce) box powdered sugar   455 g
1 (6 ounce) can frozen orange juice concentrate, thawed   175 ml
1 cup finely chopped pecans   110 g

- Combine wafers, butter, powdered sugar and orange juice
  concentrate in bowl and mix well. Form into balls and roll in
  chopped pecans. Store in airtight container. Yields 3 dozen balls.

TIP: Make these in finger shapes for something different.

• • • • •

Chocolate-Coconut Cookies

1 cup sweetened condensed milk   310 g
4 cups flaked coconut   340 g
⅔ cup miniature semi-sweet chocolate bits   115 g
1 teaspoon vanilla   5 ml
½ teaspoon almond extract   2 ml

- Preheat oven to 325° (160° C).

- Combine sweetened condensed milk and coconut in bowl. (Mixture
  will be gooey.) Add chocolate bits, vanilla and almond extract and
  stir until blended well.

- Drop teaspoonfuls onto sprayed cookie sheet. Bake for 12 minutes.
  Store in airtight container. Yields 2 to 3 dozen cookies.

• • • • •

Chocolate-Crunch Cookies

These cookies are incredibly easy.

1 (18 ounce) box German chocolate cake mix with pudding	510 g
1 egg, slightly beaten	
½ cup (1 stick) butter, melted	115 g
1 cup rice crispy cereal	25 g

- Preheat oven to 350° (175° C).

- Combine cake mix, egg and butter in bowl. Add cereal and stir until blended. Shape dough into 1-inch (2.5 cm) balls. Place on sprayed cookie sheet.

- Dip fork in flour and flatten cookies in crisscross pattern. Bake for 10 to 12 minutes and cool. Yields 3 dozen cookies.

• • • • •

Chocolate Peanut Butter Cookies

1 (18 ounce) package refrigerated, ready-to-slice peanut butter or chocolate chip cookie dough	510 g
2 (13 ounce) packages bite-size peanut butter cups	2 (370 g)

- Preheat oven to 350° (175° C). Spray mini-muffin pan. Slice cookie dough into 1-inch (2.5 cm) slices, then quarter slices. Lay 1 piece in each sprayed mini-muffin cup and bake for 8 minutes.

- While cookies are hot, gently push peanut butter cup into center of each cookie. Cool thoroughly before removing from cups and refrigerate. Serves 12.

• • • • •

Easy Peanut Butter Cookies

1 (18 ounce) package refrigerated sugar cookie dough	510 g
½ cup peanut butter	145 g
½ cup miniature chocolate chips	85 g
½ cup peanut butter chips	85 g
½ cup chopped peanuts	85 g

- Preheat oven to 350° (175° C).

- Beat cookie dough and peanut butter in large bowl until blended and smooth. Stir in remaining ingredients. Drop heaping tablespoonfuls of dough onto cookie sheet. Bake for 15 minutes. Cool on wire rack. Yields 3 dozen cookies.

• • • • •

Peanut Butter-Date Cookies

1 egg, beaten	
⅔ cup sugar	135 g
⅓ cup packed brown sugar	75 g
1 cup chunky peanut butter	290 g
½ cup chopped dates	75 g

- Preheat oven to 350° (175° C).

- Blend egg, sugar, brown sugar and peanut butter in bowl and mix thoroughly. Stir in dates and roll into 1-inch (2.5 cm) balls.

- Place on cookie sheet. Use fork to press ball down to about ½-inch (1.2 cm) thick. Bake for about 12 minutes. Cool before storing. Yields 2 dozen cookies.

• • • • •

Angel Macaroons

1 (16 ounce) package 1-step angel food cake mix	455 g
1½ teaspoons almond extract	7 ml
2 cups flaked coconut	170 g

- Preheat oven to 350° (175° C).

- Beat cake mix, ½ cup (125 ml) water and almond extract in bowl on low speed for 30 seconds. Scrape bowl and beat on medium for 1 minute. Fold in coconut.

- Drop rounded teaspoonfuls of dough onto parchment paper-lined cookie sheet. Bake for 10 to 12 minutes or until set. Remove paper with cookies to wire rack to cool. Yields 3 dozen cookies.

• • • • •

 If brown sugar has gotten hard or dry, place it in an airtight container with a slice of bread or a slice of apple and leave it for a couple of days. *This will restore the moisture.*

Chocolate Macaroons

1 (4 ounce) package sweet baking chocolate	115 g
2 egg whites, room temperature	
½ cup sugar	100 g
¼ teaspoon vanilla	1 ml
1 (7 ounce) can flaked coconut	200 g

- Preheat oven to 350° (175° C).

- Place chocolate in double boiler. Cook until chocolate melts and stir occasionally. Remove from heat and cool.

- Beat egg whites in bowl at high speed for 1 minute. Gradually add sugar, 1 tablespoon at a time and beat until stiff peaks form (about 3 minutes). Add chocolate and vanilla and beat well. Stir in coconut.

- Drop teaspoonfuls of dough onto cookie sheet lined with parchment paper. Bake for 12 to 15 minutes. Transfer cookies on paper to cooling rack and cool. Carefully remove cookies from paper. Yields 3 dozen cookies.

• • • • •

Vanishing Butter Cookies

1 (18 ounce) box butter cake mix	510 g
1 (3.4 ounce) package butterscotch instant pudding mix	100 g
1 cup canola oil	250 ml
1 egg, beaten	
1¼ cups chopped pecans	140 g

- Preheat oven to 350° (175° C).

- Mix cake and pudding mixes in bowl with spoon and stir in oil. Add egg, mix thoroughly and stir in pecans.

- Place teaspoonfuls of dough onto cookie sheet about 2 inches (5 cm) apart. Bake for 8 or 9 minutes. Do not overcook. Yields 3 dozen cookies.

• • • • •

 Don't buy cookies in the bakery *where they are more costly. It's easy to whip up a batch of cookies and bake just what you want. Freeze the rest of the dough and bake it later.*

Sand Tarts

1 cup (2 sticks) butter, softened	230 g
¾ cup powdered sugar	90 g
2 cups sifted flour	240 g
1 cup chopped pecans	110 g
1 teaspoon vanilla	5 ml

- Preheat oven to 325° (160° C).

- Cream butter and powdered sugar in bowl and add flour, pecans and vanilla. Form dough into crescents and place on cookie sheet.

- Bake for 20 minutes. Roll in extra powdered sugar after tarts cool. Yields 3 dozen.

• • • • •

Coconut Nibbles

2 cups flaky wheat cereal	60 g
1¼ cups shredded coconut	105 g
2 large egg whites	
1¼ cups sugar	250 g
½ teaspoon vanilla	2 ml

- Preheat oven to 350° (175° C).

- Combine cereal and coconut in large bowl and mix well. In separate bowl, beat egg whites on high speed until soft peaks form. Gradually add sugar and vanilla while mixing.

- Fold egg whites into cereal-coconut mixture and mix well. Drop tablespoonfuls about 2 inches (5 cm) apart on sprayed baking sheet and bake for about 8 to 10 minutes.

- Watch closely and remove from oven when they become golden brown. Do not let them get too brown on bottom. Store in airtight container. Yields 3 dozen cookies.

• • • • •

Use a large envelope to keep coupons in one place.
Review your coupons when making out your week's menus and shopping list. Be sure the expiration dates are still good.

Yummy Cookies

3 egg whites	
1¼ cups sugar	250 g
2 teaspoons vanilla	10 ml
3½ cups frosted corn flakes	155 g
1 cup chopped pecans	110 g

- Preheat oven to 250° (120° C).

- Beat egg whites in bowl until stiff. Gradually add sugar and vanilla. Fold in frosted corn flakes and pecans. Drop teaspoonfuls of mixture onto cookie sheet lined with wax paper. Bake for 40 minutes. Yields 4 dozen cookies.

• • • • •

Potato Chip Crispies

1 cup (2 sticks) butter, softened	230 g
⅔ cup sugar	135 g
1 teaspoon vanilla	5 ml
1½ cups flour	180 g
½ cup crushed potato chips	30 g

- Preheat oven to 350° (175° C).

- Cream butter, sugar and vanilla in bowl. Add flour and chips and mix well. Drop teaspoonfuls of dough onto cookie sheet. Bake for about 12 minutes or until light brown. Yields 3 dozen cookies.

• • • • •

Brown Sugar Wafers

1 cup (2 sticks) butter, softened	230 g
¾ cup packed dark brown sugar	165 g
1 egg yolk	
1 tablespoon vanilla	15 ml
1¼ cups flour	150 g

- Beat butter in bowl and gradually add brown sugar. Add egg yolk and vanilla and beat well. Add flour and dash salt and mix well.

- Shape dough into 1-inch (2.5 cm) balls and refrigerate for 2 hours.

- When ready to bake, preheat oven to 350° (175° C).

- Place dough balls on cookie sheet and flatten each cookie. Bake for 10 to 12 minutes. Yields 3 dozen cookies.

• • • • •

Lemon-Angel Bars

1 (1 pound) package one-step angel food cake mix	455 g
1 (20 ounce) can lemon pie filling	565 g
⅓ cup (⅔ stick) butter, softened	75 g
2 cups powdered sugar	240 g
2 tablespoons lemon juice	30 ml

- Preheat oven to 350° (175° C).

- Combine cake mix and lemon pie filling in bowl and stir until blended well. Pour into sprayed, floured 9 x 13-inch (23 x 33 cm) baking pan. Bake for 25 minutes.

- Just before cake is done, mix butter, powdered sugar and lemon juice in bowl and spread over hot cake. When cool, cut into bars. Store in refrigerator. Yields 20 bars.

• • • • •

Caramel-Chocolate Chip Bars

1 (18 ounce) box caramel cake mix	510 g
2 eggs	
⅓ cup firmly packed light brown sugar	75 g
¼ cup (½ stick) butter, softened	55 g
1 cup semi-sweet chocolate chips	170 g

- Preheat oven to 350° (175° C).

- Combine cake mix, eggs, ¼ cup (60 ml) water, brown sugar and butter in large bowl. Stir until it blends thoroughly. (Mixture will be thick.) Stir in chocolate chips.

- Spread in sprayed, floured 9 x 13-inch (23 x 33 cm) baking pan. Bake for about 25 to 30 minutes or until toothpick inserted in center comes out clean. Cool. Yields 20 bars.

TIP: *These bars are especially good when frosted with a prepared caramel frosting.*

• • • • •

 Always plan to shop for everything in one trip. "One item" trips to the store usually end up as impulse-buying trips. Besides, it wastes your gas and your time.

Gooey Turtle Bars

½ cup (1 stick) butter, melted	115 g
2 cups vanilla wafer crumbs	320 g
1 (12 ounce) semi-sweet chocolate chips	340 g
1 cup pecan pieces	110 g
1 (12 ounce) jar caramel topping	340 g

- Preheat oven to 350° (175° C).

- Combine butter and wafer crumbs in 9 x 13-inch (23 x 33 cm) baking pan and press into bottom of pan. Sprinkle with chocolate chips and pecans.

- Remove lid from caramel topping and microwave on HIGH for 30 seconds or until hot. Drizzle over pecans.

- Bake for about 15 minutes or until chips melt. Cool in pan. Refrigerate for at least 30 minutes before cutting into squares. Yields 20 bars.

TIP: Watch bars closely – you want the chips to melt, but you don't want the crumbs to burn.

• • • • •

Rainbow Cookie Bars

½ cup (1 stick) butter	115 g
2 cups graham cracker crumbs	210 g
1 (14 ounce) can sweetened condensed milk	395 g
⅔ cup flaked coconut	55 g
1 cup chopped pecans	110 g
1 cup M&M's® plain chocolate candies	170 g

- Preheat oven to 350° (175° C).

- Melt butter in 9 x 13-inch (23 x 33 cm) baking pan. Sprinkle crumbs over butter and pour sweetened condensed milk over crumbs.

- Top with remaining ingredients and press down firmly. Bake for 25 to 30 minutes or until light brown. Cool and cut into bars. Yields 20 bars.

TIP: If you don't have M&M's®, white chocolate bits work but you won't have the "rainbow".

• • • • •

Rocky Road Bars

1 (12 ounce) package semi-sweet chocolate chips	340 g
1 (14 ounce) can sweetened condensed milk	395 g
2 tablespoons butter	30 g
2 cups dry-roasted peanuts	290 g
1 (10 ounce) package miniature marshmallows	280 g

- Place chocolate chips, sweetened condensed milk and butter in double boiler. Heat until chocolate and butter melt, stirring constantly. Remove from heat and stir in peanuts and marshmallows.

- Spread mixture quickly on wax paper-lined 9 x 13-inch (23 x 33 cm) pan. Refrigerate for at least 2 hours. Cut into bars and store in refrigerator. Yields 3½ dozen bars.

• • • • •

Chocolate Chip Cheese Bars

1 (18 ounce) tube refrigerated chocolate chip cookie dough	510 g
1 (8 ounce) package cream cheese, softened	225 g
½ cup sugar	100 g
1 egg	

- Preheat oven to 350° (175° C).

- Cut cookie dough in half. For crust, press half dough onto bottom of sprayed 9-inch (23 cm) square baking pan or 7 x 11-inch (18 x 28 cm) baking pan.

- Beat cream cheese, sugar and egg in bowl until smooth. Spread over crust and crumble remaining dough over top.

- Bake for 35 to 40 minutes or until toothpick inserted in center comes out clean. Cool on wire rack. Cut into bars and refrigerate leftovers. Yields 3 dozen cookies.

• • • • •

 Don't forget to look at ads and coupons for drug stores. *They have some great sales on many products you ordinarily pick up at the grocery store.*

Marshmallow Treats

¼ cup (½ stick) butter	60 g
4 cups miniature marshmallows	180 g
½ cup chunky peanut butter	145 g
5 cups rice crispy cereal	130 g

- Melt butter in saucepan and add marshmallows. Stir until they melt and add peanut butter. Remove from heat. Add cereal and stir well.

- Press mixture into 9 x 13-inch (23 x 33 cm) pan. Cut in squares when cool. Yields 20 squares.

• • • • •

 # Crispy Fudge Treats

6 cups rice crispy cereal	155 g
¾ cup powdered sugar	90 g
1¾ cups semi-sweet chocolate chips	295 g
½ cup light corn syrup	125 ml
⅓ cup (⅔ stick) butter	75 g
2 teaspoons vanilla	10 ml

- Combine cereal and powdered sugar in large bowl.

- Place chocolate chips, corn syrup and butter in 1-quart microwave-safe dish. Microwave uncovered on HIGH for about 1 minute and stir until smooth. Stir in vanilla. Pour over cereal mixture and mix well.

- Spoon into sprayed 9 x 13-inch (23 x 33 cm) pan. Refrigerate for 30 minutes and cut into squares. Yields 20 squares.

• • • • •

Butterscotch Krispie Bars

1 (12 ounce) package butterscotch chips	340 g
1 cup creamy peanut butter	290 g
6 cups rice crispy cereal	175 g

- Combine butterscotch chips and peanut butter in saucepan on medium heat, stirring constantly. Stir until smooth. Remove from heat and stir in cereal and mix until mixture coats well.

- Press into sprayed 9 x 13-inch (23 x 33 cm) pan and refrigerate until firm. Cut into bars. Serves 10 to 12.

• • • • •

Milky Way Squares

4 (2 ounce) Milky Way® candy bars, chopped	4 (55 g)
½ cup (1 stick) butter	115 g
3 cups rice crispy cereal	80 g

- Melt candy with butter in saucepan on medium heat. Stir until they blend well. Stir in cereal and mix well. Pat into sprayed 7 x 11-inch (18 x 28 cm) pan. Refrigerate until firm and cut into squares. Serves 8 to 10.

• • • • •

Scotch Shortbread

1 cup (2 sticks) butter	230 g
2 cups flour	240 g
¾ cup cornstarch	95 g
⅔ cup sugar	135 g
Granulated sugar or colored-sugar sprinkles	

- Preheat oven to 325° (165° C).

- Melt butter in saucepan and stir in remaining ingredients. Press into 9-inch (23 cm) square pan.

- Bake for 45 minutes. Cut into squares immediately after removing from oven. Sprinkle with granulated sugar or colored-sugar sprinkles. Yields 2 dozen squares.

• • • • •

Hello Dollies

1½ cups graham cracker crumbs	155 g
1 (6 ounce) package chocolate chips	170 g
1 cup flaked coconut	85 g
1¼ cups chopped pecans	140 g
1 (14 ounce) can sweetened condensed milk	395 g

- Preheat oven to 350° (175° C).

- Sprinkle cracker crumbs in 9-inch (23 cm) square pan. Layer chocolate chips, coconut and pecans. Pour sweetened condensed milk over top of layered ingredients. Bake for 25 to 30 minutes. Cool and cut into squares. Yields 16 squares.

• • • • •

Praline Grahams

⅓ (16 ounce) box graham crackers (1 package)	⅓ (455 g)
¾ cup (1½ sticks) butter	170 g
½ cup sugar	100 g
1 cup chopped pecans	110 g

- Preheat oven to 300° (150° C).

- Separate each graham cracker into 4 sections. Arrange in jellyroll pan with edges touching.

- Melt butter in saucepan and stir in sugar and pecans. Bring to a boil and cook for 3 minutes. Stir frequently. Spread mixture evenly over graham crackers. Bake for 10 to 12 minutes. Remove from pan and cool on wax paper. Break up to serve. Yields 20 to 24 pieces.

• • • • •

Creamy Pecan Squares

1 (18 ounce) box yellow cake mix	510 g
3 eggs, divided	
½ cup (1 stick) butter, softened	115 g
2 cups chopped pecans	220 g
1 (8 ounce) package cream cheese, softened	225 g
3⅔ cups powdered sugar	440 g

- Preheat oven to 350° (175° C).

- Combine cake mix, 1 egg and butter in bowl. Stir in pecans and mix well. Press into sprayed 9 x 13-inch (23 x 33 cm) baking pan.

- Beat cream cheese, powdered sugar and remaining eggs in bowl until smooth. Pour over pecan mixture. Bake for 55 minutes or until golden brown. Cool and cut into squares. Yields 20 squares.

• • • • •

 When buying fresh produce, make sure it's dry. It will weigh more if it has just been sprayed.

Mincemeat Squares

1⅓ cups mincemeat	405 g
1 (14 ounce) can sweetened condensed milk	395 g
2 cups graham cracker crumbs	210 g
½ cup chopped nuts	85

- Preheat oven to 350° (175° C).

- Combine all ingredients and mix well. Spread in sprayed 9 x 13-inch (23 x 33 cm) pan and bake for 35 to 40 minutes. Cool before cutting into squares. Serves 12.

• • • • •

Nutty Blonde Brownies

1 (1 pound) box light brown sugar	455 g
4 eggs	
2 cups biscuit mix	240 g
2 cups chopped pecans	220 g

- Preheat oven to 350° (175° C).

- Beat brown sugar, eggs and biscuit mix in bowl. Stir in pecans and pour into sprayed 9 x 13-inch (23 x 33 cm) baking pan. Bake for 35 minutes. Cool and cut into squares. Yields 20 brownies.

• • • • •

Peanut Butter Brownies

1 (20 ounce) box brownie mix	565 g
1 cup peanut butter chips	170 g

- Preheat oven to 350° (175° C).

- Prepare brownie mix according to package directions and stir in peanut butter chips.

- Spoon mixture into sprayed 9 x 13-inch (23 x 33 cm) baking pan. Bake for 35 minutes. Cool and cut into squares. Yields 20 brownies.

• • • • •

Buy nuts in season (fall) and freeze in airtight containers. They will keep for months.

Dollar Days Sweets

Candies

Desserts add that special finishing touch to celebrations. They also "dress up" the simplest meal and make it into a feast.

Strawberry Candy

2 (6 ounce) packages strawberry gelatin	2 (170 g)
1 (14 ounce) can sweetened condensed milk	395 g
1 cup package flaked coconut	225 g

- Combine all ingredients and mix well. Refrigerate overnight. Shape into strawberry-size balls. Refrigerate. Serves 12 to 15.

TIP: To really take care of your sweet tooth, roll candy in sugar.

Coconut Yummies

1 (12 ounce) package white chocolate baking chips	340 g
¼ cup (½ stick) butter	55 g
16 large marshmallows	
2 cups quick-cooking oats	160 g
1 cup flaked coconut	85 g

- Melt chocolate chips, butter and marshmallows in saucepan over low heat and stir until smooth. Stir in oats and coconut and mix well.

- Drop rounded teaspoonfuls of mixture onto wax paper-lined baking sheets. Refrigerate until set. Store in airtight container. Yields 3 dozen.

Super Easy Peanut Clusters

1 (12 ounce) package chocolate chips	340 g
1½ pounds almond bark (white chocolate)	680 g
1 (9 ounce) package salted peanuts	255 g

- Melt chocolate chips and almond bark in double boiler over boiling water. Stir constantly. When melted and smooth, stir in peanuts. Drop by teaspoonfuls onto wax paper and let set until firm or refrigerate until firm. Serves 12 to 15.

Pretzels-and-Peanuts
Chocolate Candy

1 pound almond bark (white chocolate)	455 g
3 cups pretzel sticks, broken in halves	135 g
1 cup Spanish peanuts	225 g

- Melt chocolate in double boiler and stir constantly. Add pretzels and peanuts until they coat well. Spread in jellyroll pan and let stand until firm. Break into pieces. Serves 12 to 15.

Chocolate-Butterscotch Clusters

1 (6 ounce) package chocolate chips	170 g
1 (12 ounce) package butterscotch chips	340 g
1 (12 ounce) package salted Spanish peanuts	340 g

- Combine chocolate and butterscotch chips in 2-quart (2 L) glass dish. Heat in microwave on MEDIUM for 2 minutes, stir and repeat until chips melt. Watch carefully for burning. (Some microwaves have higher power. If chips melt before time given, remove immediately.)

- Stir in peanuts and drop by teaspoonfuls on wax paper. Let stand until firm. Store in airtight container. Serves 12 to 15.

Macaroon Candy

1 (14 ounce) package shredded coconut	396 g
1 (14 ounce) can sweetened condensed milk	396 g
1 teaspoon vanilla	5 ml

- Preheat oven to 375° (190° C).

- Combine all ingredients and mix well. Drop by teaspoonfuls on sprayed baking sheet. Bake for 8 minutes. Cool before removing from pan. Serves 10.

Ritzy Chocolate Balls

1 (12 ounce) jar chunky peanut butter	340 g
2 tubes buttery, round crackers	
1 (12 ounce) package chocolate chips	340 g

- Spread peanut butter layer on each cracker. Melt chocolate chips in double boiler over boiling water. Stir until smooth. Dip crackers in chocolate. Be sure to completely cover the peanut butter with chocolate. Place on wax paper to cool. Serves 8 to 12.

Peanut Butter Candy

1 (14 ounce) can sweetened condensed milk	396 g
½ cup chunky peanut butter	120 ml
½ cup chopped peanuts	120 ml

- Mix and drop by teaspoonfuls on sprayed, floured baking sheets. Bake at 375° (190° C) to 400° (205° C) for 7 to 9 minutes. Serves 8.

• • • • •

Tiger Butter

1 pound white chocolate or almond bark	455 g
½ cup chunky peanut butter	145 g
1 cup semi-sweet chocolate chips	170 g

- Line 10 x 15-inch (25 x 38 cm) jellyroll pan with wax paper. Heat white chocolate in microwave-safe bowl on HIGH for 1 to 2 minutes or until it melts. Stir until smooth.

- Add peanut butter and microwave on HIGH until it melts. Stir again until smooth. Spread mixture evenly into pan.

- In separate microwave-safe bowl, melt chocolate chips on HIGH. Pour chocolate over peanut butter mixture and swirl through with knife until you get desired effect. Refrigerate for several hours until firm. Break into pieces. Yields 2 dozen pieces.

• • • • •

Sugar Plum Candy

1¼ pounds almond bark, chopped	565 g
1½ cups red and green miniature marshmallows	70 g
1½ cups peanut butter cereal	60 g
1½ cups rice crispy cereal	40 g
1½ cups mixed nuts	210 g

- Melt almond bark in double boiler over low heat. Place marshmallows, cereals and nuts in large bowl. Pour melted bark over mixture and stir to coat.

- Drop teaspoonfuls of mixture onto wax paper-lined cookie sheet. Let stand until set and store in airtight container. Yields 3 dozen.

TIP: If you want to cut the cost of this recipe, don't add the nuts.

• • • • •

Easy Holiday Mints

1 (16 ounce) package powdered sugar	455 g
3 tablespoons butter, softened	45 g
3½ tablespoons evaporated milk	50 ml
¼ - ½ teaspoon peppermint extract	1 - 2 ml
Few drops desired food coloring	

- Combine all ingredients in large bowl and knead mixture until smooth. Shape mints in rubber candy molds and place on cookie sheets. Cover with paper towel and let dry. Store in airtight container. Yields 3 dozen mints.

Karo Caramels

2 cups sugar	400 g
1¾ cups light corn syrup	425 g
½ cup (1 stick) butter	115 g
2 (8 ounce) cartons whipping cream, divided	2 (250 ml)
1¼ cups chopped pecans, toasted	140 g

- Combine sugar, corn syrup, butter and half cream in saucepan. Bring to a boil. While boiling, add remaining cream. Cook to soft-ball stage (234°/112° C).

- Beat with spoon for 3 to 4 minutes. Add pecans and pour onto sprayed platter. Cut when cool. Yields 3 dozen squares.

• • • • •

Chocolate Drops

1 (6 ounce) package milk chocolate chips	170 g
⅔ cup chunky peanut butter	190 g
4¼ cups chocolate-flavored rice crispy cereal	115 g

- Melt chocolate chips in double boiler and stir in peanut butter. Stir in cereal.

- Press into 9 x 9-inch (23 x 23 cm) square pan and cut into squares. Yields 16 squares.

• • • • •

Chocolate Kisses

2 egg whites, room temperature	
⅔ cup sugar	135 g
1 teaspoon vanilla	5 ml
1¼ cups chopped pecans	140 g
1 (6 ounce) package chocolate chips	170 g

- Preheat oven to 375° (190° C).

- Beat egg whites in bowl until very stiff. Blend in sugar, vanilla and dash of salt. Fold in pecans and chocolate chips.

- Drop on shiny side of foil on cookie sheet. Put cookies in oven, TURN OVEN OFF and leave overnight. If cookies are a little sticky, leave out in air to dry. Yields 3 dozen cookies.

• • • • •

Chocolate Graham Cracker Drops

2 cups finely crushed graham cracker crumbs	480 ml
1 cup chocolate chips	240 ml
1 (14 ounce) can sweetened condensed milk	396 g

- Preheat oven to 350° (175° C). Combine all ingredients and mix well. Drop by teaspoonfuls onto sprayed baking sheet and bake for 8 to 10 minutes. Serves 8.

• • • • •

Butterscotch Flakes

1 cup butterscotch chips	170 g
½ cup peanut butter	145 g
2 - 3 cups corn flakes	55 - 85 g

- Melt chips and peanut butter in a double boiler and mix well. Remove from heat and stir in corn flakes. Drop by teaspoonfuls onto wax paper. Let stand until firm. Serves 12 to 15.

• • • • •

Chocolate-Marshmallow Candy

1 pound milk chocolate	455 g
1 cup miniature marshmallows	45 g
½ cup chopped pecans	55 g

- Melt chocolate in top of double boiler. Line 9 x 13-inch (23 x 33 cm) cake pan with wax paper. Pour half melted chocolate over wax paper. Cover chocolate with marshmallows and pecans.

- Pour remaining half melted chocolate over marshmallows and pecans. Let cool completely, then break into pieces. Serves 12 to 15.

• • • • •

Cocoa Puffs Candy

1½ pounds almond bark (white chocolate)	680 g
4½ cups Cocoa Puffs® cereal	160 g
1 (12 ounce) can red skin peanuts	340 g

- Melt chocolate on low heat, stirring constantly. (White chocolate will burn easily.) Stir in cereal and peanuts. Drop by teaspoonfuls onto wax paper and let stand until candy is firm. Serves 12 to 15.

Chocolate Crunch Munch

1 (12 ounce) package chocolate chips	340 g
1 (3 ounce) can Chinese noodles	85 g
½ cup chopped pecans	55 g

- Melt chocolate in double boiler and stir in noodles and pecans. Drop by teaspoonfuls onto wax paper and let stand until firm. Serves 12 to 15.

Haystacks

1 (12 ounce) package butterscotch chips	340 g
1 cup salted peanuts	150 g
1½ cups chow mein noodles	140 g

- Melt butterscotch chips in top of double boiler. Remove from heat and stir in peanuts and noodles. Drop by teaspoonfuls on wax paper. Cool and store in airtight container. Serves 12 to 15.

Tumbleweeds

1 (12 ounce) can salted peanuts	340 g
1 (7 ounce) can potato sticks, broken up	200 g
3 cups butterscotch chips	510 g
3 tablespoons peanut butter	50 g

- Combine peanuts and potato sticks in bowl and set aside. Heat butterscotch chips and peanut butter in microwave at 70% power for 1 to 2 minutes or until they melt. Stir every 30 seconds. Add to peanut mixture and stir to coat evenly.

- Drop rounded tablespoonfuls of mixture onto wax paper-lined cookie sheet. Refrigerate until set, about 10 minutes. Yields 3 dozen.

Christmas Peppermint Candy

1 (20 ounce) package white chocolate or white almond bark	565 g
1 cup crushed peppermint sticks	200 g
1 cup toasted slivered almonds	170 g

- Melt chocolate in double boiler and stir until creamy. Remove from heat and stir in crushed peppermint sticks and slivered almonds.

- Pour on sprayed baking sheet and let stand until firm. Cut into squares or break into pieces and keep in tightly covered container. Serves 12 to 15.

• • • • •

Chocolate-Covered Strawberries

30 whole strawberries with stems
1 (12 ounce) package chocolate chips   **340 g**
6 tablespoons (¾ stick) butter   **85 g**

- Place clean berries on large sheet of wax paper set on baking sheet. Melt chocolate chips in double boiler over hot water. Stir in butter and mix until it melts and blends well with chocolate.

- Dip berries in chocolate, replace on wax paper and refrigerate until chocolate is hard. Yields 30.

• • • • •

Chocolate-Covered Cherries

1 (6 ounce) package chocolate chips   **170 g**
2 tablespoons milk   **30 ml**
1 (8 ounce) jar maraschino cherries with stems   **225 g**

- Melt chocolate chips with milk in microwave or in double boiler. Pat cherries dry.

- Dip cherries into chocolate mixture and turn until they coat well. Lay cherries on baking sheet lined with wax paper and cool until firm. Yields 12 to 15.

TIP: The chocolate chip-milk mixture may be doubled or tripled.

• • • • •

Peanut Butter Fudge

1 (12 ounce) package chocolate chips   **340 g**
1 (12 ounce) jar extra chunky peanut butter   **340 g**
1 (14 ounce) can sweetened condensed milk   **395 g**

- Melt chocolate chips and peanut butter in double boiler over hot water. Remove from heat and stir in condensed milk.

- Pour into 8 x 8-inch (20 x 20 cm) pan lined with wax paper and let stand until firm. Serves 12 to 15.

• • • • •

Want an elegant dessert that's inexpensive, too?
Strawberries dipped in chocolate are so easy to do – and so impressive.

Creamy Peanut Butter Fudge

3 cups sugar	600 g
¾ cup (1½ sticks) butter	170 g
⅔ cup evaporated milk	150 ml
1 (12 ounce) package peanut butter chips	340 g
1 (7 ounce) jar marshmallow creme	200 g
1 teaspoon vanilla	5 ml

- Combine sugar, butter and evaporated milk in large saucepan. Bring to a boil over medium heat and stir constantly. Cover and cook for 3 minutes without stirring. Uncover and boil for additional 5 minutes (do not stir).

- Remove from heat, add peanut butter chips and stir until they melt. Stir in marshmallow creme and vanilla. Pour into sprayed 9 x 13-inch (23 x 33 cm) pan. Place in freezer for 10 minutes. Yields 20 pieces.

Diamond Fudge

1 (6 ounce) package semi-sweet chocolate chips	170 g
1 cup peanut butter	290 g
½ cup (1 stick) butter	115 g
1 cup powdered sugar	120 g

- Cook chocolate chips, peanut butter and butter in saucepan over low heat. Stir constantly, just until mixture melts and is smooth. Remove from heat. Add powdered sugar and stir until smooth.

- Spoon into sprayed 8-inch (20 cm) square pan and refrigerate until firm. Let stand for 10 minutes at room temperature before cutting into squares. Store in refrigerator. Yields 16 squares.

White Chocolate Fudge

This is a little different slant to fudge – really creamy and really good!

1 (8 ounce) package cream cheese, softened	225 g
4 cups powdered sugar	480 g
1½ teaspoons vanilla	7 ml
12 ounces almond bark, melted	340 g
¾ cup chopped pecans	85 g

- Beat cream cheese in bowl on medium speed until smooth. Gradually add powdered sugar and vanilla and beat well. Stir in melted almond bark and pecans.

- Spread into sprayed 8-inch (20 cm) square pan. Refrigerate until firm. Cut into small squares. Yields 16 squares.

Marshmallow Fudge

1 (12 ounce) package semi-sweet chocolate chips	340 g
1 (14 ounce) can sweetened condensed milk	395 g
1 (8 ounce) package miniature marshmallows	225 g

- Melt chocolate chips in double boiler. Remove from heat and stir until creamy.

- Mix in sweetened condensed milk and marshmallows and pour into sprayed baking pan. Cool and refrigerate until firm. Cut into squares. Serves 12 to 15.

• • • • •

 # Magic Microwave Fudge

1 (12 ounce) package semi-sweet chocolate chips	340 g
1 (14 once) can sweetened condensed milk	395 g
1 teaspoon vanilla	5 ml

- Combine chocolate chips and milk in glass dish and microwave on HIGH for 3 minutes. Stir until mixture melts and is smooth and mix in vanilla. Spread evenly into foil-lined, 8-inch (20 cm) square pan and refrigerate until firm. Cut into squares. Serves 12 to 15.

• • • • •

 Buy in bulk those items that can be stored in the pantry or freezer for later use. A warehouse club membership may be worth it even if you do not have a large family. Always compare value and price per serving.

Dollar Days Sweets

Desserts

Desserts add that special finishing touch to celebrations. They also "dress up" the simplest meal and make it into a feast.

Ambrosia Dessert

2 (11 ounce) cans mandarin oranges, drained, chilled	2 (310 g)
1 (20 ounce) can pineapple tidbits, drained, chilled	565 g
1 (7 ounce) can flaked coconut, chilled	200 g
1 cup miniature marshmallows	45 g

- In bowl with lid, combine oranges, pineapple and coconut. Fold in marshmallows. (Make sure marshmallows are separated so they do not stick together.) Refrigerate. Serves 6 to 8.

• • • • •

Cherry Crush

1 (6 ounce) box cherry gelatin	170 g
1 (8 ounce) package cream cheese, softened	225 g
1 (20 ounce) can cherry pie filling	565 g
1 (15 ounce) can crushed pineapple with liquid	425 g

- Dissolve gelatin with 1½ cups (375 ml) boiling water. With electric mixer beat in cream cheese very slowly at first. Fold in pie filling and crushed pineapple. Pour into 9 x 13-inch (23 x 33 cm) baking dish. Refrigerate. Serves 6 to 8.

• • • • •

Grape Fluff

1 cup grape juice	250 ml
2 cups miniature marshmallows	90 g
2 tablespoons lemon juice	30 ml
1 (8 ounce) carton whipping cream, whipped	225 g

- In saucepan, heat grape juice to boiling. Add marshmallows and stir constantly until they melt. Add lemon juice and cool. Fold in whipped cream and spoon into individual serving dishes. Refrigerate. Serves 6.

• • • • •

Frozen Pistachio Dessert

1 (4 ounce) package instant pistachio pudding	115 g
1 (15 ounce) can crushed pineapple with liquid	425 g
1 (8 ounce) carton frozen whipped topping, thawed	225 g
⅔ cup chopped pecans	75 g

- In bowl stir instant pudding and pineapple together. Fold in whipped topping and pecans. Pour into shallow pan, sprinkle with pecans and freeze. To serve, cut into squares. Serves 6 to 8.

Frozen Dessert Salad

1 (8 ounce) package cream cheese, softened	225 g
1 cup powdered sugar	120 g
1 (10 ounce) box frozen strawberries, thawed	280 g
1 (15 ounce) can crushed pineapple, drained	425 g
1 (8 ounce) carton frozen whipped topping, thawed	225 g

- In mixing bowl, beat cream cheese with the powdered sugar. Fold in remaining ingredients. (This will be even better if you stir in ¾ cup (85 g) chopped pecans.)

- Pour into sprayed 9 x 9-inch (23 x 23 cm) baking pan and freeze. Cut into squares to serve. Serves 6 to 8.

Divine Strawberries

This is wonderful served over pound cake or just served in sherbet glasses.

1 quart fresh strawberries, chilled	715 g
1 (20 ounce) can pineapple chunks, well drained	565 g
2 bananas, sliced	
1 (18 ounce) carton strawberry glaze	510 g

- If strawberries are large, cut in half or in quarters. Add pineapple chunks and bananas. Fold in strawberry glaze and refrigerate. Serves 6 to 8.

Candy Apples

5 red delicious apples	
1 pound caramels	455 g
2 tablespoons butter	30 ml
5 ice cream sticks	

- Remove stems from apples, wash and dry. Melt caramels and butter in top of double boiler. Stir until smooth. Push wooden ice cream stick into each apple's stem end. Dip each apple into caramel sauce and cover completely. Place apples on wax paper until they dry and caramel is hard. Serves 5.

Whipped Apple Delight

3 (2 ounce) Snickers® candy bars, frozen	3 (55 g)
2 apples, chilled, chopped	
1 (12 ounce) carton frozen whipped topping, thawed	340 g
1 (3 ounce) package instant vanilla pudding mix	85 g

- Smash frozen candy bars in wrappers with hammer. Combine all ingredients in bowl and stir very well. Refrigerate. Serves 4.

Fruit Pizza

1 (20 ounce) package refrigerated sugar cookie dough	565 g
1 (8 ounce) carton frozen whipped topping, thawed	230 g
2 - 3 cups assorted fresh fruit	350 - 525 g

- Preheat oven to 350° (175° C).

- Press dough evenly into sprayed pizza pan and bake for 25 to 30 minutes or until brown. Cool completely in pan and spread layer of whipped topping over crust. Arrange fresh sliced fruit of your choice over cookie pizza. Serves 8.

• • • • •

Sopapillas

1¾ cups flour	210 g
2 teaspoons baking powder	10 ml
2 tablespoons shortening	30 ml
Oil	
Honey	

- Mix flour and baking powder with 1 teaspoon (5 ml) salt. Cut in shortening. Add ⅔ cup (150 ml) cold water gradually. Mix and knead until smooth. Cover for 5 minutes.

- Roll into very thin rectangles. Cut in 3-inch (8 cm) squares and drop into very hot oil. Turn several times to puff evenly. Remove and drain. Serve with honey. Serves 4 to 6.

• • • • •

Mocha Pudding

1 (16 ounce) almond candy bar	455 g
1 tablespoon instant coffee granules	15 ml
1 (12 ounce) carton frozen whipped topping, thawed	340 g

- Melt candy with coffee granules in double boiler over boiling water and stir often. Remove from heat and cool completely.

- Stir in whipped topping and serve in dessert dishes as pudding. Serves 6 to 8.

TIP: You may pour into graham cracker crust to serve as a pie. Refrigerate until firm.

• • • • •

Vanilla Fruit

2 (15 ounce) cans chunky fruit (not fruit cocktail) with liquid   2 (425 g)
1 (6 ounce) package instant vanilla pudding mix   170 g
2 bananas, sliced

- Pour fruit and liquid into bowl. Add pudding mix and mix well. Stir in bananas. Spoon into dessert dishes. Refrigerate for 2 to 3 hours. Serves 6 to 8.

TIP: Add ½ cup (25 g) miniature marshmallows and/or ½ cup (55 g) chopped pecans.

• • • • •

Chocolate Ice Cream

1 (14 ounce) can sweetened condensed milk   395 g
1 (12 ounce) container frozen whipped topping, thawed   340 g
1 gallon chocolate milk, divided   3.8 L

- Fold sweetened condensed milk and whipped topping into 1 quart (946 ml) of chocolate milk. Pour into 6-quart (6 L) freezer container and add remaining chocolate milk. Freeze according to manufacturer's directions. Serves 12.

• • • • •

Chocolate Ice Cream with Raspberries

6 scoops chocolate ice cream
6 tablespoons chocolate syrup   90 ml
1 (10 ounce) package frozen raspberries in syrup   280 g

- Place 1 large scoop ice cream in each of 6 dessert bowls. Pour chocolate syrup over ice cream.

- Pour half raspberries into blender and puree. Combine with remaining berries and drizzle raspberry mixture over all. Serves 6.

Make a "bread pudding parfait" at the last minute with bread that is a few days old. Soak the bread in strong brewed coffee (add a touch of rum for the grown-ups). Melt chocolate (use up those leftover morsels and pieces) and layer the bread, chocolate, whipped cream and some chopped nuts in parfait glasses. Quick and easy!

Fancy Coffee Ice Cream Cups

1 (12 ounce) package semi-sweet chocolate chips	340 g
¼ cup (½ stick) butter	55 g
12 scoops coffee ice cream	

- Combine chocolate and butter in double boiler and heat until chocolate almost melts. Remove from water and stir rapidly until smooth and slightly thick.

- Place 12 paper liners in muffin pan. Coat inside of baking cups thickly and evenly with chocolate. Refrigerate until chocolate is hard.

- Remove paper cups from chocolate by cutting around bottom edge with tip of knife, cut up side of cup and pull paper away. Refrigerate until serving time.

- When ready to serve, fill with ice cream. Serves 12.

• • • • •

Vanilla Ice Cream

2 (14 ounce) cans sweetened condensed milk	2 (395 g)
6 cups milk	1.4 L
2 teaspoons vanilla	10 ml

- Combine all ingredients, mix well and freeze in ice cream freezer according to manufacturer's directions. Serves 12.

• • • • •

Oreo Sundae

A kid's favorite!

½ cup (1 stick) butter	115 g
1 (19 ounce) package chocolate sandwich cookies, crushed, divided	540 g
½ gallon vanilla ice cream, softened	1.9 L
1 (12 ounce) jar fudge ice cream topping	340 g
1 (12 ounce) carton frozen whipped topping, thawed	340 g

- Melt butter in 9 x 13-inch (23 x 33 cm) pan. Set aside about ½ cup (50 g) crushed cookies for top and mix remaining with butter to form crust. Press crumbs into pan.

- Spread softened ice cream over crust (work fast) and add fudge ice cream topping, whipped topping and remaining crumbs. Freeze. Serves 12.

Peanut Butter Sundae Sauce

1 cup light corn syrup	250 ml
1 cup chunky peanut butter	290 g
¼ cup milk	60 ml
Ice cream or pound cake	

- In mixing bowl, stir corn syrup, peanut butter and milk until they blend well. Serve over ice cream or pound cake. Store in refrigerator. Yields 2 cups.

• • • • •

Fuzzy Navel Milk Shake

1 cup fresh peaches, peeled, pitted, chopped	155 g
1 cup orange juice, chilled	250 ml
4 scoops vanilla ice cream	

- Combine all ingredients in blender and mix well. Pour into tall glasses. Serves 2.

• • • • •

Fudge Sauce

Great over ice cream or peanut butter ice cream pie.

1 cup evaporated milk	250 ml
1 cup miniature marshmallows	45 g
1 cup chocolate chips	170 g

- Combine evaporated milk, marshmallows and chocolate chips in saucepan. Stir until mixture melts and is smooth. Yields 3 cups sauce.

• • • • •

Apple-Spice Crisp

1 (20 ounce) can apple pie filling	565 g
1 (18 ounce) package spice cake mix	510 g
½ cup (1 stick) butter, sliced	115 g

- Preheat oven to 350° (175° C).

- Spread apple pie filling in sprayed 9 x 13-inch (23 x 33 cm) dish. Sprinkle or spread dry cake mix over fruit. Dot with butter slices and bake for 35 minutes or until cake is brown. Serves 12 to 14.

• • • • •

Quick Company Blueberry Torte

1 (20 ounce) prepared pound cake	565 g
1 (20 ounce) can blueberry pie filling	565 g
1 (12 ounce) carton frozen whipped topping, thawed	340 g

- Slice pound cake lengthwise to make 3 layers. Spread pie filling between each layer and spread whipped topping over top and sides of cake. Serves 8 to 10.

• • • • •

Cherry-Vanilla Trifle

2 (8 ounce) containers cherry-vanilla yogurt	2 (225 g)
4 (3.6 ounce) containers congealed vanilla pudding snacks	4 (100 g)
1 prepared angel food cake, torn into bite-size pieces	
1 (20 ounce) can cherry pie filling	565 g

- Combine yogurt and pudding. Layer half cake pieces, half yogurt-pudding mixture and half cherry pie filling. Repeat. Cover and refrigerate. Serves 6 to 8.

• • • • •

Pavlova

3 large egg whites	
1 cup sugar	200 g
1 teaspoon vanilla	5 ml
2 teaspoons white vinegar	10 ml
3 tablespoons cornstarch	25 g
Whipped cream	
Fresh fruit	

- Preheat oven to 300° (150° C).

- Beat egg whites in bowl until stiff and add 3 tablespoons (45 ml) cold water. Beat again and add sugar very gradually while beating. Continue beating slowly and add vanilla, vinegar and cornstarch.

- Draw 9-inch (23 cm) circle on parchment paper-lined cookie sheet and mound mixture within circle. Bake for 45 minutes. Leave in oven to cool. To serve, peel paper from bottom while sliding onto serving plate. Cover with whipped cream and top with assortment of fresh fruit such as kiwi, strawberries, blueberries, etc. Serves 12.

• • • • •

Index

A

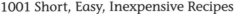

H

I

Q

R

S

Sandwiches

W

Y

Z

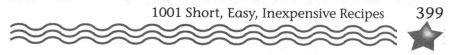

Cookbooks Published by Cookbook Resources, LLC
Bringing Family and Friends to the Table

Easy Diabetic Recipes

The Best 1001 Short, Easy Recipes

1001 Slow Cooker Recipes

1001 Short, Easy, Inexpensive Recipes

1001 Fast Easy Recipes

1001 Community Recipes

Easy Slow Cooker Cookbook

Busy Woman's Slow Cooker Recipes

Busy Woman's Quick & Easy Recipes

Easy Diabetic Recipes

365 Easy Soups and Stews

365 Easy Chicken Recipes

365 Easy One-Dish Recipes

365 Easy Soup Recipes

365 Easy Vegetarian Recipes

365 Easy Casserole Recipes

365 Easy Pasta Recipes

365 Easy Slow Cooker Recipes

Leaving Home Cookbook
and Survival Guide

Essential 3-4-5 Ingredient Recipes

Ultimate 4 Ingredient Cookbook

Easy Cooking with 5 Ingredients

The Best of Cooking with 3 Ingredients

4-Ingredient Recipes
for 30-Minute Meals

Cooking with Beer

The Pennsylvania Cookbook

The California Cookbook

Best-Loved New England Recipes

Best-Loved Canadian Recipes

Best-Loved Recipes
from the Pacific Northwest

Easy Slow Cooker Recipes (with Photos)

Cool Smoothies (with Photos)

Easy Cupcakes (with Photos)

Easy Soup Recipes (with Photos)

Classic Tex-Mex and Texas Cooking

Best-Loved Southern Recipes

Classic Southwest Cooking

Miss Sadie's Southern Cooking

Classic Pennsylvania Dutch Cooking

Healthy Cooking with 4 Ingredients

Trophy Hunters' Wild Game Cookbook

Recipe Keeper

Simple Old-Fashioned Baking

Quick Fixes with Cake Mixes

Kitchen Keepsakes &
More Kitchen Keepsakes

Cookbook 25 Years

Texas Longhorn Cookbook

Gifts for the Cookie Jar

All New Gifts for the Cookie Jar

The Big Bake Sale Cookbook

Easy One-Dish Meals

Easy Potluck Recipes

Easy Casseroles

Easy Desserts

Sunday Night Suppers

Easy Church Suppers

365 Easy Meals

Gourmet Cooking with 5 Ingredients

Muffins In A Jar

A Little Taste of Texas

A Little Taste of Texas II

cookbook ≋resources® LLC

www.cookbookresources.com
Your Ultimate Source for Easy Cookbooks

www.cookbookresources.com